book ma

THE COMIC SENSE OF
HENRY JAMES

RICHARD POIRIER

THE COMIC SENSE OF
HENRY JAMES

A Study of the Early Novels

OXFORD UNIVERSITY PRESS

NEW YORK

1960

PRINTED AND BOUND IN ENGLAND BY
HAZELL WATSON AND VINEY LTD
AYLESBURY AND SLOUGH

Contents

Preface

THE extraordinary amount of published criticism on the works of Henry James does not encourage the idea that the element of comedy in his novels is either strong or pervasive, and even those few who allude to it do not claim that the examples they have noticed, except possibly in *The American*, make any very significant sense. This book is meant to show how attention to comic expression in James's early novels can, in fact, lead us through the language to his most vitally personal meanings. Such a process ultimately allows us to recreate from qualities of his style some of the psychological identity of the author, particularly in the best of the early novels, *The Portrait of a Lady*.

When encouragement was needed that the emphasis on comedy was worth-while, it was most generously given by Douglas Bush and Kenneth B. Murdock, who were the first to read the manuscript. Albert Guerard, Jr., and Robert O'Clair made useful suggestions about style and organization, and David R. Ferry first confirmed my sense that certain oddities of expression in James were comic in their intention. To Alice Cooper and William R. Taylor, to Robert Garis, Joseph Pequigney, and William Abrahams, I am indebted for honest and amiable criticisms, and to Thomas B. Whitbread, Robert W. Coles, and my brother Philip Poirier for helping in various and kindly ways.

Criticism assumes that the questions one asks are meaningful to others, and for a sense of this I relied on those just mentioned, and on others, particularly Reuben Brower, who formed the image of an audience at once humbling and encouraging. And yet, a critical account such as this is an extremely personal undertaking. So much so that to write on a particular novelist, especially on one who was so conscious of his art as Henry James, is to feel that the necessary revelations about one's habits of response and standards of judgment are as much a part of the subject as are the novels themselves. This feeling is likely to occur at a time like the present when the criticism of fiction, particularly of American fiction, reflects in so few cases the kind of critical intelligence exemplified by James himself. In place of it we find, most frequently in the academic environment, a tendency to read novels the way Aladdin rubbed his lamp. A bit of pressure at a pre-selected point brings forth a not unfamiliar *djinn* – a cultural or psychological motif, romanticism or some other ism, an 'organic whole' into which everything can be dropped (and lost), or one of a number of dependable schemes, such as 'appearance and reality' and the European-American contrast. Any of these, and the list is easily extended, may be expected to excuse the reader from an immediate and personally involved attention to each page in its order. The genie is no page turner; he is a page and phrase selector, industriously attaching to himself that configuration of items which confirms the supposed necessity of his function, and giving a flattering illusion that what he has taken out of the work represents the experience of reading it. If he is sophisticated enough, he may even provide that dizzying substitute for critical effort – a pattern of images, soon related to an abstraction and moulded into a dazzlingly efficient key, as the saying goes, to the meaning.

But if such procedures save us labour, they also cheat us of our pleasure. To turn the pages of *The Europeans*, a consistently ignored masterpiece, and to experience the poised and resonant clarity of its style, to discover the variety of one's particular dramatic relationships to the narrative voice or the excitement of overhearing some of the wittiest dialogue in James's fiction – what has any of this to do with those mechanical schematizations about Europe and America which have invariably obscured an understanding of this sophisticated and urbanely comic book? Such a question prompted this study of James and suggested the emphasis which I have given to the rôle of comedy.

It seemed best to limit my examination to the early novels. For one thing, they have never received the consideration or, except from Mr. F. R. Leavis, the praise they deserve, having for the most part been neglected in preference to the dubiously named 'major phase' of the later works. The early fiction is especially rewarding because it shows how James, as one novel follows another, investigated and finally established the premises of his art. With *The Portrait of a Lady* and *The Bostonians* he had reached the fullness of his powers, and to see how this comes about is to discover more about his essential qualities than we could find from a study of any other group of his works. With these two novels he demonstrated how much he had learned from George Eliot and Dickens, just as, earlier, in *Roderick Hudson* and *The American*, he had assimilated Hawthorne, had conceived *The Europeans* in the spirit of Jane Austen, and shown his reverence for Balzac in *Washington Square*.

But any connections we can adduce between young James and those he admired are only symptoms of the larger fact that for him the practice of the art of fiction was an urgently personal matter. For reasons discussed in the following chapters and, particularly, in the Conclusion, James's relationship with his major characters involved a very painful moral scrupulousness. He was terribly afraid of denying to any of them the fullest opportunity for self-dramatization, of limiting their freedom of expression by defining them too categorically. And yet it need hardly be said that he is given to categorizations and to definitions of character which are close to the allegorical.

Because of this consciously felt tension between dramatic and allegorical impulses, his early fiction provides a beautifully full example of a problem that has beset almost all the great American novelists. Their works offer evidence of the persistent difficulty of using characters to illustrate ideas while at the same time investing them with a dramatic and personal vitality that breaks the bounds of any assigned representational function. Perhaps this explains why in the treatment of James, and, even more, of Hawthorne and Melville, it is conspicuously easier for critics to derive the allegorical significance of character from symbols and formal devices, abstractly considered, than from the complicated and modifying inclusion of these within the dramatic rendering of experience. This tendency is especially apparent in criticism of the greatest of contemporary American novelists, as anyone exasperated by naïve talk about Christ figures in William Faulkner will have noticed.

Though the matter is relevant to much that is important in American fiction as a whole, I have chosen to confine my inquiry to some novels of James because he is pre-eminently the greatest and most self-conscious of American writers, and because the kinds of criticism which his fiction deserves call for extensive and detailed scrutiny. In saying that discussions of American fiction too often ignore the dramatic renderings of personal experience in favour of generalities, I am not denying the importance of ideas in any particular novel. Precisely because his mind was saturated with ideas, James feared lest he used characters merely as illustrations of them. In this we find the central dilemma of the early novels. It was James's in the act of writing, and it plagues his characters in their relationships with one another. The question is felt on every page – who is exploiting the life of another human being? Or, to phrase it more relevantly within the problems I am considering, 'Am I guilty,' James seems always to be asking, 'of violating the dramatic freedom of this character in order to place him in some system of meaning?'

The comedy in these novels reveals how James met and tried to master his difficulty. It shows us the connection between the dramatic mode of the fiction and those general ideas that are usually discussed independently of it. This book is an attempt to account for the fact that the meanings I find in James come through the circuit and subterfuge, to borrow his phrase, of being often amused and continually entertained. James's comedy is usually on the very surface of the action and the language. That is perhaps why it has been ignored. Readers of his books sometimes act as if they are obliged to get beyond everything that is obvious, including their 'merely' personal reactions to it, so as to reach the supposedly deeper realms of meaning. As a consequence, the word 'meaning' has become associated not with what we experience as we read but merely with what we figure out after we are through.

My point throughout is that the meaning of these novels is apprehended only by our whole sensibility, including the simplest forms of excitement and amusement. This can be shown only by pointing to specific passages, to the workings of language first here and then there. 'Criticism,' Santayana remarks, 'is a serious and public function: it shows the race assimilating the individual.' The assimilation is a process rather than a single act, and criticism is public because the critic must always imagine himself asking a question of someone else: 'Do you hear that tone of voice?' or 'Does the language at this point make you feel as I do?'

Only after first asking such questions and then pointing to the evidence of how they might be answered can we begin to talk about themes and meanings with any assurance that these are actually part of our experience of reading. Naturally, this conviction has affected the writing and the form of this book. It might be felt, for example, that the second part of the first chapter should come first, since it offers an account of the ideas behind James's comedy and of the way his commitment to these ideas places him in a kinship with other American writers. But I have chosen to begin more barely – perhaps, to some, less interestingly – with an account of how *Roderick Hudson*, the first of James's novels, encourages the generalizations which I later make. Such a sequence is likely to protect us from a habit which James particularly feared – the habit of using knowledge to limit and circumscribe the dramatic vitality of the objects from which it was derived. Reverence for the mobility and drama of life is the particular province of Henry James; it is literally the heart of his comedy. His comic sense is his most effective weapon against the enemies of freedom, a word he uses repeatedly to point to a condition in which people and their feelings are not fixed, defined, and labelled, where life has preserved some of its dramatic tentativeness. To read his novels with an equal regard for the free movement of our own responses is but to meet the best demands which James made of himself and of those he most fondly imagined.

RICHARD POIRIER

Cambridge
Massachusetts
January 1959

Roderick Hudson

I

COMEDY in *Roderick Hudson*, which James considered his first novel, is the result, almost invariably, of the dramatic confrontation of two opposing kinds of sensibility. The first of these, most clearly seen in the character of Roderick, is egotistical and self-interested, and it expresses itself by an extravagant disregard for the feelings and needs of other people. The excessive and theatrical way in which characters with this kind of sensibility usually speak is an indication that their view of things is limited, that it is uncomplicated and unmodified by any consciousness that there are, possibly, other views. Their sensibilities allow them to express only those attitudes in which they have a vested interest, so that the style in which they speak shows little evidence of an unencumbered intelligence. Their talk, as a result, tends to caricature them, to turn them into Types. Roderick talks like the Young Temperamental Artist; Mrs. Light, like the Long Suffering Mother; Mr. Leavenworth, like the American Millionaire Abroad. Melodramatic is the term which can properly define this sensibility, and when the term is used in discussing this novel it is meant to refer to any stock expression of stylized intensity. The expression of intense feeling becomes stylized in *Roderick Hudson* because of the exclusion from it of language which would militate against the insistence of the person speaking that what he is saying is of supreme importance, even as we see, to the contrary, that it is narrow-minded and self-absorbed.

All of the characters in the novel express themselves melodramatically except Cecilia, Mary Garland, Christina Light, and Rowland Mallet. The last of these, and the most important by virtue of his being the observer of all the action in the novel, represents the kind of sensibility which is opposed to melodrama and its moral equivalents: fixity and confinement of awareness, and the self-regarding consistency of expression which never takes other possible ways of feeling into account.

Rowland is pre-eminently sane and reasonable, and he is above all selfless. His selflessness is apparent in his desire to help others, and he is clearly self-sacrificing in his attempts to preserve the engagement between Roderick and Mary, even though he is himself in love with her. Like all the admirable people in James, he is interested more in the quality of what he does than in its practical results. This, in James's view of conduct, is the ideally reasonable attitude towards experience. Those of his characters who have it are distinguished from those who do not by their indifference to the often painful consequences of an obedience to personal ideals. In this respect, Christina Light, a character of most perplexing deviousness, is yet one of the commendable figures in the novel. She tries to give up the social triumph of marriage to a Neapolitan Prince in order to satisfy herself that she is capable of doing something less palpably successful but more personally satisfying. In doing this she is motivated by the desire to emulate the integrity and fine intelligence which at their first meeting she recognizes in Mary Garland. Such characters as Christina and Rowland do not express themselves melodramatically. Indeed, they are given instead to irony and sarcasm in the attempt to expose the limited ambitions of those around them and the absurd intensity of their action and speech in pursuit of these ambitions. Because Rowland is the ever-present witness of all the action, the virtues which attend his sensibility are always conspicuous in the novel, and serve as a standard by which the expressions of the opposing and melodramatic sensibilities are rendered comic. This is true even when Rowland, who is not a remarkably witty man, makes no direct comment on what is happening. Because of him, the novel is a comic melodrama, the melodrama being inherent in most of the characters and much of the action, the comedy being a matter of our acceptance, through Rowland, of standards by which melodrama is judged as a vulgar expression of insufficient sensibility.

The plot of *Roderick Hudson* shows us the defeat, in terms of practical satisfaction, of Rowland and Christina by the forces of selfishness and irrationality with which they try to contend. This can be expressed in another way, which accurately enough describes the dramatic movement of the novel, by saying that comedy, which dominates the opening, is defeated by melodrama, which it tries to exorcise but which dominates the conclusion. The novel opens in Northampton, Massachusetts, where Rowland is visiting his cousin Cecilia before leaving for Europe. She introduces him to Roderick Hudson, a highly temperamental youth whose work as a sculptor shows such promise of genius that Rowland offers almost immediately to take him to Rome for study. In this he is at first opposed by Mrs. Hudson, Mr. Striker, the boy's employer, and Mary Garland, the girl who loves him. Rowland within a few days falls in love with Mary, but he tells no one, and when he learns on the voyage to Europe that Roderick successfully proposed to her just before sailing, he is put in a most uncomfortable position. He can make no avowal whatever of his own feeling, and he must, out of love for Mary, feel even more responsible for the emotional as well as the artistic security of Roderick. So far as Roderick's art is concerned, Rowland has little, at first, to worry about, and he has the pleasure of being the patron of the most promising young artist in Rome. He is less successful in keeping Roderick free of the damaging experiences of romantic and alcoholic escapades, however, and when Roderick meets Christina Light, presumably the most beautiful woman in Europe, he is the victim of an unmanageable infatuation which threatens to ruin his life, his art, and, though he never thinks of this, the happiness of his betrothed. Christina resembles Roderick in that a brilliant future is also being planned for her, not so much by herself as by someone else, her mother. Her position is somewhat different from Roderick's, however, in that her mother is not a selfless patron, as Rowland is, and she does not want the kind of career to which her mother is committing her. Regardless of Christina's wishes, Mrs. Light is determined to marry her to Prince Casamassima, but she succeeds in forcing Christina into the marriage only by revealing to her, with the threat of public exposure, that she is illegitimate. Her father is the Cavaliere who, for years, along with Mrs. Light and Christina's dog, has seemed merely a part, and an easily patronized one, of Christina's colourful entourage. In his extreme disappointment at the loss of Christina, Roderick suffers a moral and psychological breakdown, confirming the earlier prediction of the cynical artist Gloriani. He has to be taken to Florence for recuperation, where he is joined by his fiancée and his mother. Mrs. Hudson holds Rowland responsible for Roderick's difficulty. Dissatisfied with Florence, the party moves north to Switzerland where, by accident, Roderick meets Christina and her new husband. When he tells Rowland that he plans to follow Christina, there ensues a violent argument in which Rowland confesses his love for Mary and tells Roderick, finally, that he is an insufferable egotist. Roderick wanders off, and in the middle of a tempestuous Alpine storm falls or jumps to his death from a cliff. The novel ends with a brief account of Rowland's ennui after Roderick's death, as revealed by his sporadic trips to Northampton, where he sees Cecilia and, now and again, Mary Garland. He is, so he tells us at the very end, not restless but merely patient.

If the plot of the novel shows us the defeat, in terms of their practical utility, of those ideals of conduct and feeling which Rowland represents, it does so in no abstract, sentimental, or allegorical way. These ideals – selflessness, reasonableness, and a recognition that one's best aspirations might actually be served by practical failure – exist as part of our experience of the novel by being inseparable from our responses to the emotional complexity of the characters. In fact, they are often shown to be the result of a character's psychological incapacity. Christina's ideals, to cite an example, evolve not from any intellectual recognition or intuitive moral awareness on her part, but from deeper personal needs which tend to create that awareness. She decides to give up the Prince because she feels that this is the sort of superior action that Mary Garland, under similar circumstances, might perform. Such an act is typical of Christina's propensity, in her search for some ideal of noble self-realization, to assume different moral and dramatic postures in the way an actress might assume a given role. 'I think she's an actress,' remarks Madame Grandoni, 'but she believes in her part while she is playing it.'[1] It is, therefore, ironic that her most serious attempt to dramatize her idealism should be thwarted by the standard excuse of the theatrical villain: the excuse of the irregularity of birth. She is the victim of what Madame Grandoni calls, in the final revision of the novel, an

1 *Roderick Hudson* (Boston, 1876), p. 176. Hereafter the novel will be designated *R.H.*

obloquy which 'is now mere stage convention and melodrama.'[2] Her theatrical inclinations, which express a touching
desire to put herself in a position, even if it is a fictitious one,
which she can admire more than the merely socially exalted
position her mother wants for her, are precisely what make her
an easy victim of a threat of disgrace couched in such a conventionally theatrical way. In the characterization of Christina
at this early point in his career, James shows the logic behind
one of the most disturbing features of his work: the reason why
an Isabel Archer or a Hyacinth Robinson will *act* in a way
that seems destructive of the very ideals for which he has
eloquently declared himself. The apparent contradiction is,
we shall see, of crucial importance to a critical judgment of
James's art. As in the case of Christina, the given act has its
source in the same psychological anguish that creates the belief
in the ideal. In the novels before *The Bostonians*, however,
such a method of investing characters with ideals and of making
them the very standard-bearers of the author calls only for
our recognition or commendation and for little more. The
early novels do not reward excursions into Gestalt psychology.

None the less, it is not possible to show the nature of James's
achievement in this first novel or to demonstrate the way in
which comedy contributes to that achievement without seeing
how the standards which Rowland represents, the same
standards by which comic judgment is passed on most of the
action, have their source in his personal psychology and in
some of its misfortunes. The sort of calm reasonableness and
good sense which his continuous presence brings into every
scene provides, to repeat, a comic contrast to the pervasive
melodramatic action. But his rationality and tolerance are in
part suggestive of those 'powerless-feeling young men,'[3] in
Mr. Dupee's phrase, who preoccupy James in some of the
stories written before *Roderick Hudson*: John Ford of *The Story
of a Year* (1865), who relinquishes claim to his fiancée because
he might be killed in the war, the wealthy young artist of *A
Landscape Painter* (1866), whose wife understandably tells him
at the end of the story 'I am a woman, sir! Come *you* be a

2 *Roderick Hudson* (London, 1921), p. 369. Subsequent references to this
edition will be to *R.H.* rev.

3 F. W. Dupee, *Henry James* (New York, 1951), p. 61

man!'[4] and, most notably, Roger Lawrence of *Watch and Ward* (1871) who, like Rowland, is introduced at the very beginning with the information that one romantic disappointment has made him take a vow of celibacy, and who exhibits throughout the story an integrity which is obscurely associated with a fear of sexual and romantic involvement. It is not at all certain in these earlier efforts that James is aware of the psychological peculiarities of his heroes, and, whether he is or not, it is obvious that he can do no more than present them. They are peripherally stimulating without being substantially involved in the main meanings. Rowland's peculiarities are treated in a different way. They are so presented as to give those standards which he represents the concreteness of a specific emotional necessity. This may explain the careful and extended treatment, in the opening chapter, of Rowland's background and personality. Some explanation is apparently needed since, in what is the best early critical study of James, Joseph Warren Beach complains that the author takes nearly a dozen pages 'to tell us all he knows of Rowland Mallet and his antecedents – all he knows, and much more than we care to know at the time or shall ever have need for knowing.'[5]

The combination in Rowland of the dispassionate man, as in his toleration of Roderick, with the man of great unexpressed feeling, as in the reticence of his love for Mary Garland, the cast of mind which reveals itself in his insistence to Roderick on the connection between virtuous conduct and artistic success, and the temperament which submits itself to the life of reason as the way to the sources, if only by subsidizing artists, of creative beauty – these elements in James's characterization are made a part of Rowland's particular family inheritance. And that inheritance is, in turn, described as a part of what James knew to be a not uncommon American and European heritage. To that extent, Rowland's character is inescapable, his particular values being an expression of sentiments which are associated with the mellowest evidences of American Puritanism. James observes that he had originally sprung 'from rigid Puritan stock.'[6] In the passage

---

4 *A Landscape Painter* (New York, 1919), p. 67.
5 Joseph Warren Beach, *The Method of Henry James* (New Haven, 1918), p. 191.　　　　　　　　　　　　　6 *R.H.*, p. 9.

which follows this remark, the language ironically shows the modification, in the lives of Rowland's forebears, of what is generally meant by the word 'rigid.' The irony reveals what James, after Hawthorne, but with more urbane humour, could recognize as the complications behind Puritanical rigidity. Rowland considered his mother a saint, for example, not primarily because for years she stoically endured an unhappy marriage, but because at her death, though only then, she revealed that during her silence she had actually cultivated a 'private plot of sentiment.'[7] Her example may help to explain Rowland's inability to express his romantic attachments to Cecilia and to Mary as something more distinctly rooted in his personality than an abstract, and therefore dramatically un-vigorous, sense of honour. In the career of his maternal grand-father, however, there is even more persuasive evidence of the close connection between Rowland's standards of conduct and the inherited and largely unconscious elements in his motivation:

He had sprung from rigid Puritan stock, and had been brought up to think much more intently of the duties of this life than of its privileges and pleasures. His progenitors had submitted in the matter of dogmatic theology to the relaxing influences of earlier years; but if Rowland's youthful consciousness was not chilled by the menace of long punishment for brief transgression he had at least been made to feel that there ran through all things a strain of right and of wrong, as different, after all, in their complexions, as the texture, to the spiritual sense, of Sundays and week-days. His father was a chip of the primal Puritan block, a man with an icy smile and a stony frown. He had always bestowed on his son, on principle, more frowns than smiles, and if the lad had not been turned to stone himself, it was because nature had blessed him, inwardly, with a well of vivifying waters. Mrs. Mallet had been a Miss Rowland, the daughter of a retired sea-captain, once famous on the ships that sailed from Salem and Newburyport. He had brought to port many a cargo which crowned the edifice of fortunes already almost colossal, but he had also done a little sagacious trading on his own account, and he was able to retire, prematurely for so sea-worthy a maritime organism, upon a pension of his own providing. He was to be seen for a year on the Salem wharves, smoking the best tobacco and eying the seaward horizon with an inveteracy which superficial minds interpreted as a sign of re-

7 *R.H.*, p. 13.

pentance. At last, one evening, he disappeared beneath it, as he had often done before; this time, however, not as a commissioned navigator, but simply as an amateur of an observing turn likely to prove oppressive to the officer in command of the vessel. Five months later his place at home knew him again, and made the acquaintance also of a handsome, blonde young woman, of redundant contours, speaking a foreign tongue. The foreign tongue proved, after much conflicting research, to be the idiom of Amsterdam, and the young woman, which was stranger still, to be Captain Rowland's wife. Why he had gone forth so suddenly across the seas to marry her, what had happened between them before, and whether – though it was of questionable propriety for a good citizen to espouse a young person of mysterious origin, who did her hair in fantastically elaborate plaits, and in whose appearance 'figure' enjoyed such striking predominance – he would not have had a heavy weight on his conscience if he had remained an irresponsible bachelor; these questions and many others, bearing with various degrees of immediacy on the subject, were much propounded but scantily answered, and this history need not be charged with resolving them.[8]

The ironic comedy in this passage depends upon the implied contrast between the connotations, with all they allow us to anticipate about the subsequent statements, of the terms 'rigid Puritan' and 'primal Puritan block,' and the account of actual conduct, not only of the Captain but of the somewhat pruriently curious community of Salem. As I have suggested, this is essentially the method of comedy in the novel as a whole, though the terms of the contrast are different and, usually, sharper and more broadly comic in their application than they are here. This kind of comedy is, in a superficial way, reminiscent of Jane Austen. Her habit is often to introduce us to a character or a situation with an epithet or a sententious maxim, and then to qualify it ironically by subsequent dramatic action. The most ready example, the opening sentence of *Pride and Prejudice*, is no more ironically modified by what follows it than is the assertion here about 'rigid Puritan stock.' The passage in James involves a comic interplay between implication and the initial assertion. The purpose of this technique is to show the connection between seemingly disparate things: between the rigidity mentioned at the begin-

ning as a factor in Rowland's background, and the very unrigid
luxuriousness of the figure who is described at the end as one
of his direct ancestors. The humour derived from making this
connection comes close to turning his grandmother's *embon-
point* into a comic metaphor.

To see a similarity here to the manner of Jane Austen is to
recognize that, by and large, it is a similarity only in technique,
in verbal play, and in ironic modulation of tone. More interesting and more important is the fact that despite an affinity
between them in the use of certain resources of language and
grammar, Jane Austen and Henry James are quite dissimilar
in the points of view from which they see the comedy in any
particular act. In Jane Austen, the ironic variety of possible
interpretations is made possible by her adherence to a stable
set of social conventions. If we are to appreciate her comedy,
we must accept the structure of her society. This means not
that we have to read a book on Regency England, but that we
have to be convinced of the effectiveness, in the drama of the
novel, of the words by which Jane Austen represents that
society and its values. In doing this, she always addresses us
from inside the social conventions she presents. Her narrative
voice, usually witty, sometimes crisply derisive, and always
authoritative, reveals her confidence that social processes will
ultimately confirm and even enforce the good sense of her
judgments. Even when she uses a spokesman for her values
who suffers from a certain amount of social alienation, like
Fanny Price in *Mansfield Park*, Jane Austen's humour is never
the result of social attitudes impinging from outside the world
she creates. This is not true of Henry James. There will be
occasion later in this chapter to show that this difference
explains, in part, how those standards are created by which
James can render comic judgments, and serious judgments
which are not comic, upon the experience of his characters.
For the moment it is enough to remark, on the basis of this
passage, that James addresses us from outside any part of the
society with which he is dealing. Neither Rowland's grand-
father and his wife nor the town are spared the ironies which
are directed down on them from a point of detached social and
intellectual cosmopolitanism. James explicitly disavows, for
example, the kind of questions 'the neighbours' asked about

the grandfather's conduct: 'this history need not be charged with resolving them.' By contrast with James's attitude, the town is amusingly provincial – 'the foreign tongue proved, after much conflicting research, to be the idiom of Amsterdam,' and the propriety of its speculations is highly dubious. The style, rather than any assertion, establishes James's superiority to all the values expressed either by the town or by the objects of their scrutiny and judgment, Mr. and Mrs. Rowland. This is achieved partly by an exaggerated pomposity of language by which James makes fun simultaneously of the parochial suspiciousness of the town and of the provoking foreignness of Mrs. Rowland.

The peculiarity in Rowland's background is the more comic in that it is productive of pleasures not in what we might assume to be its opposition to Puritanical rigidity but actually through and by means of it. There is in Rowland's inheritance the custom, not unnoticed as a feature of Puritanism, of making moral and financial responsibility the agent of quietly nurtured and very private self-indulgence of feeling: 'He was seen for years on the Salem wharves, smoking the best tobacco and eying the seaward horizon with an inveteracy which superficial minds interpreted as a sign of repentance.' By following the straight and narrow, the 'rigid,' he comes into possession of 'redundant contours,' 'fantastically elaborate plaits.' It is exactly such a sequence – even the terminology is suggestive of sculpture – which Rowland recommends to Roderick for the production of art. The compassionately observed difference between Rowland and his grandfather is that the latter was able to act out for himself the seemingly contradictory impulses of his nature, while Rowland, we are told, is an 'awkward mixture of strong moral impulse and restless æsthetic curiosity,'[9] the observer who, like Ralph Touchett, must subsidize the kind of life he cannot lead. James's characterization of Rowland gives a psychological reality and a human solidity to standards of reason, intelligence, and selflessness. More than anyone else in the novel, Rowland has the indispensable virtue required of all of James's heroes: a capacity for caring more about the quality of an experience than about its practical rewards.

9 *R.H.*, p. 15.

It is now possible to show the techniques by which the qualities represented by Rowland are expressed through the comedy. A most useful instance of this occurs at the beginning of the novel during a conversation about Rome between Rowland and Cecilia. Here we see Rowland's own standards turned against him by his satirically minded cousin. During this conversation, Rowland does not live up to those elements in his character which make him useful to James as an observer of the action. The comedy is a means of correcting him, as it were. It is as if James were saying to us what the discussion of Rowland's characterization has already suggested: that as his observer Rowland stands for certain values of perception and spiritual generosity, but that he represents these not because James imposes them on him from the outside, so to speak, but because his very individual emotional complications find expression only in his adherence to these values. He discovers them as a result of his own psychological limitations. These limitations prevent him from being passionate either in conduct or in speech, and they keep him from being a very artistically creative person. When he fails to comprehend his own nature and pretends to be these things, he is himself rendered momentarily absurd by the same standards which make Mrs. Light continually absurd. The comedy directed against Rowland in this instance is a muted example of how in the rest of the novel comedy is used through him to evaluate conduct. Relevant to this is a significant addition to the conversation in the revised edition. To the second sentence of the quotation given below James adds to Rowland's remarks the line 'you must have noticed the almost priggish ecstasy with which those who have enjoyed it talk about it.'[10] 'Priggish ecstasy' is an embarrassingly apt description, as James in adding it might have meant to suggest, of Rowland's own tone as he nears the end of his little speech:

'I did a good many things when I was in Europe before, but I did not spend a winter in Rome. Every one assures me that this is a particular refinement of bliss; most people talk about Rome in the same way. It is evidently only a sort of idealized form of loafing: a passive life in Rome, thanks to the number and the quality of one's impressions, takes on a very reasonable likeness to activity.

10 *R.H.* rev., p. 6.

It is still lotus-eating, only you sit down at table, and the lotuses are served up on rococo china.

'It's all very well, but I have a distinct prevision of this – that if Roman life doesn't do something substantial to make you happier, it increases tenfold your liability to moral misery. It seems to me a rash thing for a sensitive soul deliberately to cultivate its sensibilities by rambling too often among the ruins of the Palatine, or riding too often in the shadow of the aqueducts. In such recreations the chords of feeling grow tense, and after-life, to spare your intellectual nerves, must play upon them with a touch as dainty as the tread of Mignon when she danced her egg-dance.'[11]

A combination of somewhat effeminate sententiousness and preciosity characterizes this speech. Rowland is, in the modern phrase, trying too hard, and Cecilia immediately catches the disconcerting pretentiousness of his tone:

'I should have said, my dear Rowland,' said Cecilia, with a laugh, 'that your nerves were tough, that your eggs were hard!'[12]

The significance of Rowland's remarks about Rome as a prevision of what happens there to Roderick is obvious enough, but I am primarily concerned with indicating how Cecilia's irony and laughter effectively prevent Rowland from laying claim to the intensities of feeling which his speech evokes. The feelings are, as his reference to Mignon unintentionally betrays, operatically theatrical. And theatricality suits Rowland's character, as Cecilia and as we know it, very clumsily.

The representative significance of this exchange between Rowland and his cousin is confirmed by another revision in the dialogue. James lets Cecilia clarify the point of her sarcasm by having her add that she takes exception to Rowland's talk about Rome 'with all recognition of your eloquence.'[13] Like many of James's revisions, this is by way of an interpretive comment which clarifies what is already dramatically suggested. Eloquence of speech, which James explicitly remarks upon in Roderick and Mrs. Light, is a stylistic symptom in *Roderick Hudson* of personal irresponsibility, of showing, through addiction to language too florid for ordinary sensible discourse, that a character has a deficient sense of his obligations to others and to the complexities of a given situation. The characters in

11 *R.H.*, pp. 6–7.   12 *R.H.*, p. 7.   13 *R.H.*, rev., p. 6.

this novel who speak most naturally and with little verbal flourish all have a feeling of attachment to things less obsessively selfish than, say, Mrs. Light's ambition for Christina.

In using style to dramatize varieties of egotism and selfishness, James has in mind something like a secular version of Mr. T. S. Eliot's idea in *After Strange Gods* that uncurbed self-expression can be an evidence of heretical sensibility, of 'powerful personality uncurbed by any institutional attachment, or submission to any objective beliefs.'[14] The relevance of Eliot's remark to *Roderick Hudson* is that he makes the point, for which he may be indebted to Matthew Arnold,[15] that stylistic disorders are an indication of moral and psychological ones. Yet it is even more interesting that Eliot's references to 'institutional attachment' and 'objective belief' are totally unsatisfactory as descriptions of the standards by which we judge so-called 'heretical' sensibility in James. Eliot is talking not about James but about Hardy, and while the relevance of such terms to Hardy is also, to my mind, very much in question, the irrelevance of them to James is not. For a standard such as 'institutional attachment,' James would substitute 'sensitivity,' 'intelligence,' and some word which would describe an attachment, largely, to an ideal of personal sacrifice; for 'objective beliefs' he would offer us the practice of art, very directly in this novel and in the stories of the nineties; and for the exposure of 'heretics' against these, he would give us the judgments of comedy.

In so far as they have any life in the novels, James's 'institutions' and 'beliefs' do not depend, in Eliot's sense, upon systems of value outside the work. They are, as in the case of Rowland, bound within dramatized human limitations and deficiencies. Thus Rowland's exchange with Cecilia, this early in the novel, is admirably contrived to accomplish two things at once: to reveal in Rowland the tendency towards self-indulgent theatricality, which his presence in the novel renders comical in others, and to purge him of it by way of showing him, and us, through a gentle irony, that such self-expression

14 T. S. Eliot, *After Strange Gods* (New York, 1934), p. 59.
15 Arnold's 'theory of style . . . was actually a theory of morality', according to Lionel Trilling, *Matthew Arnold* (New York, 1939), p. 159. See also pp. 30–31.

is neither natural for him nor to be expected of him. In this way Rowland becomes James's agent for bringing comedy to bear on any tendency towards egotistical feeling or its literary expression in melodramatic verbiage. Rowland, as I have already suggested, does not comment satirically or ironically on all the action that is to be so rendered. Very often he is personally responsible for comic observations and judgments, but more often he is used in the way Joyce in *Dubliners* will sometimes use his sensitive observers: he is present and we are aware, even when he stands apart from the action, of the way in which everything that is said might be measured, though Rowland might not be able to do the measuring, against the kind of sensibility we know him to have. In this way, James's subject in *Roderick Hudson* is like the subject of a painting, consisting always, as he remarks in the Preface, in 'the related state, to each other, of certain figures and things.'[16]

Possibly because *Roderick Hudson* has not been thought one of James's more demanding efforts, criticism has been curiously consistent in failing to see the character of Rowland as James asks us to see it or to agree to the importance of his function in the novel. There is a general tendency to refer to his 'solemnity,' as if it were an allegorical vice and not part of a complex character, and no one has seen that his 'solemnity,' for which I would substitute the word 'rationality,' is the means of creating not a solemn but a comic judgment on the action. Joseph Warren Beach, as a natural result of his objection to the amount of attention given to Rowland, expresses a resentment at 'being cheated of the experience of Roderick by having it shown us through the judicial optics of Rowland.'[17] Mr. T. S. Eliot, whose criticisms of the novel are accepted some thirty-three years later by Mr. F. W. Dupee,[18] complains without any regard to James's irony and critical discrimination in his characterization of Rowland, that James fails to 'see through the solemnity he has created in that character [and] commits the cardinal sin of failing to "detect"' him.[19] That the acceptance of such inadequate views of

16 *The Art of the Novel*, ed. R. P. Blackmur (London, 1950), p. 5.
17 Beach, p. 197.
18 See Dupee, *Henry James*, pp. 88–9.
19 T. S. Eliot, 'The Hawthorne Aspect,' in *The Question of Henry James*, ed. F. W. Dupee (London, 1947), p. 132.

Rowland has damaging consequences for an understanding of what is accomplished in the novel as a whole, and specifically by the uses of comedy, is apparent in a recent study by Mr. Leo B. Levy. Mr. Levy's book on James, called *Versions of Melodrama*, has many good observations on the melodramatic element in the novels and plays, but he fails to see, and so does Mr. Jacques Barzun in his article, 'Henry James, Melodramatist,'[20] that James uses melodrama more often than not with a comic intention. This is especially true in *Roderick Hudson*, largely because of the way in which James makes use of Rowland. If it were not for Rowland, the novel actually would be what Mr. Levy says it is, a work of 'simple, dramatic display' in which 'Roderick's attitudinizing produces the form of dramatic significance without the substance.'[21] He feels, as does Pelham Edgar,[22] that the wild irregularity of Roderick's genius is dramatized for its pictorial possibilities, and that the picture is not substantially conditioned by Rowland. Only Miss Cornelia Kelley[23] and Mr. F. R. Leavis[24] adequately consider the novel in the light of James's own assertion in the Preface that 'the centre of interest throughout *Roderick* is in Rowland Mallet's consciousness, and the drama is the very drama of that consciousness.'[25]

The explanation for so much critical misapprehension on this point, with the attendant assertions that Roderick is more dramatically compelling than Rowland or that Rowland is a fairly uninteresting, even priggish, man, is not to be found in the novel. Roderick's conduct, colourful and pathetic as it is, is also made repetitious and tedious, and he is so self-indulgently and theoretically will-less ('Do I succeed – do I fail? It doesn't depend on me'[26]) that he could not, like Milly Theale, struggling with her fate by 'contesting every inch of the road,'

20 See Dupee, *The Question of Henry James*, pp. 261–73.

21 Leo B. Levy, *Versions of Melodrama: A Study of the Fiction and Drama of Henry James*, 1865–1897 (Berkeley, 1957), pp. 18–19.

22 See Pelham Edgar, *Henry James: Man and Author* (Boston, 1927), pp. 232–7.

23 See Cornelia Kelley, *The Early Development of Henry James* (Urbana, 1930), pp. 182–94.

24 See F. R. Leavis, 'Henry James's First Novel,' *Scrutiny*, XIV (September 1947), 295–301.

25 *The Art of the Novel*, p. 16.

26 *R.H.*, p. 208.

provide the 'soul of drama.' That 'soul,' James remarks in the Preface to *Wings of the Dove*, 'is the portrayal, as we know, of a catastrophe determined in spite of oppositions.'[27] The 'oppositions' in *Roderick Hudson* are all of Rowland's making, and it may be that the novel would be more considerable if Roderick were intelligently enough engaged by his own problems not to be satisfied with excusing them by the remark that he is 'incomplete.'[28] Rowland tells us little more about Roderick's trouble, except that his incompleteness is a matter of his having no heart, and Roderick remains a mystery to himself and to us even at the end. He does not, therefore, remain insignificant, but his significance is a result of his stimulating the drama of Rowland's consciousness. That consciousness is itself incomplete, in the ways already indicated, in that it depends upon Rowland's accepting the fact that certain kinds of experience and the expression of certain depths of feeling are denied him. This restriction actually enhances his usefulness as the observer of the action. He becomes the dramatic centre of the novel by virtue of his feelings of incompleteness, and his attempt somehow to make up for his inadequacies is evidence of his capacity to contend with fate. His fate, like that of most Jamesian heroes, *is* his character. In his conception of Rowland, James seems to feel much the way Santayana[29] did when, in opposition to Bergson, he stated his preference for the life of reason despite its incompleteness:

a certain sort of life is shut out by reason, the sort that reason calls dreaming or madness; but he [Bergson] forgets that reason is a kind of life, and that of all the kinds – mystical, passionate, practical, æsthetic, intellectual – with the various degrees of light and heat, the life of reason is that which some people may prefer. I confess I am one of these.[30]

The denial to Rowland Mallet of a 'certain sort of life,' and his natural congeniality, given his background and tempera-

---

27 *The Art of the Novel*, p. 290.

28. *R.H.*, p. 234.

29 James, when asked if he would come to luncheon to meet Santayana, is reported by Logan Pearsall Smith to have replied: 'COME! I would walk across London with bare feet on the snow to meet George Santayana.' This report appears in *The Legend of the Master*, compiled by Simon Nowell-Smith (New York, 1948), p. 83.

30 George Santayana, *Winds of Doctrine* (New York, 1913), p. 29.

ment, with the life of reason is the burden of the ironies and the sympathetic discriminations which go into his characterization from the beginning of the novel. He is denied, quite expressly in the conversation with Cecilia, both eloquence and melodramatic self-expression, and it is this which gives him his place, among the characters in the novel, as a morally responsible individual.

This moral responsibility expresses itself comically through stringently literary means: by comic insinuations about what can be called the prose style of the people with whom Rowland is in contact. Rowland, with a certain literalness of mind, is not always intentionally funny about such matters, but by making use of this tendency towards literalness James very often contrives a double joke: at the expense of the person talking to Rowland and at the expense of the undeviatingly calm rationality of Rowland's view of things. An obvious example of this occurs when the Cavaliere visits him with the news that Christina has refused to marry the Prince:

'Miss Light has committed a great crime; she has plunged a dagger into the heart of her mother.'
'A dagger!' cried Rowland.
The Cavaliere patted the air an instant with his fingertips. 'I speak figuratively. She has broken off her marriage.'[31]

Quite often, however, Rowland himself should be given the credit for the ironic wit with which exaggerated expression is treated in the novel. This is especially true in his dealings with Roderick. When Roderick first appears, for example, he makes the sort of utterance which soon becomes characteristic of him: 'I can't be slow if I try,' he tells Cecilia, who has merely remarked that he walks too fast, 'there's something inside me that drives me. A restless fiend!'[32] The ironic comedy to which this remark is submitted is fairly broad, but this is not uncharacteristic of the comedy throughout the novel. Nor is it uncharacteristic that the counterpoint should be in this case between verbal exaggeration and a contrasting unintimidated calmness. The contrast is given particular emphasis by the fact that while Roderick is speaking Rowland is reclining in a hammock, pretending to allow Cecilia's child, Bessie, to rock

31 *R.H.*, p. 353. 32 *R.H.*, p. 19.

him to sleep. When he hears Roderick's evocation of the fiend, he attempts to get up – 'I want to see the gentleman with the fiend inside of him,' he tells Bessie – only to be told by the child that 'It's only Mr. Hudson.'[33]

The scene on the porch in Northampton is the first of many similar instances in which James elicits an amused scepticism towards Roderick's attitudinizing. We are encouraged to take a comic, though tolerant, view of him by the very fact that Rowland continues to do so even after he begins to express great admiration for his talent. His admiration, like Cecilia's, does not prevent his responding, with his own version of Cecilia's 'long, light, familiar laugh,' to any 'peculiarly striking piece of youthful grandiloquence.'[34] Part of the justification for Rowland's inability to take Roderick's grandiloquence seriously – to take it, that is, as an indication of dangerous egocentrism – is to be found not only in his natural tolerance of Roderick's youthfulness but also in the fact that Roderick himself seems to see the comedy inherent in his own extravagance of feeling and in the hyperbole of his expression. This is clearly the case when he tells Rowland about the interview with his mother in which he informed her of his plans to go to Rome:

'She had the advantage of me, because she formerly knew a portrait-painter at Richmond, who did her miniature in black lace mittens (you may see it on the parlor table), who used to drink raw brandy and beat his wife. I promised her that, whatever I might do to my wife, I would never beat my mother, and that as for brandy, raw or diluted, I detested it. She sat silently crying for an hour, during which I expended treasures of eloquence.'[35]

Throughout the early part of the novel and until the beginnings of Roderick's dissipation in Rome, such utterances as these are comic partly because we do not believe that they actually express anything substantial about Roderick. They reveal an excess of youthful spirit and his tendency to tell, in the manner of a boy, tall stories about himself. When he describes his parting with Mr. Striker – 'I bid good-by here, with rapture, to these four detested walls – to this living tomb' – Rowland is described as 'correcting a primary inclination to

33 *R.H.*, p. 19.   34 *R.H.*, p. 23.   35 *R.H.*, pp. 39–40.

smile.'[36] Rowland later comes to recognize that Roderick's verbal exaggeration is not a joke, a bit of gulling, but evidence instead of a deeply troubled personality and an 'extraordinary insensibility to the injurious effects of his eloquence.'[37] It does not follow as a consequence of this insight that Roderick's melodramatic speech ceases to be comically rendered, or that Rowland withholds his irony when he is confronted with it. The comedy remains essentially the same, but, as the novel continues, its significance is modified by developing dramatic circumstances. From being largely a commemoration of Roderick's 'eloquence,' as an evidence of his youthful protest about the cramping circumstances of Northampton, the comedy becomes satirically derisive of it, as an evidence of his submission to the equally cramping circumstances of his own temperament:

'Pity me, sir; pity me!' he presently cried. 'Look at this lovely world, and think what it must be to be dead in it!'
'Dead?' said Rowland.
'Dead, dead; dead and buried! Buried in an open grave, where you lie staring up at the sailing clouds, smelling the waving flowers, and hearing all nature live and grow above you! That's the way I feel!'
'I am very glad to hear it,' said Rowland. 'Death of that sort is very near to resurrection.'[38]

In this exchange Rowland is the man of literal imagination by an act of choice: his first response – 'Dead?' – has the ring of his reply to the Cavaliere's statement about Christina's plunging a dagger into her mother's heart, but here he is, as it were, exploiting his native tendency towards literalness in the interests of a sarcastic judgment upon Roderick's feeling. His final response becomes witty because he pretends to 'believe' what Roderick tells him, calmly insisting, however, on a different and equally absurd interpretation of it.

Rowland's comedy, a matter of putting his rationality at the service of dramatic irony, is similarly used to expose the theatrical verbalizations of Mrs. Light. She asks his help in forcing Christina to accept the Prince, and while doing so she describes Christina's characteristic way of handling her fiancé:

36 *R.H.*, pp. 41–2.   37 *R.H.*, p. 391.   38 *R.H.*, pp. 424–5.

'Christina has treated him as you wouldn't treat a dog. He has been insulted, outraged, persecuted! He has been driven hither and thither till he didn't know *where* he was. He has stood there where you stand – there, with his name and his millions and his devotion – as white as your handkerchief, with hot tears in his eyes, and me ready to go down on my knees to him and say, "My own sweet prince, I could kiss the ground you tread on, but it ain't *decent* that I should allow you to enter my house and expose yourself to these horrors again."'[39]

With the same tone of satiric and urbane rationality used in his replies to Roderick, the tone of a sophisticated man making very wide and innocent eyes, Rowland can only respond to Mrs. Light with the observation that 'It would seem, then, that in the interest of Prince Casamassima himself I ought to refuse to interfere.'[40]

Generally, however, it is Christina whose irony serves, in a more direct fashion than Rowland's, to expose the pretentiousness of her mother's speech and the fraudulence of the sentiments behind it. She has, in James's description, a 'languid, imperturbable indifference,'[41] which presents itself to us as a cynical and seductive version of Rowland's intelligent imperturbability. When she is sitting for Roderick, to give an instance, he remarks that Rowland had shown his disapproval of an earlier work by looking as if he were wearing a pair of tight boots. Mrs. Light immediately takes the opportunity to remark to Christina:

'Ah, my child, you'll not understand that. You never yet had a pair that were small enough.'
'It's a pity, Mr. Hudson,' said Christina gravely, 'that you could not have introduced my feet into the bust. But we can hang a pair of slippers round the neck!'[42]

The explicit expression by Rowland, and to a lesser extent by Christina, of wit and irony as a response to melodramatic speech so habituates us to the process that James can depend upon our finding comedy in exaggerated uses of language even when no one directly points it out to us. This is usually the case when a character is acting so much in defiance of reasonable and natural manners that he becomes a grotesque.

39 *R.H.*, p. 364.   40 *R.H.*, p. 365.
41 *R.H.*, p. 137.   42 *R.H.*, pp. 165–6.

In the characterization of Mrs. Light, James shows her development towards comic grotesqueness as she becomes more and
more imbued with the absolute primacy, to the exclusion of all
moderation, of her ambitions for Christina. When Christina
opposes her she complains to Rowland:

'If ever a woman was desperate, frantic, heart-broken, I am that
woman. I can't begin to tell you. To have nourished a serpent, sir,
all these years! To have lavished one's self upon a viper that turns
and stings her own poor mother! To have toiled and prayed, to
have pushed and struggled, to have eaten the bread of bitterness,
and all the rest of it, sir – and at the end of all things to find myself
at this pass. It can't be, it's too cruel, such things don't happen, the
Lord don't allow it. I'm a religious woman, sir, and the Lord
knows all about me. With his own hand he had given me his
reward! I would have lain down in the dust and let her walk over
me; I would have given her the eyes out of my head, if she had
taken a fancy to them. No, she's a cruel, wicked, heartless, unnatural girl.'[43]

This speech needs no ironic observation from Rowland or
Christina to have its comic absurdity made obvious to us. It is
a burlesque of the feelings it expresses, a fact noticeable in the
sudden failure of verbal inspiration ('and all the rest of it, sir'),
and in the obvious parodies of Biblical language. Her evocations of martyrdom and heavenly reward do more than
satirize the hysteria and pretensions of a woman corrupted by
her ambitions. They reveal something like Eliot's description
of the 'heretical sensibility' as one which is not bound in its
exorbitant self-expression to any 'institutional attachment.'
But we have seen that such phrases do not have much to do
with James, and no one would consider the comedy in Mrs.
Light's religiosity significant merely because it is blasphemous.
We are back to the question of what does give the comedy its
significance.

If Mrs. Light is a grotesque figure, then by what standards?
To say that she is grotesque by the standards of what we know
about life is not a literary judgment. The 'life' exists only in
the novel, if it is to be a part of that organized experience by
which the author makes anything resembling the complex
distinctions about conduct of which comedy is capable. This,

43 *R.H.*, p. 362.

essentially, would be James's view of the matter, and it would explain why Mrs. Light is not, by his definition, a grotesque figure in the Dickensian sense. Writing about *Our Mutual Friend* in 1865, he observes that Dickens does not, as does James himself, reveal the grotesqueness of a character by contrasting it *within* the world of the novel with representations of 'sound humanity.' The implication is that if we are to respond to the eccentrics in Dickens's novel, we ourselves must do the job of relating them to a reality which we experience not in the novel itself but in the world outside it:

What a world were this world if the world of *Our Mutual Friend* were an honest reflection of it! But a community of eccentrics is impossible. Rules alone are consistent with each other; exceptions are inconsistent. Society is maintained by natural sense and natural feeling. We cannot conceive a society in which these principles are not in some manner represented. Where in these pages are the depositaries of that intelligence without which the movement of life would cease? Who represents nature? Accepting half of Mr. Dickens's persons as intentionally grotesque, where are those exemplars of sound humanity who should afford us the proper measure of their companions' variation?[44]

'A community of eccentrics is impossible' – such a proposition is the essential *raison d'être* of *Roderick Hudson*. It explains why Rowland's consciousness is the centre of the drama; why, as it is remarked at the beginning, the comedy in the novel is given its significance by the measuring of one kind of sensibility by another, and why, finally, within each kind of sensibility James is careful to discriminate, again by the use of comedy, the kinds and degrees of 'sound humanity.'

II

Any larger observations about the significance of comedy in *Roderick Hudson* involve an account of James's relationship to an important problem in American and English fiction. This problem involves the creation in a given novel of a society

44 Unsigned review of Dickens's *Our Mutual Friend*, *The Nation*, I (December 21, 1865), 787. The review is reprinted in a very useful collection of James's essays and reviews, *The Future of the Novel*, ed. Leon Edel (New York, 1956), pp. 75–80.

which will adequately bear a resemblance to life as we know it, and which will, at the same time, be capable of involving itself in actions which give us the dramatic experience of certain values or ideas. It is possible, in terms of this problem, to make a general distinction between American and English fiction. To begin with, it is worth remarking on the uniqueness of George Eliot's announcement in 1871 that the subject of *Middlemarch* had to do with a 'certain spiritual grandeur ill-matched with the meanness of opportunity.'[45] Before George Eliot the English novel, with the exception of Charlotte Bronte,[46] did not question the belief that aspiration could be satisfied within a society that in its fictional existence was an image of society as it actually did exist, with its tranditions, manners, and suppositions about the virtues of one kind of conduct as against another. The situation in the major American novelists of the nineteenth century can be stated quite differently: individual aspiration requires for its expression a society which is only tangentially connected with the kind of society within which English novelists could dramatize the personal destinies of their heroes and heroines. As a result, the most significant body of American fiction, as it was produced by Hawthorne, Melville, and Twain, has been romantic in the sense adduced by Hawthorne in his Preface to the *Blithedale Romance* in 1852. He remarks that his

present concern with the socialist community is merely to establish a theatre, a little removed from the highway of ordinary travel, where creatures of his brain may play their phantasmagorical antics without exposing them to too close a comparison with the actual events of real lives.[47]

Hawthorne's 'theatre, a little removed' is observable even in some of his works which are involved directly with social and historical propositions, as in the best of his short stories, 'My Kinsman, Major Molineux,' where the young boy becomes aware of his American identity through a series of dream-like

45 George Eliot, *Middlemarch*, (Everyman ed.), I, xv.
46 See the excellent discussion of Charlotte Brontë in an article by George Armour Craig, 'The Unpoetic Compromise', *English Institute Essays*, 1955, ed. Mark Schorer (New York, 1956), pp. 31–41.
47 Nathaniel Hawthorne, *The Blithedale Romance*, in *Hawthorne's Works* (Boston, 1883), V, 321.

experiences and by witnessing a real but seemingly phantasmagorical pageant. Hawthorne's 'theatre' is not unlike James's
'balloon of experience' which, in his definition of 'romance'
in the Preface to *The American*, he pictures as 'tied to the earth'
by 'a rope of remarkable length.'[48] Such a conception of the
romantic removal of experience to a position where it will not
be exposed to 'too close a comparison with the actual events
of real lives' explains in large part the 'raft' of *Huckleberry Finn*,
the Pequod of *Moby Dick*, the screened 'office' within an office
of Melville's *Bartleby*, and, later, the 'woods' in *The Bear* and
the 'bull-ring' in Hemingway. Each of these places of removal
sets the stage for a reordering of the social hierarchies which
exist outside it. The reordering is accomplished in terms of
aspirations and achievements which cannot express themselves
in a society based upon practical utility and traditional manners.
In every case, however, the 'removed stage' of action, the
'balloon' is, in fact, tied to earth, to a society in the novel
which is a reproduction of the kind of society in which the
characters would ordinarily live. Huck's raft is not, for
example, cut off from civilization. He carries inside him the
vocabulary and the values of that civilization, and the dramatic
excitement of the novel is partly a linguistic one. There is a
question of Huck's being so caught up in other people's words
that he will forfeit that freedom of feeling which his idyllic
existence with Jim has given him. The novel is, in that sense,
about Huck's enslavement to the kind of world to which his
'balloon,' his raft, is tied in the hard knots of words and
phrases, and their attendant values, which bewilder him whenever he tries to unravel his impulses.

Ideally, Hawthorne's description of the method of *The
Blithedale Romance* did not mean that the experience in a work
of fiction so removed itself from comparison with 'real lives'
that the result was allegorical, with the characters disengaged
from the kinds of responsibility which would ordinarily attach
to their actions. It was a fear of this, however, which explains
why in his study of Hawthorne, published in 1879, the year
of his first extensive revision of *Roderick Hudson*, James expresses certain objections, which Miss Cornelia Kelley very
adequately describes,[49] about the tendency in Hawthorne

48 *The Art of the Novel*, p. 33.   49 See Cornelia Kelley, pp. 250–6.

towards romantic allegory. He complains, for example, that the characters in *The House of the Seven Gables* are 'figures rather than characters' and that they are 'all types, to the author's mind, of something general.'[50] James's reservations about allegory and about the grotesques in Dickens are of a piece: 'Who represents nature?'[51] This takes us to James's own literary practice. In a novel like *Roderick Hudson* he attempts to deal with the kind of experience which American fiction customarily dramatizes by removing the theatre of action from the 'highways of ordinary travel' and, at the same time, to give a strongly realistic image of society as it is normally conceived and experienced. It is my contention that in the attempt to put these two kinds of society in conjunction – the romantically removed and the realistically presented – James naturally found himself involved in the writing of comedy.

The equivalent in James of 'the theatre, a little removed' is the society of what we can call the elect, of those people of high intelligence and selflessness of whom Rowland is an example. He stands for certain qualities, it has been shown, not in any sense allegorically but as they exist in and because of distinctly realistic human frailties. His idealistic faith in the 'essential salubrity of genius'[52] is shown to be not an absolute standard, unfortunately impossible of achievement, but a delusion bred of his need to believe it. This does not make his ideal less commendable, but only the less romantic, the less 'removed' from that 'natural feeling and natural sense' which James commends in the comment on Dickens. For this reason it does not seem true in this novel, or in the world of James as a whole, that he is, in Joseph Warren Beach's phrase, like 'some visionary Platonist, [content] to refer each item of conduct to an absolute standard of the good and the beautiful.'[53] The thing that makes James's work slightly different from most of those in the idealistic and romantic tradition of Emerson, Hawthorne, and Melville, and relates him, though eccentric-ally, to Jane Austen and George Eliot, is that his 'absolute standards' can only be called 'visionary' in a very indirect way.

James is most intellectually congenial not with the aspiring visionaries, like Roderick or Isabel, but with those people who,

50 *Hawthorne* (New York, 1879), p 121.   51 See footnote 44.
52 *R.H.*, p. 47.   53 Beach, p. 149.

made wise rather than cynical by experience and by their own limitations, are optimistically dedicated to helping them out. Rowland, Valentin in *The American*, and Ralph in *The Portrait*, all occupy a middle ground between the detached visionaries, the people who are, so to speak, actually up in James's 'balloon,' and the systematized society down on the ground. Through them we see the latent ironies of the one and the comic stupidities of the other, and are witness to the tragedy which attends the necessary failure of the visionaries in their attempt to give something more than merely imagined existence to their ideals. In the consciousness of a man like Rowland – the man of many travels, the man who makes his own society, the cosmopolitan – we are shown the struggle between those who excite his imagination, as they excite James's, by seeming for some brief while really to achieve an individual fulfilment of their ideals, and those who represent conventionality and who measure individual fulfilment by the standards of social and economic practicality. The struggle is such that the excesses on either side can become comic, as in the case of Roderick, with his contempt for the suggestion that he is responsible to anything *except* his ideal. The visionaries can become as comically limited in their view of experience as those whom we might call the utilitarians. As Roderick observes of himself, in the revised edition, 'I'm an ass unless I'm an angel.'[54]

James's comedy in *Roderick Hudson* results, in large part, from his attempt to keep the 'balloon of experience' tied to the earth, to keep what he considered the necessary conjunction of the 'free' world and the 'fixed' world. The terms 'free' and 'fixed' are James's own. They occur in a passage from the Preface to *The Spoils of Poynton*, in which there is a clear indication of the connection in James's mind between comedy and the social structures which he creates in his novels:

Thus we get perhaps a vivid enough little example, in the concrete, of the general truth, for the spectator of life, that the fixed constituents of any reproducible action are the fools who minister, at the particular crisis, to the intensity of the free spirit engaged with them. The fools are interesting by contrast, by the salience they acquire, and by a hundred other of their advantages; and the free spirit, always tormented, and by no means triumphant,

54 *R.H.* rev., p. 204.

is heroic, ironic, pathetic or whatever, and, as exemplified in the record of Fleda Vetch, for instance, 'successful', only through having remained free.[55]

The terms in this passage are helpful only if we keep in mind that they should not be used for statically schematic descriptions of the way James places his characters in relation to one another. They help us to describe what is going on at 'the *particular* crisis,' and to be aware of the polarities between which, in the dramatic movement of the novel, his characters may move. The one dependably placed character is the moderate man in the middle, though we have seen in the case of Rowland that even he can be made to look foolish when he talks unlike himself. In *Roderick Hudson*, then, the term 'fixed' can apply at the beginning to Mr. Striker and to Mrs. Hudson, in the sense that they represent conventional repressions upon Roderick's freedom of movement and do so by expressing themselves in a 'fixed' and, therefore, comic way: Mr. Striker is clearly a kind of humour, the New England man of practical good sense, and Mrs. Hudson exploits all the conventions of the deserted mother. By introducing these two people with somewhat disrespectful comic phraseology, James quite literally 'fixes' them in certain peculiarities to which they, and James, are to remain confined. We take too much pleasure in Mr. Striker's oddity ever to want him to express anything but that oddity. He is described as having 'interminable legs' with which he every so often kicks the air, at the same time that he comments on the proposed advantage of Roderick's using Italian models with the observation that 'I suppose they're no better made than a good tough Yankee,'[56] and, a bit later, on Rowland's generous offer of help to Roderick, with the remark that 'I'm a self-made man, every inch of me!'[57] Similarly, Mrs. Hudson is introduced as 'empty-handed save for the pocket-handkerchief in her lap, which was held with an air of familiarity with its sadder uses.'[58] These pictorially comic introductions occur in the scene in Northampton in which the very subject of Roderick's freedom – his trip to Rome – is being discussed. The use of Mr. Striker and Mrs. Hudson as 'fixed constituents' who 'minister to the free spirit

55 *The Art of the Novel*, pp. 129–30.   56 *R.H.*, p. 55.
57 *R.H.*, p. 58.   58 *R.H.*, p. 47.

engaged with them' is a matter not only of their moral stand on Roderick's departure, but of their actual literary existence, the comic 'fixity' which James imposes upon them. Because they are as they are, Roderick, in this particular scene, is a 'free spirit,' and it is in seeing him in the context of the particular 'fools' of Northampton that Rowland can justifiably overlook his friend's excessive expressions of freedom from conventional social behaviour.

Roderick Hudson is by way of a comment on both American and English fiction with respect to their various ways of dramatizing the relationships between aspiring characters and the conventions of the society in which they live or from which they try to escape. Does a novelist, under these circumstances, merely adopt the values of the romantic rebel? And, if he does that, will he not forfeit the necessary presence in the novel of sound and realistic intelligence by which the actions of such characters can be seen with compassion but also with discrimination? Or is he to accept the conventions of a society, reproduced in the particular novel from actual life, and from that point of view regard the actions of his romantic heroes? Were he to do that, then his imagination would not even be engaged by the aspirations of such characters, by their desire to escape what George Eliot calls the 'meanness of opportunity' which traditionally constituted society has to offer. In *Roderick Hudson*, James sets the pattern for his later works by using a character like Rowland – a Mr. Allworthy who is not a country squire but a world wanderer who makes his own society wherever he happens to visit. James puts him very much in the middle, using his intelligence and his freedom from all commitments, except those of reason and selfless benevolence, as the standards by which he can direct irony in both directions, either at fixed society on the one hand or aspiring romantics on the other.

Society, as an organized pattern of conventions and of assumptions about what is worth striving for, is reduced in this novel to comic fixity – in Mr. Striker, Mrs. Hudson, Mr. Leavenworth, who is described with a comic picturesqueness not unlike that used on the latter two, and in Mrs. Light. Mrs. Light is as much a grotesque as Mr. Striker because she is equally undeviating, though more impassioned, in her belief in the value of those practical rewards which are an expression of traditional social hierarchies. On the other hand, the aspiration of a character like Roderick exerts a great appeal on James and on his elected observer, particularly when it exercises itself within the confinements by which the socially 'fixed constituents' threaten, often with good intention, to stifle it. But such aspiration is in itself the subject of comedy: of gentle and admiring irony at the innocent optimism with which it can at first express itself and of more satiric irony when it becomes egotistical self-assertion. When this happens, aspiration becomes grotesque because it violates those standards of 'natural sense and natural feeling' which James considers necessary, in his remarks on Dickens, to 'the maintenance of society.'[59] 'Society' on those terms is a very uncomplicated thing. Henry Fielding often talks about 'natural feeling,' but he also talks about affection and amiability within the limits of social status and conventions, and he does so in a way which we never find in James, unless, as in *The American*, he is being satiric. 'Natural sense and natural feeling' exist in James not in society, as it is thought of usually in the English novel, but rather in those select individuals who gather together in wholly extemporised and usually expatriate groups to form a 'society'. This 'society' exists to serve, if only by subsidy or by good talk, the cause of freedom in its disengagement from fixity, of romance in its attempt to impose itself upon realism. And it exists, too, to consider patiently why at the end of each novel the cause of freedom has somehow failed.

The two characters, Rowland and Christina, whom I have previously shown to be responsible for most of the direct verbal sarcasm and irony in the novel, are also the two who represent, in humanly fallible form, the absolute standards of full consciousness and of willingness to be selfless in the interest of an ideal. Their presence as well as their own verbal expression sets the standard by which comedy can exist in this novel. In summation of this there is a passage in the Preface to *The Princess Casamassima* which gives a clue to James's own awareness that his comedy might operate in the way I have described. James's method, to recapitulate briefly, is to have all the characters measured by their relationship to an ideal of aware-

59 See footnote 44.

ness and selflessness. While showing that even in the best of
them there are deficiencies in these virtues, he gives to those
who come closest to the ideal in any given novel the function
of providing a rationale, a pattern of feeling and intelligence,
which is like that supplied in Jane Austen by coherent social
values. By their distance from the 'society' of these highly
endowed individuals, the other characters are rendered relatively more or less comic and, at the extreme distance, grotesque. In his Preface, James is commenting on the value of
having his characters in a state of 'bewilderment,' of not having
them even at their best 'too *interpretative* of the muddle of fate,
or in other words too divinely, too priggishly clever.'[60] None
of the characters can be ideally conscious of what is going on
around him and remain humanly and dramatically useful.
But there are degrees of 'bewilderment,' and there is a kind
of stupidity which means that a character may not be 'bewildered' at all, the stupidity which keeps him from being
conscious of more significance than he can handle. Mr. Striker
is thereby less 'bewildered' by Roderick than Rowland is,
and he is perfectly right in his predictions that Roderick will
succeed no better in Rome, finally, than he did in Northampton.
Mr. Striker is right, but he is also, by James's standards,
'stupid.' James relates all this very specifically to comedy, and
gives us what, so far as I know, is his most explicit account of
the way in which his comedy reflects the seriousness of his
intentions:

The whole thing comes to depend thus on the *quality* of bewilderment characteristic of one's creature, the quality involved in the
given case or supplied by one's data. There are doubtless many
such qualities, ranging from vague and crepuscular to sharpest and
most critical; and we have but to imagine one of these latter to see
how easily – from the moment it gets its head at all – it may insist
on playing a part. There we have then at once a case of feeling, of
ever so many possible feelings, stretched across the scene like an
attached thread on which the pearls of interest are strung. There are
threads shorter and less tense, and I am far from implying that the
minor, the coarser and less fruitful forms and degrees of moral
reaction, as we may conveniently call it, may not yield lively
results. They have their subordinate, comparative, illustrative

60 *The Art of the Novel,* p. 64.

human value – that appeal of the witless which is often so penetrating. Verily even, I think, no 'story' is possible without its fools – as most of the fine painters of life, Shakespeare, Cervantes and Balzac, Fielding, Scott, Thackeray, Dickens, George Meredith, George Eliot, Jane Austen, have abundantly felt. At the same time I confess I never see the *leading* interest of any human hazard but in a consciousness (on the part of the moved and moving creature) subject to fine intensification and wide enlargement. It is as mirrored in that consciousness that the gross fools, the headlong fools, the fatal fools play their parts for us – they have much less to show us in themselves. The troubled life mostly at the center of our subject – whatever our subject, for the artistic hour, happens to be – embraces them and deals with them for its amusement and its anguish: they are apt largely indeed, on a near view, to be all the cause of its trouble. This means, exactly, that the person capable of feeling in the given case more than another of what is to be felt for it, and so serving in the highest degree to *record* it dramatically and objectively, is the only sort of person on whom we can count not to betray, to cheapen or, as we say, give away, the value and the beauty of the thing. By so much as the affair matters *for* some such individual, by so much do we get the best there is of it, and by so much as it falls within the scope of a denser and duller, a more vulgar and more shallow capacity, do we get a picture dim and meagre.[61]

To be 'capable of feeling in the given case more than another of what is to be felt for it' is to be 'free' in the best sense, 'free' from the different forms of self-absorption which are to be found in all the characters in this novel except Rowland, Christina, and Mary. They are the only ones capable of that 'enlargement' of consciousness which permits them to see that their own conduct and other people's involves complex responsibilities to an ideal of selflessness which, by the standards of most other characters in the novel, is impractical. The deeply felt expression of this ideal neutralizes what might otherwise be considered melodramatic absurdity. As a result, Rowland, without engaging our comic sense, can risk his neck climbing a rock to pick a flower for Mary when such an act, attempted earlier by Roderick for Christina, appeared madly theatrical and self-dramatizing. And so, too, we are given nothing to laugh at in the extremely melodramatic circumstances of Roderick's death – in dark and storm on the Swiss

61 *The Art of the Novel*, pp. 66–7.

Alps while his distraught and hysterical mother swoons at his absence. Even at the moment when he has at last come to see the injuriousness of his egotism, he becomes the victim of tempestuous forces which seem, as they destroy him, also to dignify, in some ultimate way, his destructive submission to the forces of irrational feeling inside him. In mourning for him, Rowland 'the most rational of men was for an hour the most passionate.'[62] The conclusion of the novel shows us how, in their imagination of what Roderick *might* be, James no less than Rowland reveals a 'consciousness subject to fine intensifications and wide enlargement.'

The ideals which are the positive standards behind the comedy are also those which allow us to be finely aware of the pathos of Roderick's death, to get the most out of it. To do that we must see beyond the excitement of the death itself to something more important: the effect upon the consciousness of Rowland Mallet. It pays to express the matter brutally – that what happens to Rowland in life is more important than Roderick's death – because James is a novelist of extraordinary toughness in giving the lie to the notion that we are obliged to 'feel' for things because they demand it of us in a loud and conventional voice. The lamentations of Mrs. Hudson at the disappearance of her son are, for example, rendered in a way that makes her coarseness of mind and emptiness of head more rather than less offensive. 'We care,' James writes in the Prefaces, 'our curiosity and our sympathy care, comparatively little for what happens to the stupid, the coarse and the blind.'[63] We pity Roderick at the end of the novel because, though he is at times all these things, he yet leaves recorded on the consciousness of Rowland Mallet some of his fineness and his promise. But the ending of the novel is such that we finally 'care, our curiosity and our sympathy care,' for what happens to Rowland. The last sentence of the novel adequately explains what happens to him: 'I assure you,' he tells Cecilia, 'I am the most patient.'[64] It is not clear whether he is patient in the expectations, which clearly will not be realized, of Mary Garland's love, or whether he is 'patient' because he expects nothing. As we shall see, this is the final plight of the characters who matter most in each of the novels

62 *R.H.*, p. 480.   63 *The Art of the Novel*, p. 62.   64 *R.H.*, p. 482.

through *The Portrait of a Lady.* It is a patience akin to death, in which fineness of impulse loses confidence in its social efficacy. This, parenthetically, explains why so many of James's good people are unmarried and remain so. That is the destiny of the hero of James's next novel, *The American,* and it is significant that there, as in *Roderick Hudson,* much of the comedy comes from the fact that at the centre of the action is a man who has such confidence in the effectiveness of his good intentions that it can be said of him, as of Rowland, that he is betrayed by his sense of humour, his willingness to suffer 'fools' because he cannot imagine that they might contaminate the value and the beauty of things in which he trusts and believes.

II

The American

I

JAMES began *The American* in Paris, the scene of the novel, in the winter of 1875, during the months when *Roderick Hudson* was ending its run in the *Atlantic Monthly*. These circumstances are important to an understanding of the similarities and differences between the two novels. It is not surprising that both, coming so close to one another in time, reveal in their comedy essentially the same biases about established society and individual aspiration. In *The American*, as in *Roderick Hudson*, comedy results, for the most part, from the dramatization of the conflict between what have been called in the previous chapter the 'free' and the 'fixed' characters. Those who are 'free,' in this case Newman, Valentin, Claire, and, to an extent, Mrs. Tristram, are people who are still exploring the possibilities of their own characters and whose perceptions are not warped by social allegiances or blighted by self-absorption. The 'fixed' characters, though they may be relatively genial, like Tom Tristram, or intelligent and sophisticated, like Madame de Bellegarde and her son Urbain, are contented with what they have, taking particular satisfaction, in the case of the Bellegardes, from a place in a conventionally constituted society. They do not endanger their self-satisfaction by any 'fine intensification or wide enlargement'[1] of consciousness such as James describes in the Preface to *The Princess Casamassima*. This sharp contrast in types of character is modified by the minor plot of the novel, but only to make the satire on Parisian society the more devastating and general. Noémie is presented as a corrupt version of a 'free' spirit – she escapes the limitations of her social and economic status by becoming a *lorette* – and her father is an ironic version of a 'fixed' one – he pretends to restrict his daughter's activity at the same time that he accepts a living from it.

Both *Roderick Hudson* and *The American* are about ambition

1 *The Art of the Novel*, p. 67.

and futility, and in each case the ultimate frustration of an ambitious ideal is mysterious and melodramatic. Roderick cannot understand why he loses Christina any more than Newman can understand why Claire must refuse to marry him. Each woman submits to the will of her mother, while in both cases the force of maternal coercion is assisted by something intimidating out of the past. This includes the irregularity of Christina's birth as well as Claire's sense not only that she is obliged to obey her mother but also that she is fated by the history of her family to accept a lifetime of unhappiness. James allows for the inference in both cases that the factors which cause the failure of hope and ambition are distinctly European – they are associated with the mysteries of tradition or, in Christina's case, with the polite form of the oldest profession. At the same time the ambition of the 'free' characters is made peculiarly American – it is a matter of securing the future by possessing the 'ideal' in some palpable form, so that Christina is the human embodiment of that 'ideal beauty' which Roderick tries to represent in his sculpture, and Claire is the necessary evidence that Newman's life has been a success. 'To make it perfect, as I see it,' he remarks with a minimum of jocularity, 'there must be a beautiful woman perched on the pile, like a statue on a monument.'[2]

The two novels are alike, finally, in the kinds of literary expression which result from the contrasts which I have briefly described. Comedy exposes and evaluates the difference between 'free' and 'fixed' characters, while melodrama results from the self-assertions of would-be 'free' characters whose ambitions are being thwarted or 'fixed' by forces over which they have no control. But here we come to an important difference between the two novels. The melodrama in *The American* is not satirized at any point, as it continually is in *Roderick Hudson*. This is but one reason why the two novels, despite their many similarities, are quite different in the *kinds* of comedy they include and in the particular emphasis which it is allowed to give to experience.

2 *The American* (Boston, 1877), p. 48. Hereafter, the novel will be designated *Am*. James revised Newman's remark only to make it even more extravagant: 'There must be a lovely being perched on the pile like some shining statue crowning some high monument,' in *The American* (London, 1921), p. 43. Subsequent references to this edition will be to *Am*. rev.

The comedy in *The American* has very little to do with melodrama, conceived as any theatrically stylized and self-indulgent expression. A character and his way of expressing himself are treated comically because of some representative social characteristic. Even when melodrama does occur in the novel it is treated in the sympathetic way that is reserved in *Roderick Hudson* only for the melodrama of Roderick's death at the end. There, and in *The American* as a whole, melodrama is accepted as a legitimate response to the reality of mystery and evil. In the chapter in which Newman has his final interview with Claire, for example, he gives 'a powerful thump with his clenched fist on his knee,'[3] delivers a 'great rap on the floor with his stick, and a long, grim laugh,'[4] sits 'looking at her with a long inarticulate murmur,' which in the revision becomes a 'wail,'[5] and strikes his heart, declaring that 'what I feel here is a glowing fire!'[6] Such conduct on Roderick's part over the loss of Christina was the object of some of James's and Rowland's wittiest irony, while in *The American* the laughter comes not from the reader or the observer, but from the very character who is being melodramatic. He is laughing 'grimly' at the discovery that reality itself is apparently melodramatic in its ultimate expressions. There is nothing approaching satiric comedy in the presentation of Newman's intensity of feeling.

This deference on the part of James to his hero is, we shall see, fully justified by the dramatic movement of the novel. But it is also a symptom of the most obvious fact about the uses of comedy in *The American*. Whenever we find it, even when it affectionately makes fun of Newman in the early scenes, it is always used to enhance the hero's character or to abuse those who fail to recognize his value. Their failure to do so, however, is made more important as a revelation of the way a fixed social position, rather than personal incapacity, has limited their sensibilities. Individuals as such are not grotesques in this novel. Society, as it is represented by Parisian aristocracy or the demi-monde of Noémie, is the grotesque image in the reflected light of which James sees certain individuals as more or less comic.

3 *Am.*, p. 358.   4 *Am.*, p. 361.
5 *Am.*, p. 366. Cf. *Am.* rev., p. 367.   6 *Am.*, p. 363.

Comedy in *The American* is almost entirely social satire. Unlike *Roderick Hudson*, where the emphasis is explicitly not upon a social or national type but upon an individual personality, *The American* is concerned with the public identity of its characters, their nationality, and their relationship to an historically observable and hierarchical Parisian society. The failure of hope and ambition in *Roderick Hudson* have nothing to do with social status or with one's being an American. Roderick's failure is a failure of character. Newman has no failings, or at least none which accumulate to determine his fate. His defeat is ascribed to the sinister workings of social cultism, not to the limitations of his intelligence. Rather than innocent or unaware, he is, to use James's terms in the Preface, 'beguiled' and 'betrayed'.[7] It cannot be called a failure of awareness that he refuses to accept the pretensions of the Bellegardes, since in James's comedy there is the evidence that we, too, are to doubt the reality of their superiority. Even his one deficiency is a part of his virtue. Because of the healthiness of his own mind he has none of the imagination which would let him see in the foreground of social manners the decadence and evil which lurks, to his ultimate undoing, in the background. He possesses the high principles of Rowland, but because, as Mr. Dupee observes,[8] he also has the animal spirits of Roderick, along with considerably more strength and confidence of will, he feels, as Rowland never does, an absolute optimism in the effectiveness of his own ambitions.

Newman, therefore, cannot reflect for us, as Rowland could, the subtleties of other people's actions and the complicated moral possibilities behind their manners. As a result, James himself is a very active character in the novel, his satiric voice being in evidence whenever his hero is treated shabbily. It thunders to his defence through the niceties of Parisian social decorum, never more characteristically than during the party given by Madame de Bellegarde to signify Newman's engagement to her daughter:

M. de Bellegarde then presented his prospective brother-in-law to some twenty other persons of both sexes, selected apparently for their typically august character. In some cases this character was written in a good round hand upon the countenance of the

7 *The Art of the Novel*, p. 22.   8 Dupee, *Henry James*, p. 98.

wearer; in others Newman was thankful for such help as his companion's impressively brief intimations contributed to the discovery of it. There were large, majestic men, and small demonstrative men; there were ugly ladies in yellow lace and quaint jewels, and pretty ladies with white shoulders from which jewels and everything else were absent. Every one gave Newman extreme attention, every one smiled, every one was charmed to make his acquaintance, every one looked at him with that soft hardness of good society which puts out its hand but keeps its fingers closed over the coin. If the marquis was going about as a bear-leader, if the fiction of Beauty and the Beast was supposed to have found its companion-piece, the general impression appeared to be that the bear was a very fair imitation of humanity. Newman found his reception among the marquis's friends very 'pleasant'; he could not have said more for it. It was pleasant to be treated with so much explicit politeness; it was pleasant to hear neatly turned civilities, with a flavor of wit, uttered from beneath carefully-shaped mustaches; it was pleasant to see clever Frenchwomen – they all seemed clever – turn their backs to their partners to get a good look at the strange American whom Claire de Cintré was to marry, and reward the object of the exhibition with a charming smile.[9]

Although Newman is himself aware that he is possibly 'behaving like a d—d fool,' he cannot reflect in any way adequate to James's purposes either the insidiousness of manner in this social occasion or the resentments which, from the style of the passage, James himself seems to feel. The word 'pleasant,' as Newman uses it, has none of the sneering bitterness that it accumulates as James repeatedly applies it to subtly inappropriate objects. The tone is strident largely because of the pattern of repetitions, not only of words but of grammatical structure. Thus, in the style itself there is a mocking exaggeration of the way in which the patronizing manners of these people depend upon the reiteration of customary form. James's tone in this brings to mind one of Dr. Sloper's reactions to Lavinia's irony: 'My dear Lavinia, do you call that irony? I call it pugilism.'[10] No one in this novel is consistently deputized, as Rowland is in *Roderick Hudson* and Ralph in *The Portrait of a Lady*, to provide a standard in the presence of which obtuseness and oddity are *rendered* comically absurd without our being told about it. As a result, James enters the fray himself, and temporarily sacrifices that detachment and superior uninvolvement which customarily distinguishes his point of view. In comparison with the comedy we find in the other early novels, even when it is openly satiric, the comedy at this point and at others in *The American* is exceptionally crude. James seems to be personally involved, even personally vengeful, and, hovering as he does in this passage on the edge of diatribe, he reveals a conspicuous though momentary failure of the emotional security which Mr. R. G. Soderberg[11] aptly describes as a defining quality of his humour. This leads to the speculation, for which there is considerable evidence, that there is a large element of self-identification in James's treatment of Newman and of his experience in Parisian society.

This is to contradict Miss Cornelia Kelley's remark, which fairly represents the views of critics before and after her, that *The American* 'is not at all autobiographic.'[12] Her notion of the relevance of autobiography to the novel is limited, however, to the verifiable facts about James's life as compared with the fictional facts of Newman's. In such a comparison it is perfectly obvious that Newman is as unlike James as it is possible for him to be. He has made his own fortune in wash-tubs and leather, he has been close to vagrancy, he is not an artist, he is not from a well-to-do family, and he is very untutored. No one would deny, however, that writers, like other men, often choose to see themselves precisely in those people whose personal histories are most unlike their own. It is part of a commendable human vanity which leads one to feel that people very different from oneself probably suffer from the same hurts or take delight in the same pleasures. So it is that Newman's obvious differences from his creator could make James the more anxious to associate himself with his particular social difficulties in Paris. What is known of James's life in that city before and during the composition of *The American* helps us to understand why his comedy is so actively and personally expended on the side of his hero. In fact, it is possible to observe in James's account of Paris and of French writers some of the explanations not only for the tone of his satire but also for

11 R. G. Soderberg, *The Comic Element in Henry James*, unpublished dissertation (Leeds University, England), p. 2.

12 Cornelia Kelley, *The Early Development of Henry James*, p. 238.

the metaphors which help to characterize the victims and the benefactors of it.

II

James went to Paris in the autumn of 1875 with the intention of settling there for several years, perhaps permanently, and he left in the autumn of the following year disgruntled with Parisian social and literary life. Two elements in any culture – social style and literary style – are always closely connected in James, even to the point where, as we see in *Roderick Hudson*, the style in which characters speak is the best indication of their moral sense of the world around them and of their place in it. There are so many suggestions of this sort in the writings of the early period that it could have been predicted in 1876 that James would at some later time (1899) explicitly observe that 'the future of fiction is intimately bound up with the future of the society that produces and consumes it.'[13] In the light of this, James's attitude towards Paris is closely connected with his view of French literature and of his own vocation. He never denies that the society of Paris had for him, as for any sensitive American, the appeal of an historically developed and richly sophisticated civilization. More often than not, however, he comments on the social atmosphere of Paris in order to show that it contributes to the moral superficiality which he finds in most of the French literature in vogue during the 1870's.

His experience in Paris is a combination of literary and social dissatisfactions, and he describes them as if they were the same thing. Writing to Howells in May 1876, he admits that he has seen almost nothing of the literary fraternity 'and there are fifty reasons why I should not become intimate with them. I don't like their wares, and they don't like any others; and besides, they are not *accueillants*.'[14] In later years, when he is remembering what it was like to talk with Flaubert, he is

13 'The Future of the Novel,' in *The Future of the Novel*, ed. Leon Edel, p. 37. Notice also James's remark in his note on Charles de Mazade, *The Nation*, XXI (December 30, 1875), 419: 'the people who put up with a corrupt government are the sort of people who write poor books.'

14 *The Letters of Henry James*, ed. Percy Lubbock (New York, 1920), I, 49.

led to the general observation that the French are 'the people
in the world one may have to go more of the way to meet
than to meet any other; and this, as it were, through their
being seated and embedded, provided for at home. . . .'[15]
Here, as in any passage in James in which people are metaphorically said to be in a fixed position ('seated and embedded'), it is suggested that the self-sufficiency of French
society and of French literary culture is not a sign of its inclusiveness but of its provincial exclusiveness. On one occasion,
as an example of this, he speaks of hearing Turgenev and
Flaubert discussing Daudet's *Jack*, and sarcastically observes,
despite his intense affection for Turgenev, that 'none of the
three had read, or knew enough English to read, *Daniel
Deronda*.'[16] So complicated are his feelings about Paris and its
preponderance of manner and artfulness that he is reported
to have warned Edward Marsh, when the latter was going
on his first trip to that city, not to be 'put off by its superficial
and external aspect,' and then to have explained that the '*true*
superficial and external aspect of Paris has a considerable
fascination,' and that Mr. Marsh is, therefore, only to be wary
of 'what I may call the superficial and external aspect *of* the
superficial and external aspect of Paris.'[17] He probably meant
to say that in his own experience he found it a fairly dangerous
place for an Anglo-Saxon, particularly for one less perceptive
than himself, like Christopher Newman.

During the period of 1875–6, while he was working on
The American, objections of this kind to the literary and social
aspects of Paris were actively forming in James's mind. Three
months after his letter to Howells, in which he seems relatively
unbothered by the fact that the literary fraternity are not
accueillants, he tells his brother William that

my last layers of resistance to a long-encroaching weariness and
satiety with the French mind and its utterance has fallen from me like
a garment. I have done with 'em, forever, and am turning English
all over. I desire only to feed on English life and the contact of
English minds – I wish greatly I knew some. Easy and smooth
flowing as life is in Paris, I would throw it over tomorrow for an
even very small chance to plant myself for a while in England. If

15 *Notes on Novelists* (New York, 1914), p. 72. 16 *Letters*, I, 42.
17 This conversation is reported in *The Legend of the Master*, p. 99.

I had but a single good friend in London I would go thither. I have got nothing important out of Paris nor am likely to. My life there makes a much more succulent figure in your letters, my mention of its thin ingredients as it comes back to me, than in my own consciousness. A good deal of Boulevard and third-rate Americanism: few retributive relations otherwise. I know the *Theatre Francais* by heart![18]

This letter was written in July 1876, a month after the first nstalment of *The American* had appeared in the *Atlantic Monthly*. It may help to explain why James is so actively sympathetic with Newman during his worst confrontations with French society, and why, to push the matter too specifically perhaps, when all of his hero's 'retributive relations' lie in ruins, it occurs to him to let Newman retire from Paris to the more Anglo-Saxon atmosphere of London and the English countryside. But the relevance to the novel of James's experience in Paris is of importance to criticism less for what it reveals about James's prejudices than for its effect on his literary expression.

A few examples have indicated that it is possible to describe James's attitude towards French literature and towards Paris, in the mid-seventies, in exactly the same terms. It might be put this way: that he respected the manner in which the French expressed themselves even as he deprecated the moral superficiality behind or within the manner. As Mr. Morris Roberts suggests in his excellent study of *Henry James's Criticism*, James had a deep admiration 'for those things in which [the French] have always excelled, technical curiosity, the exploration of the possibilities of art, critical and self-conscious discussion and experiment.'[19] Technical ingenuity for its own sake might be considered a version in the arts of highly polished manners in society. James was sensitive to the charm of both of these. Indeed, the effectiveness of technical trickery in the drama was so appealing as to make him wonder during the Paris dramatic season of 1873 if 'to become a wholesome and grateful spectacle, even the ugliest possibilities of life need anything more than rigorous exactness of presentation.'[20]

18 *Letters*, I, 51.
19 Morris Roberts, *Henry James's Criticism* (Cambridge, Mass., 1929), p. 38.
20 *Transatlantic Sketches* (Boston, 1875), p. 107.

None the less, he goes on to assert that in France as he then found it 'novel and drama alike betray an incredibly superficial perception of the moral side of life.'[21] During the intermissions of *La Dame aux Camélias* he reports that he had to take refuge in the street to laugh 'at my ease over its colossal flimsiness.'[22] James felt that what he regarded as the moral triviality of contemporary French literature was especially evident to American perceptions. In the sometimes blustering manner of his early reviews he remarks in 1868, speaking of a novel by Octave Feuillet, that 'like those of most of the best of the French romancers, his work wears, morally, to American eyes, a decidedly thin and superficial look. Men and women, in our conception, are deeper, more substantial, more self-directing.'[23] Throughout *French Poets and Novelists*, published in 1878, a year after *The American* appeared in book form, there is in almost every essay a variation on the accusation found in the unperceptive assertion that Baudelaire 'offers a rare combination of technical zeal and patience and of vicious sentiment.'[24] James ascribes this, interestingly enough, to that 'provincialism of spirit' which he thinks is characteristic of the advocates of 'art for art'. He finds a similar provincialism in those elements of French society which in *The American* believe in manners for the sake of manners, and he points to an equally vicious sentiment behind them. The imagery in some of this criticism is suggestively similar to that which will be observed in the novel. It puts an emphasis on the enclosure of morally vapid or treacherous significance within outward forms of apparent grace and beauty. Writing in December 1875 about Charles de Mazade, the literary critic for the *Revue des Deux Mondes*, he asserts that in French literature during the time of Napoleon III 'everything ran to form, and the successful books were apt to resemble little vases, skilfully moulded and chiselled, into which unclean things have been dropped.'[25]

To recall his saying that French littérateurs were not

21 *Ibid.*   22 *Ibid.*, p. 108.
23 Unsigned review of a translation of Octave Feuillet's *Camors*, *The Nation*, VII (July 30, 1868), 92–3.
24 *French Poets and Novelists* (London, 1878), p. 81.
25 Unsigned note on Charles de Mazade, *The Nation*, XXI (December 30, 1875), 419.

accueillants, that they offered few 'retributive relationships,' that they were, as in the case of Flaubert, 'embedded,' is to see why in James's opening descriptions of Newman he refers to him as 'relaxed and lounging' and as having in his face a 'blankness which is not simplicity, that look of being committed to nothing in particular, of standing in an attitude of general hospitality to the chances of life.'[26] James has in mind exactly such a figure as Newman when, in contrast to the 'seated' and 'embedded' people of Flaubert's society, he remarks with obvious pride that

We at least of the Anglo-Saxon race, more abroad in the world, perching everywhere, so far as grounds of intercourse are concerned, more vaguely and superficially, as well as less intelligently, are the more ready by that fact with inexpensive accommodations, rather conscious that these themselves forbear from the claim to fascinate, and advancing with the good nature that is the mantle of our obtuseness to any point whatever where entertainment may be offered us.[27]

In his description of the one man in the group around Flaubert who might qualify as his literary hero in the way Newman is his social hero, James uses a terminology which puts a very sharp emphasis on his largeness and openness of mind and his freedom from any fixity or confinement of view. Turgenev is made into an 'American' type, and in his essay on him in *French Poets and Novelists* he goes to some pains to stress the similarity of the Russian and American national experience. 'Russian society, like our own, is,' he remarks, 'in the process of formation.'[28] Then, too, Turgenev's novels have that 'deep moral note'[29] which James identifies with the American as distinguished from the French sensibility. By contrast, the conviction that holds Flaubert, Daudet, Zola, and de Maupassant together is 'the conviction that art and morality are two perfectly different things, and that the former has no more to do with the latter than it has with astronomy or embryology.'[30] Turgenev, whose free intelligence could not be bound by 'mere neatness of formula,'[31] felt as James did that even to ask the question about morality and art indicated a

26 *Am.,* p. 7.   27 *Notes on Novelists,* pp. 72–3.
28. *French Poets and Novelists,* p. 281.   29 *Ibid.,* p. 284.
30 *Partial Portraits* (London, 1888), p. 302.   31 *Ibid.,* p. 303.

constricted and limited view of human beings. The great artists, James remarks in his essay on Baudelaire, 'feel that the whole thinking man is one, and that to count out the moral element in one's appreciation of an artistic total is exactly as sane as it would be (if the total were a poem) to eliminate all the words in three syllables.'[32] Failure to see human character as massively as this explains why there is 'something ungenerous in [Flaubert's] genius,'[33] while Turgenev seems 'to care for more things in life, to be solicited on more sides, than any novelist save George Eliot.'[34] In his writing Turgenev contrives situations which are '*morally* interesting,' and when James uses the term moral he is thinking not of Turgenev's commitment to ethical principles but his 'deeply sympathetic sense of the wonderful complexity of our souls.'[35] Morality for James is a kind of educated cosmopolitanism of the spirit.

In summation, James's account of the social-literary life of Paris indicates that he had the direct experience of being involved within that contrast of 'fixed' and 'free' sensibilities which is the ideological basis for much of the comedy in his novels. Out of the accumulation of references from letters and from reviews written at the time of *The American* and afterwards, a picture emerges of the group around Flaubert and of Turgenev's part in it which is a duplication in actual and historical life of the relationships we find continually in the novels. Thinking of Turgenev within the literary coterie of Paris, James remarks that

It was this air that he carried about with him of feeling all the variety of life, of knowing strange and far-off things, of having an horizon in which the Parisian horizon – so familiar, so wanting in mystery, so perpetually *exploité* – easily lost itself, that distinguished him from his companions. . . . The French capital was an accident for him, not a necessity. It touched him at many points, but it let him alone at many others, and he had, with that great tradition of ventilation of the Russian mind, windows open into distances which stretched far beyond the *banlieue*.[36]

Turgenev's admirably wide and unencumbered way of looking at things is associated in James's mind with the most

32 *French Poets and Novelists*, p. 81.   33 *Partial Portraits*, p. 319.
34 *French Poets and Novelists*, p. 276.   35 *Ibid.*, p. 277.
36 *Partial Portraits*, pp. 304, 322.

admirable use anyone can make of his potential individual freedom from all forms of fixity and provinciality. Milly Theale, on the Alpine height where we first meet her, is in a 'state of uplifted and unlimited possession'[37] which from the first to the last novel, whether in a character, like Isabel Archer, or in the voice of the narrator, is always a represented ideal. It is the ideal position from which to deal with experience in life or in art, and life becomes an art for those characters who achieve it. Turgenev and James attained it in almost the same way, by being able to appeal to something beyond the circumscriptions of English and particularly of French cultivated society. They both can look beyond these to the mystery and promise of their own vast and unfinished countries. James never makes an explicit recognition of this resemblance, but it is implied in everything I have been quoting and in the similarity between the language he uses about Turgenev and the language he uses about himself. In *Partial Portraits* he says of Turgenev that 'Cosmopolite that he had become by force of circumstances, his roots had never been loosened in his native soil,'[38] and in describing to William his sense of superiority to most Englishmen he uses almost exactly the same terms about himself: '. . . to be – to have become by force of circumstances – a cosmopolitan is of necessity to be a good deal alone.'[39]

From this elevated aloneness he can see, as Turgenev can, over the 'horizons' of people who belong to established coteries, either social or literary. As a consequence, he is prone to use his comedy in defence of the romantic attitude and of individual 'freedom.' The object of the comedy may be the people who misuse or contaminate this 'freedom,' and since the idealistic aspiration for it is, in James, customarily thwarted, some of his irony, often affectionately and even begrudgingly used, is directed at such characters as Roderick, Newman, Isabel Archer, Hyacinth Robinson, and Milly Theale. But the full force of James's comedy, his broadest humour and most emphatic satire, is saved for those people, like the Bellegardes,

37 *The Wings of the Dove* (London, 1923), I, 111.
38 *Partial Portraits*, p. 292.
39 *Letters*, I, 55. This conjunction of quotations is also noticed by Daniel Lerner, 'The Influence of Turgenev on Henry James,' *Slavonic Review*, XX (American Series I, 1941), 31.

who hamper the impulse towards 'freedom' of James's heroes
and heroines. In the case of the Bellegardes, James's comedy is as
virulent as it is because his attitude towards them draws upon
a great deal of personal feeling about their representative
quality. It might be conjectured, on the basis of the account
given of his life in Paris, that the Bellegardes are to Newman
what parts of Paris were to James. Newman's attitude towards
the judgment of the society within which he must have his
own value recognized is an echo of what we have seen to be
James's own. This is especially apparent when, with every
good intention, Valentin promises not to make any unkind
allusions to what, for him, is the anomaly of a tub manufacturer
proposing to his sister, the Countess Claire de Cintré:

I do not know whether, in renouncing the mysterious opportunity to which he alluded, Bellegarde felt that he was doing something very generous. If so, he was not rewarded; his generosity
was not appreciated. Newman quite failed to recognize the young
Frenchman's power to wound his feelings, and he had now no
sense of escaping or coming off easily. He did not thank his companion even with a glance. 'My eyes are open, though,' he said,
'so far as that you have practically told me that your family and
your friends turn up their noses at me. I have never thought much
about the reasons that make it proper for people to turn up their
noses, and so I can only decide the question off-hand. Looking
at it in that way, I can't see anything in it. I simply think, if you
want to know, that I'm as good as the best. Who the best are I
don't pretend to say. I have never thought much about that either.
To tell the truth, I have always had rather a good opinion of myself; a man who is a success can't help it. But I will admit that I was
conceited. What I don't say yes to is that I don't stand high – as
high as any one else. This is a line of speculation I should not have
chosen, but you must remember you began it yourself. I should
never have dreamed that I was on the defensive, or that I had to
justify myself; but if your people will have it so, I will do my best.'[40]

Newman sounds socially naïve in this passage. But it is
apparent from the masculine clarity of his utterance and the
complete absence of anything like small-minded aggressive-
ness in the way he talks that we are to respect his overly simple
view of social distinctions. Indeed, James's ironic observations
at the beginning of the passage take Valentin to task even

40 *Am.*, pp. 146–7.

before his hero can, but essentially from the same point of view.

The only difference between Newman and James in response to the pretensions of the Bellegardes is the difference between a natural man of the world and a 'cosmopolitan by force of circumstances.' Valentin at one point tells Newman that he envies above all 'a sort of air you have of being thoroughly at home in the world.'[41] And his subsequent remark that this was the air which people are supposed to recognize in the Bellegardes partly confirms the irony, implicit in the whole novel, that Newman and not the Bellegardes represents true aristocracy both in his manners and in his sensibility. Valentin describes Newman's 'air' by using an image which has already been discussed: 'You strike me, somehow, as a man who stands at his ease, who looks at things from a height.'[42] For all this, however, he does not know what it is that he literally as well as figuratively overlooks. As with most of James's heroes, Newman's fate is sealed by his incapacity to be short-sighted. James's position is somewhat different and more secure than his hero's. In addition to having Newman's superior view of things, he also has the experience on the other side of which he can feel his superiority as a part of knowledge as well as of character. Indeed, it is the getting of such knowledge that confirms the character or destroys it. That is the choice of Newman at the end of the novel when he can either besmirch himself by telling all he knows about the Bellegardes, and so ruining them, or, in an act of profound and noble contempt, destroy his information. Until that point, however, James feels it necessary to bring his own knowledge to the defence of his hero. He does so very often in the brusque satiric manner observable, we have seen, in his description of Madame de Bellegarde's party. James's personal involvement is also apparent in the uses of metaphorical language and in the handling of comic dialogue, and this calls for a fuller consideration of the connection between literary expression in the novel and James's own Parisian experiences outside it.

III

In James's own response to Paris there is an intensely felt differentiation between its admirable but highly constricting

41 *Am.*, p. 125.   42 *Am.*, p. 126.

emphasis on social and literary techniques and, opposing this, those more humanly inclusive and aspiring qualities which he found in Turgenev and in himself. This differentiation is apparent everywhere in *The American*, but most clearly in the almost allegorical rigidity with which James places his characters in relationship to one another. It is extremely important to notice, however, that he initially assigns certain values to characters mostly through the verbal comedy with which he introduces them. James's comedy in his introductory descriptions of a character's personal appearance accomplishes two almost contradictory things: it emphasizes the representational significance of a character, but, at the same time, it prevents us, by making us laugh, from being immediately moralistic in our reactions. This is quite different from, say, the allegorical tendencies in Trollope. In *Barchester Towers* Trollope engages our interest in a very limited social issue by making us, through his descriptions of character, partisans of the 'good' side. He does so, however, with little of the modifying and complicating comedy one finds in James. Indeed, part of the pleasure in Trollope is in the ease with which we can have an uncomplicated antipathy: Harding, we are told, 'did not hate the chaplain as the archdeacon did, and as we do.'[43] In *The American*, old Madame de Bellegarde and her son Urbain, whose names make us wonder if James was not forgetting himself when he accused Trollope of being primitively satiric for calling one of his characters Quiverful,[44] are both placed in static moral positions from the moment we meet them. But James's stylistic ingenuity in describing them makes us take pleasure in those very features of their characterizations which, as the plot will reveal, are actually poisonous. Comedy is thereby a means of temporarily suspending our desire to make moral generalizations. In a way, this use of verbal surface is an imitation, in James's art, of manners in Parisian society. By using his literary art to take us in, as it were, James makes it less likely that we will misunderstand how easily Newman is deceived by social art. Like Newman, we later see that in allowing ourselves to be entertained we had missed seeing enough.

43 Anthony Trollope, *Barchester Towers* (Oxford, 1953), I, 171.
44 *Partial Portraits*, pp. 117–18.

When James dislikes a character in *The American* he does so with verbal flamboyance, particularly in his revisions of the novel, and with a colourful and hyperbolic abuse. As I have been saying, he thereby deflects those responses of disapproval which the point of the description would seem to allow. A similar use of language in characterization is what induces us in American frontier literature to admire the scoundrels, like Johnson J. Hooper's Simon Suggs, or, in Dickens, to be sometimes delighted by the characters who most appal us. Mr. H. R. Hays, if his comments on satire in the late novels are any indication, would call this 'cheating by way of technique,'[45] by which he means that James tries to hide his 'shaky values' by trickery. Such a view of the matter could only be held along with an extremely naïve conception of fiction. Dramatic literature exists only because it does 'cheat,' as philosophy does not. It does not 'reveal' attitudes to us or affirm values, it makes us *experience* certain kinds of action by making us respond to certain kinds of language. And above all it is meant to entertain us. Fiction makes us feel, if anything, the necessity of moral uncertainty when confronted with a dramatic imitation of life. This is particularly apparent if one responds to the comedy in an action. A comic description substantially lessens, though it does not remove, the tendency towards moral strictures. The reason for this is that comedy is in itself an evidence that the object or the person being dealt with is under control. There is less worry about a villain when he is the object of a jest. This may explain why in the revisions of his novels James tends to increase and heighten the comedy which he imposes on those he does not like. Having securely tied them down some years earlier, he proceeds to decorate his victims for our entertainment. Consider, for example, the initial descriptions of Tristram. In the first edition he is said to be

corpulent and rosy, and though his countenance, which was ornamented with a beautiful flaxen beard, carefully divided in the middle and brushed outward at the sides, was not remarkable for intensity of expression, he looked like a person who would willingly shake hands with any one.[46]

45 H. R. Hays, 'Henry James, the Satirist,' *Hound and Horn*, VII (April–June, 1934), 517.   46 *Am.*, p. 20.

[he] was a rather degenerate mortal. . . . People said he was sociable, but this was as much a matter of course as for a dipped sponge to expand.[47]

After the final revision, Tristram is

large, smooth, and pink, with the air of a successfully potted plant, and though his countenance, ornamented with a beautiful flaxen beard carefully divided in the middle and brushed outward at the sides, was not remarkable for intensity of expression, it was exclusive only in the degree of an open door of an hotel – it would have been closed to the undesirable.[48]

[he] had somehow found means to be degenerate without the iridescence of decay. People said he was very sociable, but this was as much a matter of course as for a dipped sponge to expand.[49]

The comparisons in this description are extravagant, especially in the revisions, where the changes may be regarded as indicating a clarification by exaggeration of what James originally implies. The revision does not suggest that James intended to change the substance of what he had originally written, but only that he wanted to intensify the comic response which is elicited by both versions. Each of them emphasizes the absurdity and vulgarity of Tristram's sociability. Indeed, part of Tristram's significance in the novel is in the way he lets us discriminate about the otherwise highly valued quality of responsiveness and openness. The metaphors, particularly in the revised form, have in common the suggestion of unintelligent absorption of whatever is offered: he is compared to a 'plant,' the 'open door of an hotel,' and a 'sponge.' His sense of what is 'undesirable' is, like that of the objects to which he is compared, determined not by intelligence but by the most simple-minded and predetermined discrimination.

The analysis of the meaning of these comic metaphors is as tiresome, even, perhaps, as unconvincing, as the analysis of most jokes. To admit this is a way of stressing the point that in the act of reading, in experiencing these passages with proper attention and excitement, we do not very seriously acknowledge the significance which analysis allows us to see in these metaphors. We do not, and James does not want us

---

47 *Am.*, p. 40.   48 *Am.* rev., p. 16.   49 *Am.* rev., p. 36.

to do so. Conceiving of a metaphor as having two parts, one of which is the picture that entertains and the other the significance that instructs, we can say that James wants us to laugh at the first rather than be solemnly concerned with the second. The significance is inescapably suggested when we look for it, particularly after the dramatic action has encouraged us to a retrospective analysis. But it is important to admit that it is retrospective. By the end of the novel our amusement at the picture has exhausted itself, and we are left with the bare meaning in its full dramatic force – Tristram's tiresome social coarseness. All the flabby promiscuity of his incomprehending mind comes out with comic outrageousness in his final remarks to Newman after Claire has been irrevocably lost:

'If I express myself strongly it is all because I love you so much; and from that point of view I may say I should as soon have thought of making up to that piece of pale high-mindedness as I should have thought of making up to the Obelisk in the Place de la Concorde.'[50]

The picture in the metaphors I have been discussing is comic to the point of slap-stick. Even the rhythm of the sentences in which the metaphors occur is that of a man who is not worried about scoundrels and who enjoys keeping them in line for us by making them look foolish. Only later are the implications of the metaphors brought into focus by the dramatic action.

The relationship between dramatic action and metaphorical patterns in this novel is, therefore, a delicate one. To analyse a metaphor at a given moment in the novel, to assign it a significance in some metaphorical pattern garnered from the novel as a whole, and then to claim as a result that the experience of that particular moment is the same as the significance heaped upon the metaphor is too pervasive a practice in literary criticism to need illustration. It is a result of such analytical procedure that comedy in James has been ignored. It has been ignored by critics who ask not 'what is it like to be reading this' but 'what does this mean,' and by 'mean' they customarily have in mind something like the content usually and properly

50 *Am.*, p. 447.

associated with non-dramatic discourse, philosophy, or sociological psychology. In talking about comedy, it is necessary to stress that in dramatic literature the primary concern of literary criticism is the *way* we apprehend the meaning, our experience of it rather than the meaning itself, abstractly considered. *The American* is in many ways both shrill and superficial in its handling of character and in the exclusion of moral and psychological complications from the kind of life which it organizes. It is saved from being wholly superficial not by its philosophical meanings but by the way in which we are allowed to apprehend them. It is made into an experience that mature readers can appreciate by its comedy, and this will become more apparent in a further discussion of its metaphors and their dramatic function.

The basic dramatic conflict is, essentially, between Newman's way of looking at life and Madame de Bellegarde's. The nature of the conflict, as well as the partisanship of James, is apparent in the descriptions of personal appearance. These descriptions are, first of all, invariably comic, though they differ as to the kind of comedy, and, second, they all involve metaphors either of seclusion, for the Bellegardes, or hospitality, for Newman and his allies. The thematic expression of things that are 'fixed' and 'free' has already been discussed as a basic feature of James's comedy. At this point in James it is not merely a principle behind his characterizations, as in *Roderick Hudson*. It is also an explicit part of his comic vocabulary. In *The American*, as I observed previously, the notion of 'free' and 'fixed' characters is expressed largely in terms of openness and enclosure, of largeness and expansion as against smallness and contraction. Madame de Bellegarde's mouth is first described as a

conservative orifice, a little pair of lips at once plump and pinched, that looked, when closed, as if they could not open wider than to swallow a gooseberry or to emit an 'Oh, dear, no!' [51]

And although the figure of Urbain is described as noble and majestic, he is said to have 'small opaque eyes,'[52] and in the revised edition his 'thin smile' is made into the comic picture of 'a smile that affected [Newman] as the scraping of a

51 *Am.*, p. 168. 52 *Am.*, p. 173.

match that doesn't light.'[53] In his habit of walking up and down the room he is compared to 'a sentinel at the door of some smooth-fronted citadel of the proprieties.'[54] Similarly, their house in Paris has a face 'as impassive and as suggestive of the concentration of privacy within as the blank walls of Eastern seraglios – it answered to Newman's conception of a convent.'[55] There are many such comparisons in the novel, all of them in sharp contrast to the impression we are given of Newman, who, in the first page, is lounging 'with legs outstretched' in the spacious Salon Carré of the Louvre. Unlike the Bellegardes, he confidently offers to let the world 'go ahead and try me,' a phrase of which he is extremely fond. He can wittily remark to Tristram, who selected Newman's rooms with an eye to the latter's social standing, that 'I didn't know I "stood" socially at all – I thought I only sat around informally, rather sprawling than anything else.'[56] Such images, when they have to do with Newman, are like those which help characterize the good Americans in *The Ambassadors*, where Maria Gostrey describes her expatriate countrymen by the humorously deprecating remark: 'We're abysmal – but may we never be less so!'[57]

The calculation with which James discriminates between characters in terms of 'open' and 'closed' sensibilities, and the way in which these discriminations are made initially by his metaphorical descriptions of appearance, is apparent in the introductions of Claire and Valentin. Both share this quality of 'openness,' of 'general hospitality to the chances of life,' which characterizes the hero in the first scene of the novel. They are, as it were, imprisoned Americans, and Newman tries literally to set them both free. James's comedy in describing them is unlike that in his descriptions of the older Bellegardes. Comedy in this instance is not satiric, and it is not meant to make us laugh. But like James's satiric comedy it has its source in highly energetic verbal exaggeration. The metaphors are periphrastic, and there is a delight in their extreme inventiveness and oddity. Akin to this sort of comedy

53 *Am.*, p. 203. Cf. *Am.* rev., p. 197.   54 *Am.*, p. 229.
55 *Am.*, pp. 56–7.   56 *Am.* rev., p. 93. See also *Am.*, p. 98.
57 *The Ambassadors* (London, 1923), II, 117. For a discussion of this particular image in the later James see Frederick C. Crews, *The Tragedy of Manners* (New Haven, 1957), p. 40 *passim*.

is the comic pleasure, even sometimes the laughter, produced by any display of exorbitant human dexterity. There is a kind of gay sportiveness in the metaphors by which James expresses his pleasure in Claire and Valentin. In his descriptions of Tristram and the older Bellegardes, the extravagance of metaphor absorbs morally serious implications in comic absurdity. Similarly, when James likes a character in this novel his hyperboles tend to take us beyond discriminations about him and into a pleasurable idealization. In these instances, as in the satiric characterizations, James's revisions indicate that he enjoyed extemporizing on distinguishing features which he had essentially created in the first edition. As an example, Claire's grey eyes in the first edition are said to be 'gentle and intelligent,'[58] and they become in the final revision 'like a brace of deputed and garlanded maidens waiting with a compliment at the gate of a city.'[59] Such a change once again puts a stress through metaphor on 'hospitality,' the repeatedly emphasized characteristic of the 'American' figures in the novel. Later, Claire's openness, her capacity for experience, is contrasted explicitly with her mother's stultifying completedness of character in a metaphor which makes it plain that, for Newman, Claire is a kind of American:

Madame de Cintré's face had, to Newman's eye, a range of expression as delightfully vast as the wind-streaked, cloud-flecked distance on a Western prairie. But her mother's white, intense, respectable countenance, with its formal gaze, and its circumscribed smile, suggested a document signed and sealed; a thing of parchment, ink, and ruled lines.[60]

Valentin is also associated with America in the hero's mind because Newman thinks it a shame that his friend's movements should be confined to the intertwining streets of Paris 'when over there in America one's promenade was a continent,'[61] and he tries to arrange things so that Valentin will have an American future as surely as Claire will. As Newman sees him, he resembles his sister

not in feature, but in the expression of his clear bright eyes, completely void of introspection, and in the way he smiled. The great

58 *Am.*, p. III.
60 *Am.*, p. 168.
59 *Am.* rev., p. 106.
61 *Am.*, p. 301.

C.S.H.J.—5

point of his face was that it was intensely alive – frankly, ardently, gallantly alive. The look of it was like a bell, of which the handle might have been in the young man's soul: at a touch of the handle it rang with a loud, silver sound. There was something in his quick, light brown eye which assured you that he was not economising his consciousness. He was not living in a corner of it to spare the furniture of the rest. He was squarely encamped in the centre and he was keeping open house.[62]

This passage and others like it illustrate a quality in James which is customarily ignored. Everyone knows that he is delicately complex in what he says, but it is seldom observed that we are led to respond to the refinements of his sensibility by very loud and broad verbal effects. It can be said of his language, particularly of his images, what he himself said of the 'vibration' which he felt from a meeting with George Eliot:

It was doubtless even excessive in proportion to its cause – yet in what else but that consisted the force and the use of vibrations? It was by their excess that one knew them for such, as one for that matter only knew things in general worth knowing.[63]

The excessiveness in James's style, particularly in his images, is in part expressive of that melodramatic inclination which many, especially Mr. Leo B. Levy and Mr. Jacques Barzun, have noticed. It has not been noticed, however, that this same excessiveness tends to satirize the melodrama it creates, as in *Roderick Hudson,* or that its effect on the evaluation of character in *The American,* even when its final implications are most serious, is, in our immediate response, largely comic. While Mr. Dupee is essentially correct in observing that James's 'remarkable metaphors'[64] proliferate in the period of the 1890's, it should be observed that the tendency and very often the practice begins in the novels of the seventies. It is hard to forget Fleda's response in *The Spoils of Poynton* to one of Mrs. Gareth's speeches about Owen, 'as if it had been the shake of a tambourine borne toward her from a gypsy dancer.'[65] But it

62 *Am.,* pp. 118–19.
63 *Henry James Autobiography,* ed. Frederick W. Dupee (New York, 1956), p. 577.
64 Dupee, *Henry James,* p. 193.
65 *The Spoils of Poynton* (London, 1922), p. 194.

should also be remembered that in the first edition of *Roderick Hudson* Mr. Leavenworth's face 'bore a certain resemblance to a large parlor with a very florid carpet, but no pictures on the walls.'[66] Such images, and those which either occur in the first edition of *The American* or are implicitly there ready to be coined in the revision, spring from a very diverse literary tradition.

Miss Constance Rourke's account of the literary traditions available to James at the time of *The American* is well known and highly respected. It involves, however, a number of rather surprising errors. She remarks, for example, that James's originality resides partly in his showing 'that defeat had become at last an essential part of the national portraiture,' where 'triumph had hitherto been the appointed destiny.'[67] All of Melville, Hawthorne, and the best of Twain is, by this proposition, disregarded. Furthermore, it is apparent from what has been said so far about James's involvement in the literary world of Paris and London that it is unnecessary and unprofitable to look for the sources of his literary expression wholly in American literature. Miss Rourke explains his comedy as if it were indebted mostly to popular American humour and some of its raciness to the spectacular displays put on by Barnum. I am not questioning the fact that James was aware of the literary enormities practised by writers in his native idiom. But awareness is no guarantee that he was substantially influenced by them. His knowledge of frontier idiom is apparent in a review of *Marian Rooke*, where he accuses Henry D. Sedley of 'using a form of the traditional Sam Slick dialect, in which all the humorous quaintness is omitted and all the extravagent coarseness is retained.'[68] And he explains Newman's ability to 'top' Valentin's anecdotes by the fact that

Newman had sat with Western humorists in knots, round cast-iron stoves, and seen 'tall' stories grow taller without toppling over, and his own imagination had learned the trick of piling up consistent wonders.[69]

66 *R.H.*, p. 173.
67 Constance Rourke, *American Humor* (New York, 1931), pp. 255–6.
68 Unsigned review of Henry D. Sedley's *Marian Rooke*, *The Nation*, II (February 22, 1866), 248.   69 *Am.*, p. 130.

Given what we know about James's taste and reading, however, it is likely that he was influenced more by Dickens than by American popular humour in his creation of highly imaginative images. There is also a good chance that he learned a lot about descriptive exaggeration from Swift. In 1874, reviewing a novel by J. W. de Forest, he quotes an example of what he considers 'color laid on not exactly with a camel's-hair brush':

his pulpy pink face wore an air of abiding perplexity which rivalled that of his Dundrearyish friend Ironman. At times it seemed as if his large watery features would decompose entirely with irresolution, and come to resemble a strawberry-ice which has been exposed to too high a temperature.

Of this James remarks that

The author's touch, in this and similar cases, has more energy than delicacy, and even the energy aims rather wild. Did Mr. de Forest refresh his memory of Swift before writing the adventures of John Vane? He would have been reminded that though the great master of political satire is often coarse and ferocious, he is still oftener keenly ingenious.[70]

James himself is 'keenly ingenious' in the manner of Swift. As applied to Swift, the term means, for one thing, that *Gulliver's Travels* may be read as a fanciful and amusing children's book or as a serious allegory. Ideally, it is read as both simultaneously. Essentially the same kind of ingenuity is apparent in the workings of James's metaphors. The *point* of what he says in a particular figure comes to life after we have been entertained by it. He is more like Swift and less like Dickens in this particular use of language, because there always is a point behind the entertainment offered by his hyperbole. I have already commented on the effect of this in the working out of the plot of *The American* and in the control of our reactions to characters until that plot evolves. The profit of James's technique – of inviting us more to the enjoyment at a given point of the excessiveness of his descriptions than to solemnity about their significance – is clear enough when we think of Madame de Bellegarde and her friends.

70 Unsigned review of J. W. de Forest's *Honest John Vane*, *The Nation*, XIX (December 31, 1874), 441.

While we recognize their malevolence from the moment they appear, we do not know whether to take it as part of a comedy of manners or as a portent of disaster. Both possibilities are there in the language, the first in the picture of the metaphors which we 'get' as we read along; the second, in the significance of the metaphors which we fully grasp only when the action is completed. If it is to be a comedy of manners, the novel will be about the achievement of romantic ambition; if it is to be a tragedy of manners, to borrow a phrase from Mr. Frederick C. Crews,[71] it will be about the futility of ambition. The progress of the novel is from the one to the other, which is to say that the novel moves from comic emphasis on the entertaining aspects of the metaphors to seriously melodramatic emphasis on their portentous significance. The function of James's comedy is to keep us in suspense much of the time as to which of these outcomes is the more likely. Looked at another way, the novel is about the conflict between the predominance of the pleasant images about openness and the threatening images about enclosure. The images of contraction and withdrawal which invest every description of the Bellegarde family and their properties lend an almost warlike quality to Newman's desire 'to expand, without bothering about it – without shiftless timidity on one side, or loquacious eagerness on the other – to the full compass of what he would have called a "pleasant" experience.'[72] In doing so within the Bellegarde family, Newman provides what Valentin tells him at the outset will be an 'entertaining' spectacle. We can now turn to that – to the comedy in the novel which depends less on James's metaphors than on dialogue and dramatic confrontation.

The comic scenes and dialogue in the novel result in large part from the dramatic conflict between Newman's self-confident frankness and the adroit and devious sophistication of the Bellegardes, or, to repeat the terms, between 'open' and 'closed' social behaviour. Much of the comedy and, through it, some of the most attractive expressions of Newman's character occur because he is too spontaneously and innately superior to be able to recognize the evidences in social conduct of contrived and devious nastiness. When Valentin tells him that his inability to recognize aristocratic social superiority will make his attempts to win Claire 'something of a spectacle,' he replies, ironically, that 'it *is* a pity that I don't understand you. I shall lose some very good jokes.'[73] At the outset, the 'spectacle' reveals the capacity of the Bellegardes for witty and pointed conversation, and even when their perfidy is most apparent, near the end of the novel, the irony and sarcasm in which they and their friends indulge remains highly polished and controlled.

The even tone of comic social discourse in the novel, even though there is a progressive intensification of feeling behind it, suggests a number of things. In the first place it illustrates in the French characters the beguiling artfulness of persistent social custom and manner. Newman admires this in Madame de Bellegarde even as James admired the technique of Flaubert, though he found the substance wanting. When Newman confronts her with evidence that she is a murderer, she merely gives a small cough, 'a piece of dissimulation which struck Newman as really heroic,' and which brings from her less impressive elder son the question, 'Dear mother, does this stuff amuse you so much?'[74] In the second place, the consistency of social poise in the Bellegardes and their circle, with its attendant conversational witticisms, has almost the same effect on the reader as the use of comic metaphors. It keeps us from feeling certain that we really do know what is going on behind it. The discrepancy between manners and reality in the social action of the novel is like the discrepancy between the comic suggestions in James's descriptions of Madame de Bellegarde and the dangerous realities behind them. Thus, the comedy which comes from dramatic dialogue contributes as much as the comedy in the metaphors to putting us off, as it were, and to making what finally does happen into a 'mystery' which is only less surprising to us than to Newman. In illustration of this, there are three scenes involving witty social discourse which reward attention. They occur roughly at the beginning, the middle, and the end of the novel, and there is little variation between the first and the third, even though the conditions of the action have radically changed.

The first of these scenes occurs when Valentin introduces

Newman to his mother, his brother, and his sister-in-law. For us, as for Newman, the centre of interest is the old Marquise, Madame de Bellegarde. Newman has been warned by Valentin not to expect to purchase her favour by being funny: 'Take warning by me,' he cautions his friend, 'she never laughs.'[75] The effect of her constraining influence is apparent less on Valentin, whom she considers Newman's *amuseur*, than on her older and favourite son Urbain. 'He is much better than this one,' she tells Newman, 'but he will not amuse you.'[76] The fact that neither Urbain nor his mother is very responsive to other people's humour no more prevents them from being comic themselves than it prevents Jaggers in *Great Expectations*, a man who never laughs. However, their humour is of a particular kind. Notably in the case of Urbain, the characteristic wit accepted in the Bellegarde household has the taint of being the product of punctiliously learned, but slightly defensive, high social manner. He and his mother object especially to the comic tone of Valentin. For them, he is a kind of 'lord of misrule' because he can so freely and pointedly adopt what Santayana defines as the 'comic mask – the irresponsible, complete, extreme expression of each moment.'[77]

Madame de Bellegarde's objection to spontaneous and free comedy finds expression in her own considerable wittiness. Indeed, she uses comedy in defence of the fixity of her position, and she satirically 'bristles,' as James might say, to fend off the comic improvisations by which Valentin and Newman display their different kinds of irreverence for her social posturing. The meeting between Newman and Madame de Bellegarde is therefore a contrast of the comic attitudes which are characteristic of the two types of characters that have been discussed, the 'fixed' or 'closed' characters and the 'free' or 'open' ones. The result of the meeting is a social victory for the Bellegardes and a moral victory for Newman. She effectively keeps him in place, but, compared with his expansive good nature and his impressive indifference to making fun of himself, which is a sign of his considerable strength, her self-assured witticisms are stagy and theatrical. It is as if she were addressing not this particular man but a version of

75 *Am.*, p. 166.   76 *Am.*, p. 172.
77 George Santayana, *Soliloquies in England* (New York, 1922), p. 137.

him which she might have found in a bad satiric novel, a
'literary' version of the untutored man of business who is
something even odder, an American.

Some of Madame de Bellegarde's wit is the effect of a pretended vagueness, by which she implies that she cannot really
believe in Newman's reality:

'You are an American?' she said presently. 'I have seen several
Americans.'

'There are several in Paris,' said Newman jocosely.

'Oh, really?' said Madame de Bellegarde. 'It was in England I
saw these, or somewhere else; not in Paris. I think it must have been
in the Pyrenees, many years ago. I am told your ladies are very
pretty. One of these ladies was very pretty! such a wonderful com-
plexion! She presented me a note of introduction from some one –
I forget whom – and she sent with it a note of her own. I kept her
letter a long while afterwards, it was so strangely expressed. I used
to know some of the phrases by heart. But I have forgotten them
now, it is so many years ago. Since then I have seen no more
Americans. I think my daughter-in-law has; she is a great gad-
about, she sees every one.'[78]

Madame de Bellegarde is certain of only one thing: that she
could not have met an American in Paris, the same Paris
where for James the literary people were not *accueillants*. For
the rest she is very uncertain: 'I think,' 'I am told,' 'I used to
know,' 'I have forgotten.' This is very different from her
customary idiom, especially from the way she talks later in the
scene when Newman expresses his desire to marry her daughter.
She responds to this proposition with impressive brevity, by
merely shaking her head and pronouncing a soft 'no,' while to
his reminder that he is very rich she simply articulates 'how
rich?'

Madame de Bellegarde is a worthy opponent for a man
who has seen a free-fight in Arkansas. She is a woman of for-
midable personal force and intelligence, and her vagueness in
this conversation, like all her gestures, is a calculated effort
to make people feel her powerful self-sufficiency. She means to
suggest to Newman the extraordinary peculiarity, so far as she
is concerned, of anyone's being an American, and she also
means to suggest that the peculiarity is of no interest to her.

It is simply not an imaginable part of her world. Americans, so the rhythm and substance of her comment implies, are hard to remember because no civilized society (she saw her last American in the mountains of the Pyrenees) has anything that resembles them. By the time she is finished with her references to 'these', 'your women', and 'strangely expressed', Americans have become anthropological specimens. She thereby lends weight to the later suppositions of her friends that in his court-ship of her daughter Newman is the 'beast' in a re-enactment of 'Beauty and the Beast'. Newman's willing participation in the comedy, his 'jocosity', defeats the implication that he is a barbarian, though his humour is slightly barbaric when measured against the brilliant dramatic skill of Madame de Bellegarde. Her talk is evidence of highly developed cultiva-tion, even though it is put to the uses here of an imperturbable and polished bitchery. It is a social version of that 'technical' skill which James admired in French literature.

In the conversation just discussed James manifests in his use of dialogue the same intention which he shows in his use of comic metaphors. Because we enjoy Madame de Bellegarde and because James contrives to make us find her entertaining, we tend to suspend moral disapproval of the way she treats Newman. To appreciate the value of this scene largely as entertainment is to have that 'want of "moral reaction"'[79] of which Newman himself is accused by Babcock. Babcock, who anticipates the Wentworths in *The Europeans*, and is treated with an equally tender satire, cannot bear what he considers Newman's 'gross intellectual hospitality'.[80] Just such hospitality lets us, no less than Newman, enjoy Madame de Bellegarde in spite of our suspicions about her ultimate culp-ability. She is marvellously clever and entertaining at the same time that she is making insinuations which are to be the very justifications for her ultimate rejection of the hero.

This brings us to a point of some importance. Comedy as it is being used here has the function of forestalling our con-cerns about the morality of characters, conceived of as in-dividuals, while it stimulates our interest in them as repre-sentatives of certain kinds of social conduct. The psychology of Madame de Bellegarde is no less superficially created than

79 *Am.*, p. 86.   80 *Ibid.*

that of the other characters in *The American*. But this does not mean that her status, her embodiment of a social type, is to be experienced with anything less than a complex variety of reactions. We might say that we think less of her than of the rôle she plays, and that our admiration results from the highly intelligent comedy which she creates. She is not meeting a man named Newman, she is playing a part in the social *occasion* of meeting an American millionaire. James's comedy as well as her own draws attention to her social as distinguished from her psychological identity. Our interest is engaged more by her manners, which seem to have the weight of a whole society behind them, than by any of her more personal eccentricities. We are made willing to be morally deferential because such a scene as this is presented less as a dramatic meeting which is significant for the individuals involved than as a show-piece put on to illustrate their permanent social differentiations. It is not unlike watching a morality play, wholly secularized and then presented as a musical comedy.

Despite the satire to which Newman is submitted by Madame de Bellegarde's remarks, and despite his inability to grasp fully the abusiveness of her wit, Newman emerges from this conversation and from the one that follows it in this secne even more of an idealized American than before. This may seem odd on the face of it, since if, as James puts it in *The Lesson of Balzac*, we 'accept the color of the air' with which 'the author suffuses his picture',[81] we must accept James's own high estimation of witty conversation. We admire Newman, as a result, not because he is impressive in his own salon, but because he is impressive in the Bellegardes'. The fact that we are asked to appreciate Madame de Bellegarde necessarily disposes us to respect relatively supple responses to conversational ragging. That Newman emerges unscathed is partly to be ascribed, ironically, to his incomprehension. His own self-expression is never warped by a mean-minded suspiciousness that he is being insulted. As a result he appears to be indifferent in a grandly aristocratic way. He interprets all of the carefully contrived jibes as pleasant and even silly jokes.

In the scene being discussed, then, both Newman and the Bellegardes have their most attractive capacities fully engaged.

81 *The Question of Our Speech, The Lesson of Balzac* (Boston, 1905), p. 80.

The result, as the scene nears its conclusion, is one of the most charming conversations in the novel. Newman has just indiscreetly remarked to this family of unemployed aristocrats that he is sometimes conscious of having too much time on his hands. He is unfortunately not proficient in literature, he tells them, and he is accustomed in any case to daily business activity: 'I began to earn my living when I was almost a baby.' And he adds, without any intentional sarcasm, that 'elegant leisure comes hard.' This speech is followed by an understandable and profound silence, after which the conversation continues:

'You began to earn your living when you were a mere baby?' said the marquise.

'Hardly more – a small boy.'

'You say you are not fond of books,' said M. de Bellegarde; 'but you must do yourself the justice to remember that your studies were interrupted early.'

'That is very true; on my tenth birthday I stopped going to school. I thought it was a grand way to keep it. But I picked up some information afterwards,' said Newman reassuringly.

'You have some sisters?' asked Madame de Bellegarde.

'Yes, two sisters. Splendid women!'

'I hope that for them the hardships of life commenced less early.'

'They married very early, if you call that a hardship, as girls do in our Western country. One of them is married to the owner of the largest india-rubber house in the West.'

'Ah, you make houses also of india-rubber?' inquired the marquise.

'You can stretch them as your family increases,' said young Madame de Bellegarde, who was muffling herself in a long white shawl.

Newman indulged in a burst of hilarity, and explained that the house in which his brother-in-law lived was a large wooden structure, but that he manufactured and sold india-rubber on a colossal scale.[82]

Newman's 'burst of hilarity' is not ours. He laughs at what he takes to be the marquise's European gullibility about the wonders of the American West, or at least that is a way of taking his unnecessary explanation that the houses are wooden. We, on the other hand, laugh at the sophisticated play of

[82] *Am.*, pp. 176–77.

mind, the vaudevillian inventiveness by which the Bellegardes
not unpleasantly make fun of him. Nor is the fun entirely
without point on James's part, when we notice that the dramatic conflict is adroitly characterized within the terms of the
metaphor of 'open' and 'closed' by the juxtaposition of the
expanding American rubber house with the 'muffled' daughter-
in-law of the Marquise.

While we see in the comedy the essential and profound
differences between Newman and the Bellegardes, he sees only
those differences which might be explained away. The reader's
view of social differentiations is, thereby, essentially Valentin's.
He is a partisan of Newman, but with a clear sense of the
comedy of his position. Even though in temperament he is
similar to Newman, he first calls on him, because, given their
backgrounds, they are 'too different to quarrel'.[83] At first he
will not take his desire to marry Claire seriously. 'You are not
noble, for instance,' he remarks, to which Newman exclaims,
'The devil I am not'![84] In finally agreeing to further his friend's
cause, he is expressing as much positive aversion for his mother
and brother as fondness for the American intruder. His motive
is partly in the anticipation of the amusement he will find in
observing the encounters between people who are so abrasively
dissimilar. In this respect he is like Mrs. Tristram who, in first
suggesting the match, did so, she rather cruelly admits at the
end, out of 'curiosity' as to 'whether such a marriage could
actually take place'.[85] Both Mrs. Tristram and Valentin have a
strong sense of personal futility, of the waste of their own lives,
which tends to make them want to experiment with the lives
of other people.

Even for those who are most anxious to help him, therefore,
Newman is, as it were, on stage when he confronts the heads
of the Bellegarde family and their friends. All his friends are
more aware than he is of what is going on. Being a part of the
world of sophistication to which we, through James's style,
are given an entrance, they support Newman but want also
to see if he will measure up to the test. The test is met in such
scenes as this first meeting with the Bellegarde family. In the
next meeting to be considered, the issues of the confrontation
are more sharply apparent than in the first. But if the wit is

83 *Am.*, p. 122.   84 *Am.*, p. 143.   85 *Am.*, p. 448.

slightly more sarcastic it is only because Newman, with the aid of Valentin, has to deal with Urbain, a son much less clever and self-assured than his mother. For the most part, the general tenor of the social comedy remains essentially what it was in the in the first scene, despite the fact that Newman would like to get beyond mannered talk and into plain speech.

In this meeting Newman is told that the Bellegardes will allow Claire to listen to his proposals. Only Valentin, Newman, and Urbain are present, with Valentin acting as a comic *raisonneur*. During their conversation, he continually translates Urbain's snobbish insinuations into language plain enough to expose their potential vulgarity. This naturally infuriates the elder brother, since to indicate the necessity for clarification, as Valentin does, is to grant that Newman is justified in being confused by the mystique of social 'differences'. It is to suggest that the elaborate manners of the Bellegardes do not necessarily express any objective reality. To put the matter generally, if we do not accept the validity of a claim to superiority, then all expressions of it become comic. This is especially true when a person's unjustified confidence is so smug as to make him assured that everyone will naturally recognize his superiority. With such presumption to status comes the comic illusion that it need only be *suggested* to be realized, and that the proof of one's security of position lies in the very indirection of high social manners. To those who do not allow the claim in the first place the manners seem foolishly affected.

This is roughly what Fielding has in mind in *Joseph Andrews* when he observes that 'the only source of the true Ridiculous (as it seems to me) is affectation,' and that the causes of affectation are either vanity or hypocrisy.[86] Both of these emerge during this scene as particular characteristics of Urbain, but they are revealed to us not by Newman but by Valentin. He is aware, as Newman could not be, of what aristocracy could mean and has meant in his ancient family. More to the point, he is also aware that Urbain's willingness to accommodate Newman is a matter of very cold and vulgar reality, the desire, in this old but impoverished family, for a fortune. As the conversation begins Valentin tells Newman that at the family conference in which his proposal to Claire was discussed:

86 Henry Fielding, *Joseph Andrews* (Oxford, 1934), p. 5.

My mother and the marquis sat at a table covered with green cloth; my sister-in-law and I were on a bench against the wall. It was like a committee at the Corps Législatif. We were called up, one after the other, to testify. We spoke of you very handsomely. Madame de Bellegarde said that if she had not been told who you were, she would have taken you for a duke – an American duke, the Duke of California. I said that I could warrant you grateful for the smallest favors – modest, humble, unassuming. I was sure that you would know your own place, always, and never give us occasion to remind you of certain differences. After all, you couldn't help it if you were not a duke. There were none in your country; but if there had been, it was certain that, smart and active as you are, you would have got the pick of the titles. At this point I was ordered to sit down, but I think I made an impression in your favor.[87]

The comedy in this speech derives from its extravagant unreality. In addition, the casual rationality of Valentin's tone makes the absurdities he is describing even more ridiculous, the consequence of a comic technique which owes something to Swift's *A Modest Proposal*. In the dialogue which follows, Urbain's manner of speech presumes, with quite uncalculated comic results, to give reality to the unreal pretentiousness of attitude already parodied by Valentin:

'The novelty has not quite worn away, I confess,' the marquis went on; 'perhaps it never will, entirely. But possibly that is not altogether to be regretted,' and he gave his thin smile again. 'It may be that the time has come when we should make some concession to novelty. There have been no novelties in our house for a great many years. I made the observation to my mother, and she did me the honor to admit it was worthy of attention.'

'My dear brother,' interrupted Valentin, 'is not your memory just here leading you the least bit astray? Our mother is, I may say, distinguished for her small respect for abstract reasoning. Are you very sure that she replied to your striking proposition in the gracious manner you describe? You know how terribly incisive she is sometimes. Didn't she, rather, do you the honor to say, "A fiddlestick for your phrases! There are better reasons than that"?'

'Other reasons were discussed,' said the marquis, without looking at Valentin, but with an audible tremor in his voice; 'some of them possibly were better. We are conservative, Mr. Newman, but we are not also bigots. We judged the matter liberally. We have no doubt that everything will be comfortable.'

. . . 'Comfortable?' [Newman] said, with a sort of grim flatness of intonation. 'Why shouldn't we be comfortable? If you are not, it will be your own fault; I have everything to make *me* so.'

'My brother means that with the lapse of time you may get used to the change' – and Valentin paused to light another cigarette.

'What change?' asked Newman in the same tone.

'Urbain,' said Valentin, very gravely, 'I am afraid that Mr. Newman does not quite realize the change. We ought to insist upon that.'

'My brother goes too far,' said M. de Bellegarde. 'It is his fatal want of tact again.'[88]

Valentin plays the part in this, as in other scenes, of the wise clown; as Urbain says in the revised edition, he has 'no nice sense of what shouldn't be said.'[89] By his irony he indicates that he sees the asininity of Urbain's attempt to patronize Newman, and that he realizes, too, that Newman's inability even to imagine what Urbain is talking about prevents him from sufficiently discomfiting his adversary. The comedy in the earlier scene involved a series of jokes by which Newman was characterized by the Bellegardes as almost anthropologically peculiar. He was, for them, unreal. The comedy in this scene is similarly based on a conception of Newman's originality, the 'difference' with which Urbain and his mother must try to be 'comfortable'. But Valentin's irony reveals that the unreality is in the pretensions of Urbain and not in Newman. Newman does not understand what Urbain is talking about, and the reader is encouraged by Valentin's comic renditions at least to pretend not to understand it either.

There is a sense in which Urbain's absurdity puts us off as much as it does Newman. It is not yet apparent that Urbain and his mother take their pretensions with a fateful seriousness. If Newman fails to recognize the portentousness of their manners, out of his sublime self-assurance that they cannot in any way affect the fate of a healthy and strong-willed man, so do we fail of a similar recognition, out of the assurance, given by the comedy, that Newman and Valentin can sufficiently control even the ugliest manifestations of Urbain and his

88 *Am.*, pp. 203–4.   89 *Am.* rev., p. 198.

mother. The comedy has the function of giving us a false sense of security in Newman's success. As a result, the reader of the novel reacts pretty much as Newman does when he hears from Claire, in the presence of Urbain and Madame de Bellegarde, that she must give him up: 'This sort of thing can't be, you know. A man can't be used in this fashion.'[90]

The barrier between Newman and the Bellegardes cannot be removed by verbal explanations. They cannot possibly tell one another about the nature of the difference between them. The Bellegardes are impervious not only to the force of Newman's eloquence but even to the threat that he will expose them to public shame, using the document supplied by the old family maid, Mrs. Bread. Newman himself becomes aware of this when, confronting them with the evidence that Madame de Bellegarde murdered her husband, he finds her so inexpressively defiant. When he visits the Duchess, whom he met at his engagement party, with the intention of telling his secrets, he comes for the first time to understand just what Madame de Bellegarde's impenetrableness can rely on as a positive strength. While the whole atmosphere of the novel becomes darkened, and even as the plot moves towards the ultimate defeat of Newman's hopes, we are given in this scene with the Duchess an example of urbane and mannered comedy, a dramatic presentation of the elegant social play to which Newman at the beginning of the novel was exposed in his first meeting with the Bellegardes. This is James's way of pointing out the undisturbed continuity of poise which Newman cannot disrupt and which does not even allow him the opportunity to try.

Newman's inability to complete his errand results partly from his refusal to take cheap and immediate advantage, a characteristic of him revealed early, in the anecdote of his refusing to make a substantial profit on a man who had at one time subjected him to a calculated meanness. It is equally important, however, that the dramatic movement of the scene and the quality of the Duchess's social discourse actually give him no chance to tell his story even if he should finally decide to do so. Before his visit gets under way it is interrupted by the arrival of the Prince, who is described with the comic

90 *Am.*, p. 322.

grotesqueness that customarily invests characters who do not contribute to the success of James's heroes:

> The Prince was a short, stout man, with a head disproportionately large. He had a dusky complexion and a bushy eyebrow, beneath which his eye wore a fixed and somewhat defiant expression; he seemed to be challenging you to insinuate that he was top-heavy.[91]

There is a good deal of animus in the introduction of the Prince, and more so when James changes the phrase 'he was top-heavy' to 'he might be hydrocephalic.'[92] The vitality in the portraiture seems the more curious when we consider that the Prince has a place in the novel only in this scene, a matter of no more than two pages. When he is announced, the Duchess asks Newman to remain. The Prince is a bore, so she claims, and she desires his visit to be short. We are surprised, therefore, when her conversation with him takes the amusing and even delightful turn that it does. The Duchess, a woman of extraordinarily theatrical corpulence – she earlier reminded Newman of the 'Fat Lady at a fair'[93] – begins her talk with the Prince by a description of the 'sentimental vicissitudes of the Princess X,' and this leads

> to a discussion of the heart history of Florentine nobility in general; the duchess had spent five weeks in Florence and had gathered much information on the subject. This was merged, in turn, in an examination of the Italian heart *per se*. The duchess took a brilliantly heterodox view – thought it the least susceptible organ of its kind that she had ever encountered, related examples of its want of susceptibility, and at last declared that for her the Italians were a people of ice. The Prince became flame to refute her, and his visit really proved charming.[94]

We are entertained by this exactly at the point when our hero is most exasperated. This odd state of affairs can be explained by observing once again that James's social comedy at the expense of the Parisians depends upon our not taking them seriously as individuals. They are grotesque representations of people we expect to find only in the theatre, and the scene itself is managed as if it were an entr'acte. They intend that their subject of conversation should be unreal in the sense

91 *Am.*, p. 442.   92 *Am.* rev., p. 443.
93 *Am.*, p. 278.   94 *Am.*, p. 443.

that neither is responsible for more than the sheer pleasure of contriving playful and pleasurable dialogue. To make the matter even more comically theatrical, James shows both of them as physical freaks, so that the romantic nature of their remarks is, in its intensity, both theoretical and amusingly artificial. Though no point is made of it in the language of this scene, the dramatic circumstances of the novel let us imagine that Newman's sense of exclusion at the loss of Claire is especially painful at this moment in that the discussion of love and passion assumes a world in which these things are frivolously public and very much a matter of delightful flamboyance. It is not surprising, in view of this, that Newman takes no part in the talk, that he 'was naturally out of the conversation.'[95] This experience gives him more of a clue to the impossibility of his position – he leaves almost immediately for England – than has any of his encounters with Madame de Bellegarde or Urbain:

The duchess help him – that cold, stout, soft, artificial woman help him? – she who in the last twenty minutes had built up between them a wall of polite conversation in which she evidently flattered herself that he would never find a gate.[96]

A combination of pleasure and distaste emanates from the handling of this and the earlier scenes. Such were James's feelings about the society which he creates in the novel and about the Paris which he knew while writing it. The expression of this is in the kinds of comedy that have been observed, both in metaphorical uses of language and in comic dialogue. This comedy is at the same time committed to the defence of Newman because it shows that the social environment in which he is active has sufficient charm and attractiveness to deceive us as well as him. It can be said, as a consequence, that comedy tends in all of its uses to idealize the hero.

The attractiveness which is given to Madame de Bellegarde by her witty social adeptness is, by the end, like the outside of those little vases, already mentioned, to which James compares French literature written after 1848, 'skillfully moulded and chiselled,' but hiding from view the 'unclean things' that are inside. The conversation between the Prince and the Duchess excludes Newman as by a 'wall of polite conversation' through which he cannot find a gate, and it suggests how the grotesque circumscription, which has entrapped Claire and which keeps Newman from saving her, arches out from the Bellegarde family to encompass the whole society of which they are a part, connecting even with the wall of the convent behind which Claire has for ever disappeared. Her retreat into the Carmelites is a public confirmation, of which her brother does not approve, that behind the ever tightening 'closeness' of her family and their society is the reality of death instead of life, of death posing as life. The metaphorical suggestions of this from the earlier part of the novel are confirmed by the dramatic action and by the progressive exclusion of Newman from those conversations in which artificiality of manner serves as well as any physical barrier to make him feel the futility of his efforts. His vigil outside the house of the Carmelites in which Claire has begun her life of silence and abnegation is described in a way that implies that the place is a symbol for a whole society. The language gathers up the metaphors which have characterized that society since the beginning of the novel and finally ratifies their full significance:

Newman found himself in a part of Paris which he knew little – a region of convents and prisons, of streets bordered by long dead walls and traversed by few wayfarers. At the intersection of two of these streets stood the house of the Carmelites – a dull, plain edifice, with a high shouldered blank wall all round it. From without Newman could see its upper windows, its steep roof and its chimneys. But these things revealed no symptoms of human life; the place looked dumb, deaf, inanimate. The pale, dead, discoloured wall stretched beneath it, far down the empty side street – a vista without a human figure.[97]

Newman's plans for Claire had been imagined by him and by James in terms quite unlike this. When Newman first proposes, James remarks that Claire has the 'air of a woman who has stepped across the frontier of friendship and, looking around her, finds the region vast,'[98] and when she seems oppressed by melancholy family secrets Newman reflects that 'what he offered her was, in fact, above all things a vast, sunny immunity from the need of having any.'[99]

97 *Am.*, p. 467.   98 *Am.*, p. 160.   99 *Am.*, p. 218.

The brutal sharpness of contrast in the images of hope and futility, of imagination and deadness indicate something of critical importance about the organization of this novel. Because of the combination of elaborate manners on the part of the Bellegardes with Newman's preternaturally healthy lack of suspiciousness, the revelation of their treachery comes with an unannounced dramatic shock. What had been comedy of manners suddenly becomes a melodrama in which all the excesses of expression naturally accruing to it are to be taken not comically but as an adequate response to the nature of things. This does not mean that no humour is involved in the melodrama, but that there is no satiric humour. James subscribes to Newman's violent and enraged feelings by agreeing with him that the betrayal of the Bellegardes is nothing that he could have anticipated and nothing that makes realistic sense. The question for criticism is whether in representing this James does not reveal weaknesses in his plot and his characterization.

The plot of *The American* turns on a mystery, on the refusal of Claire de Cintré to marry Christopher Newman. She cannot explain to him how this has happened, and she does not seem to understand it herself: 'It's like a religion. There's a curse upon the house. I don't know what – I don't know why – don't ask me.'[100] The novel does not allow us to feel any less shocked than Newman by Claire's inconstancy. When he expresses his reaction to it, he does so in terms that might well serve the literary critic in assessing the movement of the plot: 'It was too strange and too mocking to be real; it was like a page torn out of a romance, with no context in his own experience.'[101] It has very little context, for that matter, in the experience offered by the novel. There is nothing in what has been given about the characters to explain the extraordinary choice of the Bellegardes.

Claire, for example, barely exists at all outside the schematization in which she plays the part of a European whose qualities are innately American. During most of the conversations at the Bellegardes' she says nothing, and what we know about her comes from the descriptions in which James puts an emphasis on the suggestive openness of her facial expressions. The

100 *Am.*, p. 363.   101 *Am.*, p. 419.

characterizations of Urbain and Madame de Bellegarde are fuller, but there, too, the details are largely absorbed into representational definition. The making of this definition is mostly comic, the comedy carrying the implication not only that Newman cannot appreciate what the Bellegardes stand for but also that there is something vile behind their high manners. The corruption, when it is finally revealed, involves the fact that several years earlier Madame de Bellegarde's unscrupulous determination to make a profitable marriage for her daughter impelled her to murder her own husband. To discover also that their manners include such extraordinary idealism that they must forbid Claire to marry an American millionaire is, therefore, to feel more than a little cheated. It is, of course, possible to imagine characters who are capable of such apparently paradoxical action, but James does not give body to them in this novel, and it is his rather than our job to do so. He is, as we have seen, committed, for purposes of social satire, to exactly the opposite kind of character.

In James's Preface to *The American*, written some thirty years after the first publication of the novel, he sees it as a weakness that he does not definitely place the clue to Claire's conduct in the hands of the reader, and that he fails to account for the proposition that the Bellegardes would obviously prefer Newman's fortunes to the seclusion of their only daughter in a Carmelite convent. The assumption behind James's criticism is that a clue *could* have been given, that the plot and the characterization might have taken the direction that they do, and that an explanation might somehow have been added. But given the kinds of characterization that are found in *The American*, it would not have been possible, short of writing quite another kind of novel, to have provided such explanations. Neither in the characterizations of individual members of the Bellegarde family, none of whom is given a complicated psychology, nor in the society which they are made to represent is there provision for the impractical renunciation of the Bellegardes at the end. Renunciation, a term reserved for the selfless reactions of James's heroes, is a proper way to describe the rejection of Newman by these villains. It is a completely profitless act unless measured by standards of romantic idealism, and these are not the standards, it need hardly be said, which have motivated the Bellegardes at any point. Their renunciation is not entirely in the tradition of Jamesian heroes, of course, since, while acting as they do, they break a solemn vow, and in that they are treacherous. Only the treachery itself is not surprising. It would have been predictable if they had forced Claire to give up Newman in order that she might marry Lord Deepmere. An act of cynical self-interest, disguised as a desire to have Claire marry in her own class, would be wholly in character. Precisely for that reason it is incomprehensible that their treachery should be at the service of intangible social principles which they easily violated by allowing the engagement in the first place.

The comedy in the novel depends to a considerable extent on the fact that behind the social manners of the Bellegardes there exists not the positive prejudices of an aristicratic coterie but an eye for the main chance and an old-world capacity to scheme in order to achieve it. The rejection of Newman involves the assertion of ideals for which practical sacrifices must be made, and this is not the kind of thing which could unfold from character as this novel has created it in the Bellegardes. One cannot feel in *The American*, to paraphrase what James remarks of good fiction in general, that character is the determination of incident and incident is the illustration of character.[102] Once the characters are 'placed' in the categories which allow for James's satire, there is nothing that can be called development in characterization. Instead of it there is only a dramatic intensification of the differences between the categories. This intensification is expressed mostly through modulations in James's satire on the pretensions of the Bellegardes. It is not related in any way to a dramatization of a change of heart, developing with the action, by which the Bellegardes are moved to reject Newman. There is no dramatization of this, there is merely the announcement that it has occurred.

The flatness of characterization, which allows for the comic descriptions and comic dramatic dialogue in the novel, prevents James from dramatizing the moral and psychological complications involved in his plot. This is evident in the characterization not only of the Bellegardes, who cause the complica-

102 *Partial Portraits*, p. 392.

tion, but also of Newman, who stimulates them to act as they do. There are times, in fact, when James's treatment of Newman indicates that he may have been trying to give the novel more satisfying coherence than it has.

This is to say that there are suggestions here and there of the hero's legitimately objectionable qualities. Had these been developed, the comedy would have been more subtly discriminating than it is and his rejection by the Bellegardes would have been at least understandable as a reaction to things in him which the reader had also recognized. James's seeming reservations about Newman can be summed up by saying that he is a man without imagination. In his simplistic view of Europe he is to be distinguished from Isabel Archer or from Roderick Hudson. It could not be said of either of these, as it is of Newman, that the complex Parisian world 'neither inflamed his imagination nor irritated his curiosity.'[103] His coarseness of observation is made part of his charm, however, as when, in the opening scene, he admires the painting of the marriage feast at Cana by Paul Veronese because 'it satisfied his conception, which was ambitious, of what a splendid banquet should be.'[104] On the other hand, there are a few instances where it is less clear that James means us to see Newman's potential vulgarity in so favourable a light. He tells us, for example, that Newman 'had already begun to value the world's admiration of Madame de Cintré, as adding to the prospective glory of possession,'[105] and, even more ambiguous, he gives Newman the remark that while he should like his wife to interpret him to the world, he is worried that 'when the instrument was so perfect it seemed to interpose too much between you and the genius that used it.'[106] Had the implications of such passages been developed in any dramatically coherent way, they would have allowed for a closer relationship in the novel between character and the development of plot. Though the action of the Bellegardes might still be called a 'mystery' or an expression of a kind of 'religion,' it would at least be apparent that something considerable in Newman had provoked them to it.

But whatever qualifications are made about Newman are

103 *Am.*, p. 39. 104 *Am.*, p. 19.
105 *Am.*, p. 165. 106 *Am.*, p. 152.

localized ones scattered here and there. What seem to be personal defects are transmuted into delightfully natural characteristics, so that responses which might be taken as simple-minded become instead an evidence of the healthy and boyish American incapacity to take social hierarchy as seriously as it asks to be taken. Consider, for example, James's observation about Urbain's reaction to Newman. It points with a good deal of suggestiveness to the effect on the Bellegardes of Newman's lack of imagination. As usual, however, the suggestions are dissolved by satiric jibes in the hero's favour:

His tranquil unsuspectingness of the relativity of his own place in the social scale was probably irritating to M. de Bellegarde, who saw himself reflected in the mind of his potential brother-in-law in a crude and colorless form, unpleasantly dissimilar to the impressive image projected upon his own intellectual mirror.[107]

Newman cannot conceive of any values but his own, and he is not joking when, in response to Claire's accusation that he is only using Valentin for amusement and 'would not like to resemble him,' he replies: 'I shouldn't like to resemble anyone.'[108] The ground is laid, a piece here and a piece there, for a conflict between the Bellegardes and Newman which would involve definitions of personality and of social value less superficial than those we discover in *The American*. The novel rests instead on other grounds, those defined and for the most part limited by the conception of character and experience discussed under the rubric 'open' and 'closed.' As a result, the novel does not encourage any qualifications to Newman's expression of dismay at the loss of Claire, even though the terms of his expression blatantly contradict those others which I have been adducing:

'Why should you object to me so – what's the matter with me? I can't hurt you, I wouldn't if I could. I'm the most unobjectionable fellow in the world. What if I am a commercial person? What under the sun do you mean? A commercial person? I will be any sort of a person you want.'[109]

It could be argued that this speech is dramatically effective in showing how Newman misconceives the effect he makes on people dedicated to social proprieties, and it could also be

107 *Am.*, p. 220.   108 *Am.*, p. 228.   109 *Am.*, p. 326.

said that for this reason it is proper that there should be a contradiction between James's feelings about Newman's unimaginativeness and Newman's willingness to imagine himself into any rôle that is needed. But James is only sporadically critical of Newman's incapacity to place himself in the position of other people. James's failure ever to qualify the touching and seductive eloquence of his speeches, the reiteration that the reasons for his rejection cannot but be unreasonable, and the satiric insistence on the superficiality of the Bellegardes – these elements in the novel do not suggest that we are to make any discriminations against Newman's evaluation of himself. The weight of idealized characterization very nearly obliterates the kind of potential qualification to which I have been pointing. Being the open-minded, generous-spirited American, he need be respectful only of the ideal of his own good-humoured prosperity, and such an ideal not only can overlook social standards at all alien to it but even differentiations of a technical order, like foreign languages. Though a knowledge of these is not customarily given a man merely because he is a fine fellow, James tells us that Newman

found his way in foreign cities by divination, his memory was excellent when once his attention had been at all cordially given, and he emerged from dialogues in foreign tongues, of which he had, formally, not understood a word, in full possession of the particular fact that he had desired to ascertain.[110]

Why indeed *should* the Bellegardes find such a man objectionable? It is no wonder that the social comedy in the novel invariably involves the exposure of different kinds of European unreality, either their inventive and charmingly absurd talk about rubber houses and Dukes of California or, later, the unreal and self-parodying social exclusiveness of Urbain.

The comedy at the end, once all the social machinations have been exhausted, shows the effects of having the plot turn upon a motive for the Bellegardes which to Newman, and to us, does not grow out of the dramatization of conduct and character earlier in the novel. The comedy becomes macabre. It registers Newman's sense of the irrationality of experience, and his recognition, when Valentin's failure is placed within

110 *Am.*, p. 81.

the context of his own, that the very nature of things is in all likelihood perversely fateful. Violence and futility dominate not only the conclusion of Newman's relationship with Claire but also of Valentin's affair with Noémie. These two plots are carefully synchronized to suggest the presence in quite different lives of seemingly unnatural calamity. Valentin remarks to Newman of himself and Noémie that 'it's a striking contrast to your noble and virtuous attachment – a vile contrast!'[111]

James's attempt to put the two romances in juxtaposition is unmistakable: the news of Noémie's being 'launched' as a courtesan is announced in the same chapter with the news of Newman's engagement;[112] Valentin observes that 'her ideal has been satisfied'[113] at a time when Newman is most exultant about his own good fortune; at the end of Chapter XII Valentin leaves for Geneva and the duel in which Noémie's fickleness has involved him, and Chapter XIII witnesses Claire's departure from Paris on orders from her mother; Newman hears almost simultaneously that his engagement has been broken and that Valentin has been wounded;[114] and, finally, he witnesses Valentin's funeral in the same chapter in which he is told that Claire is going to a living death in the convent. The advantage of making such a series of close parallels between apparently contrasting relationships is described adequately enough by James himself in a review of *Middlemarch*. He there comments on the 'balanced contrast between the two histories of Lydgate and Dorothea':

Each is a tale of matrimonial infelicity, but the conditions in each are so different and the circumstances so broadly opposed that the mind passes from one to the other with the supreme sense of the vastness and variety of human life, under aspects apparently similar, which it belongs only to the greatest novels to produce.[115]

The two plots in *The American* do not, of course, take place 'under aspects apparently similar,' but except for that James's remark on George Eliot helps us to see what he was about in his own novel. The relationship between the two plots might

111 *Am.*, p. 266.   112 *Am.*, p. 213.
113 *Am.*, p. 253.   114 *Am.*, p. 330.
115 'George Eliot's *Middlemarch*,' in *The Future of the Novel*, ed. Leon Edel, p. 86.

be conceptualized by thinking of Newman as defeated by the forces of restriction and seclusion, while Valentin is defeated by what James in another review once referred to as the 'irregular society in France that has become so extensive and aggressive.'[116] Noémie represents social freedom gone astray – a 'free spirit', as she is called in the revised version.[117] But while she is outside the social exclusiveness of Parisian high society, her position is one conventionally established for its convenience. This is Valentin's excuse for her to the sometimes disgusted Newman. Her profession plays almost as much a part in the world of manners as the social cultism of the Bellegardes. Both Newman and Valentin are defeated by corrupt manifestations of a firmly established social order, and it is therefore dramatically right that the one should die simultaneously with the death of the other's hopes. Duelling, which kills Valentin, is a mystery to Newman just as are the social customs which deprive him of Claire, and both are founded upon history and tradition. Newman's violence of expression in the last eight chapters of the novel is caused by his discovery that neither his healthy decisiveness nor his practical good sense can do anything about the mysterious forces which seem to determine his destiny as well as Valentin's. As he sits with his dying friend, he thinks of his own plight in a way which could as easily refer to either of them:

What had happened to him seemed to have, in its violence and audacity, the force of a real calamity – the strength and insolence of Destiny herself. It was unnatural and monstrous, and he had no arms against it.[118]

Newman's sense of the unreality of the disasters which occur at the end of the novel is the basis for much of the comedy which we find there. The general nature of it may be illustrated by the reaction of Mrs. Bread to Newman's melodramatic speech about his suffering and his intention to destroy her employers. Newman tells her:

'I want to bring them down – down, down, down! I want to turn the tables upon them – I want to mortify them as they mortified me. They took me up into a high place and made me stand there

116 Unsigned review of *Modern Women, and What is Said of Them, The Nation*, VII (October 22, 1868), 333.

117 *Am. rev.*, p. 74.   118 *Am.*, p. 339.

for all the world to see me, and then they stole behind me and pushed me into this bottomless pit, where I lie howling and gnashing my teeth! I made a fool of myself before all their friends; but I shall make something worse of them.'[119]

'Something worse,' he continues, might include the hanging of Madame de Bellegarde. At this point Mrs. Bread expresses the innocently concerned reaction that 'it would break up the family most terribly, sir!'[120]

The comedy in this exchange results from the reminder of the distance between common experience and Newman's. This is accomplished, in part, by the use of the stock phraseology of ordinary domestic trouble. Mrs. Bread does not intend to be funny – she is as good, and about as interesting, as good bread. But her remark is comic because it represents the ridiculous inappropriateness to Newman's feelings of ordinary statements and the language that goes with them. His is the language of an archangel expelled from heaven, from the 'high place' which Valentin refers to early in the novel, and hers is of some uncomprehending spinster lady into whose prim garden he has fallen. The Satanic comparison is appropriate enough, given James's language, and is made more so as we watch Newman proceed, with devilish clairvoyance into the nature of her pride, to seduce Mrs. Bread into betraying her employers. To do so he tries to infuse into her complaints some of the intensity of his own, especially in the final version of the novel. Mrs. Bread recounts, for example, that when Madame de Bellegarde suspected her of having an affair with her husband 'she said that if I'd sit in her children's school room I should do well for a penwiper! When things have come to that I don't think I need stand on ceremony.' To this Newman rejoicingly exclaims, 'I never heard of anything so vicious! Go on, Mrs. Bread.'[121]

The comedy as the novel progresses changes from jokes about ordinary social matters, made by highly imaginative uses of language, to jokes about extraordinary experiences, such as Newman's rejection, made by juxtaposing them with relatively flat and habitual uses of language. Comedy of this latter kind occurs in James when an aspect of reality totally different from the one which we are momentarily accepting

119 *Am.*, p. 387.   120 *Am.*, p. 388.   121 *Am.* rev., p. 391.

interjects itself. Such comedy can be truly called philosophical, and it has versions which include the final scene of Chaplin's *City Lights*, when a flower-pot falls on the head of the comic hero as he tearfully takes a flower from the blinded heroine, as well as the last scene of *King Lear*, in the peculiar effectiveness of Lear's remarking just before he dies, 'Pray you undo this button. Thank you, sir.' Such comedy is to be found not only in Newman's interview with Mrs. Bread and the subsequent scenes in which he deals with Urbain, but also in the death scene of Valentin. In attendance, aside from Newman, is Valentin's aptly named friend M. Grosjoyaux and another, M. Ledoux, who remarks, after Valentin has received the last rites, that hope for his recovery is mistaken kindness, since 'when a man has taken such excellent measures for his salvation as our dear friend did last evening, it seems almost a pity he should put it in peril again by returning to the world.'[122] Valentin, in an echo of Mercutio, expresses a movingly courageous and comic view of his own death when, to Newman's 'And how are you getting on?' he replies 'Oh, I'm getting off! They have quite settled that; haven't they?'[123] The concluding chapters have much of this odd gaiety, some of it coming directly from James, as in his paraphrase of Newman's feelings about Claire's decision to enter the Carmelites: 'How could she fail to perceive that his house would be much the most comfortable sort of convent?'[124] The highly comic scene with the Duchess and the Prince occurs even after this, at a point when Newman has completely given up hope.

There is nothing extraordinary about the use of comedy at the culmination of a series of distressing and very uncomic actions. Under such circumstances the kind of comedy involved in Valentin's remark on his death is a way of reminding oneself that existence goes on beyond the periphery of one's own disaster. It is a way of affirming that though your situation is killing you, you still have the capacity to recognize that life is going on outside it. Comedy in these circumstances is a form of courage and vanity. This explains why the wit of Madame de Bellegarde when Newman confronts her with his evidence makes him admit to a grudging admiration for her 'magnificent pluck'.

122 *Am.*, p. 336.   123 *Am.*, p. 339.   124 *Am.*, p. 372.

James's comedy in *The American* usually multiplies the versions in which the object in front of him can exist. It reminds us of other aspects of the experience with which he is dealing, of the multiplicity of possible responses even to events so calamitous that they seem to predetermine the way we are to react to them. A somewhat peculiar illustration is in the remark of Madame Urbain to Newman just after his frustrating visit to the Carmelite convent: 'Poor Claire – in a white shroud and a big brown cloak! That's the *toilette* of the Carmelites, you know. Well, she was always fond of long, loose things.'[125] That we can find this funny under the circumstances in which it is said testifies to the liberality of mind which James's comedy can induce. Because of this, he might have made his characterizations more complex than they are, and have thereby avoided the problem in the plot which he himself recognizes in the Preface.

None the less, the courage and largeness of view implied in this use of comedy does anticipate Newman's final reaction to the shocking incoherence of his experience. By burning the evidence with which he might ruin the Bellegardes, he proves his superiority to them and affirms that exalted view of the possibilities of human conduct which he and James found wanting in an uncongenial Parisian world. James, by his comedy, defies Fate no less than Newman does by his conduct. In neither case is there a willing submission to conventional assumptions about human reactions, either to the claims of old civilization or even, where reaction is more apparently predetermined, to social treachery and personal disaster. In *The American*, the heroics of Newman's final action and of James's art are one, offering, thereby, a confirmation of the autobiographical significance discussed at the beginning of this chapter.

125 *Am.*, p. 423.

The Europeans

The Europeans appeared in 1878, a year after the publication of *The American*. The contrast between the titles is a blatant indication of differences of emphasis and attention. More important, however, is the fact that *The Europeans* is radically unlike *The American* in its modes of perception and in the views of experience which derive from them. The nature of the comic involvement of 'open' and 'closed' characters, for example, reveals an extreme complication of James's earlier standards. This results both from a more sympathetic view of manners than he has hitherto shown and a more intensive concern for the connection between social conduct and individual psychology. The descriptions of the Wentworths and their surroundings tend to be metaphorical in a way that places them with the 'open' or 'free' characters found in the previous novels. The dramatic action, however, which includes their conversation, reveals that they are charmingly fearful of even the possibilities of freedom and opportunity.

By contrast, Eugenia, Mr. Wentworth's theatrically European niece, is as mannered as the Bellegardes and equally deceptive. But again, the dramatic action reverses the expectations to which the imagery of the earlier novels has perhaps disposed us, and by the end, her manners are an indication not of a self-protective limitation of view but of a desire to take advantage of the promise she sees in the American world. This European and, to an extent, her brother Felix, is ironically more American, by Christopher Newman's standards, than the New England relatives she is visiting near Concord, Massachusetts. *The Europeans* is an impressive example of the fact that while a scheme of imagery or of the ideas that attach to it can be extemporized from any novel or even from a group of them, it cannot be imposed statically on yet another one. We must look first and last not at motifs and themes in the abstract but at the immediate and particular dramatization of these. Indeed, James's development from *The American* to *The Europeans* is in the direction of making his characters less subservient to 'type' and in showing that their personalities are often at variance with the 'types' to which they would ordinarily be assigned.

I call this a development, rather than a change, because it involves a treatment of character which is to become sacred to James's art and the central dramatic circumstance of his fiction. Both in his creation of characters and in their treatment of one another, virtue resides in not using other people in a way that is unjust to the potential fullness of their personalities. More than any novel so far, *The Europeans* shows a concern for letting at least the main characters define themselves. This means, essentially, that it is the most dramatic of the novels we have considered, the least indicative of the two ways in which a novelist can limit the freedom of his characters: by non-dramatic analytical intrusions or by allegory.

It has not been the practice to praise this novel, which for its size could be called a novella, as highly as it deserves. There has been an almost unanimous critical slighting, beginning with the patronizing comments of William James and the equally disparaging replies of Henry. That he did not include it in the New York edition does not, of itself, mean much. *The Bostonians* was also left out, though he would have liked to include it, and some other works which, as he writes to Howells, were 'crowded out by want of space and by the rigour of the 23 vols., and 23 only, which were the condition of my being able to arrange the matter with Scribners at all.'[1] It is likely, however, that *The Europeans* was one of 'the things pretty numerous' which were omitted 'from deep-seated preference and design.'[2] Far from expressing any affection for it, Henry James seemed anxious to abuse it. His brother stimulated this by objecting at the time of publication to what he considered its superficiality. In reply, Henry made the excuse that at most it was an 'artistic experiment' for which he did not want to 'run the risk of wasting or gratuitously using big situations.' He was willing to adopt William's own terminology, calling it 'thin' and 'empty,' and summed up the matter by saying that he was 'aware of its extreme slightness.'[3]

Henry James's feeling about *The Europeans* is understandable. The plot, for example, never allows for any substantial doubt that things will work out as they do, and that this will make everyone happy, or at least allow everyone to appear so. Only Eugenia feels disappointed, a matter, for all the other characters at least, which is irrelevant to the easy pleasantness of the general social atmosphere. Her own impeccable decorum would, in any case, have preserved the placidity of the conclusion.

As the novel opens, she and her brother Felix have just arrived in America to visit their only living relatives, the Wentworths. They are also, it appears, in search of a fortune. Felix's imperturbable gaiety, an assurance that he will not get involved in any serious complications, is a guarantee of his eventual success, while Eugenia, it can be predicted, will never overcome the suspicions of her relatives. The latter are, for one thing, uncertain about the meaning of her 'morganatic' marriage to a noble, and they are put off by the deviousness of her conduct. She fails to convince even the most worldly member of the community, Robert Acton, that she is to be trusted, so that he neglects to propose to her even though she had been given reason to suppose he might. There are marriages enough at the end, however, to give the story the aspect of a fairy tale. Felix proposes to Gertrude, forcing Mr. Brand, who thought he himself was in love with her, to recognize that it is Charlotte whom he actually loves. Clifford Wentworth, after Eugenia indulges in some farcical flirtations with him, proposes, as it was assumed he would, to Lizzie Acton, and the final lines of the novel remark that Robert Acton eventually marries 'a particularly nice young girl.'[4] Four marriages and the way they are brought about, none of them involving a very complicated effort, account well enough for the plot. There are, of course, impressive moments that bear little relationship to the marital situations, but most of these, like the scene when Mr. Wentworth sits to Felix for his portrait, could be shifted about with little change in the significance of the action. This scene, like others, is a detachable vignette dramatizing some aspect of the comic disparity between European and New England points of view.

The simplicity of the main action is reason enough, no

4 *The Europeans* (London, 1921), p. 209. Hereafter the novel will be designated *Eur.*

doubt, to make James refer to the novel as 'slight,' but he probably was more displeased by the fact that around the main action there is practically no contingent life. This would indeed be a failing in a novelist who, within two years, would be encouraging Howells to become the American Balzac so that he might give a full appreciation to the 'paraphernalia' of life.[5] The matter meant so much to James that some of his severest criticisms of other writers is focused upon their failure to show characters within what he calls 'an accumulation of secondary experience.' He is speaking of Maupassant, and he goes on to say that a novel can be superficial by lacking, as does *Une Vie*, 'the miscellaneous *remplissage* of life.'[6] Such bareness in *The Europeans*, however, is combined with the beautiful lucidity of James's early style. This is perhaps what makes particular details so surprisingly vivid: the immense triangle of cake and the Madeira wine which Gertrude serves Felix on his first visit, or the 'dove-colored freshness' and sunny whiteness of the Wentworth house, neither description, it is always remarkable to discover, occupying more than a few lines. One of the results of this, as later discussion will show, is to encourage a maximum alertness to the slightest nuance in characterization or physical detail. Such a technique is especially useful in a novel so consistently dramatic. By encouraging us to imaginative speculations it absolves James of responsibility for pointing things out to us, as he does by his intrusions into the drama of *Roderick Hudson* and *The American*. There is yet another reason for the absence of direct analysis or philosophical psychologizing in *The Europeans*, one which, however, tends to confirm James's own estimation of the novel. Here we come upon a fact peculiar to all of the characters.

With the exception of Eugenia, none of them is allowed to suffer, and what we assume to be her suffering is completely cloaked under the ample garment of her own sophistication. This is of considerable significance to the uses of comedy. In many respects the comedy in *The Europeans* is similar to that in the other novels so far discussed. It serves to point out and define any kind of unnatural feeling. This was true of the pretension of the Bellegardes, which was shown by the comedy

to be so unnatural that it could not include the imagination of
love, and of the melodramatic expressiveness of Roderick and
Mrs. Light, subjected to a parody that exposed their lives of
theatrical self-delusion. In each of the first three novels, comedy
is the instrument for the laying bare of reality such as James
found missing in *Nana* owing, he remarks, to the absence in
Zola of a sense of humour.[7] There is a variety of Jamesian
comedy, however, which we do not find in *The Europeans*.
In its absence a kind of reality with which he customarily
deals is also less strongly affirmed. This, again, is the reality of
suffering. It will be recalled that in the earlier novels there is
always a certain amount of macabre humour, particularly near
the end, when the action is most nearly tragic. The hero, like
Newman or Rowland, will become almost giddy by being at
last face to face with the reality which was before hidden from
him. The condition of such a hero is apparent in comic remarks
made at the most intense moments of suffering both by the
characters and by James. As we have seen in *The American*,
such comedy has the effect of affirming the objective reality
of kinds of experience which have nothing to do with the
personal grief of the hero. Under these circumstances, comedy
reveals a philosophical humility before aspects of life to which
one's intensities are irrelevant. In terms of literary art, comedy
becomes a way of rejecting melodrama and the self-absorbed
expression which brings it into dramatic existence.

Besides this aspect of comedy, *The Europeans* lacks the
philosophical meaning that goes with it, the pathetic recognition of the essential indifference to individual fate of the
customary order of things. Rather, the superficial optimism
of Felix in the opening scene appears, at least, to be confirmed
by the subsequent action as a more realistic attitude towards
life than Eugenia's somewhat sardonic expectations. With the
exception of *Confidence*, the most undistinguished of James's
longer works, all the novels from *Roderick Hudson* to *The
Portrait of a Lady* show the ultimate failure of romantic love
and the frustration of its social fulfilment in marriage. At least
on the face of it, *The Europeans* also seems to be an exception
to this pattern. Everyone at the end is settled in a way that is

7 'Review of Zola's *Nana*,' *The Parisian* (Paris), No. 48 (February 26, 1880),
9. *The Future of the Novel*, ed. Leon Edel, p. 95.

most natural to him and to us. This is achieved because all the characters, except Eugenia, come into possession of what is necessary for their happiness, as distinguished from what they thought they needed and wanted. As in the case of Brand, this can involve the end of self-deception, and his romantic career is symptomatic of how the whole community adjusts to its happiest possibilities by casting off all that disguises or complicates the right order of things. Thus, Eugenia's departure is by way of an exorcism. She is the lady of disguises, of manners, of artfulness. It is possible to see the novel in this light, and to agree with Miss Elizabeth Stevenson that its theme is the necessary acceptance of triviality in the interests of happiness.[8] If that is what the novel means, however, then it is itself trivial, and while triviality may please James's characters, it cannot be expected to satisfy his readers. Against the apparent logic of the plot and what it suggests, against Miss Setvenson's conception of the theme, and against James's own estimation of the novel stands one thing that this account has yet to consider, the character of Eugenia and her significance in the whole design.

Eugenia's presence in the novel calls James's estimation of its superficiality into question by making a substantial difference in the relative importance of the other characters. Her full name is Eugenia-Camilla-Dolores, the Baroness Munster of Silberstadt-Schreckenstein. This is a spectacular name, the sort that might be found in some operatically romantic story about exotic people or, more likely, in a farcical comedy about minor nobility. Silberstadt-Schreckenstein brings to mind an odd combination of wealthy glamour and impoverished fear, while in her personal name there are successively evoked a queen, recently deposed in France, a courtesan, made almost a mythic figure by Dumas *fils*, and the traditional lady of the sorrows.[9] The suggestion of a complicated and even contradictory variety of personal roles is thoroughly appropriate to Eugenia's character and to her place in the novel. She

8 Elizabeth Stevenson, *The Crooked Corridor* (New York, 1949), p. 121.

9 The name Eugenia may suggest 'eugenics,' as Joseph McG. Bottkol thinks it does (Joseph McG. Bottkol, 'Introduction,' *The Aspern Papers* and *The Europeans* [New Directions, 1950], xix). But the word was not coined from the Greek until 1883, four years after the publication of *The Europeans*, by Francis Galton.

represents a configuration of attributes which the society of the Wentworths cannot comprehend. She is too big for her setting, exceeding the dimensions of Mr. Wentworth's benevolent but constricted understanding no less than she overburdens the small cottage he lets her use and in which she seems, with her large element of 'costume,' like a dowager queen living in a doll's-house. Ultimately, if we choose to think of *The Europeans* as merely a charming pastoral, she is too large a figure for the novel itself.

But if *The Europeans* is a pastoral, it is a satiric one. This is apparent, in miniature, in the conversation between Felix and Gertrude after his preliminary visit to their relatives. Describing the Wentworth household as primitive and patriarchal, Felix observes that 'it's the *ton* of the golden age.' Eugenia's immediate reply suggests that we are to witness the confrontation of the pastoral with the artfully witty: '. . . and have they nothing golden but their *ton*? Are there no symptoms of wealth?'[10] Through her sophisticated presence and the attitudes towards experience which she expresses, the simple pastoral becomes part of a comedy of manners. The plot may lend credence to the opinion that the novel is about frivolity as a necessary prerequisite for happiness, but the comedy suggests that the state of happiness which has no room for the likes of Eugenia is not, in James's mind, a very inclusive human accomplishment.

In so far as James is positively disposed to the pastoral qualities of the Wentworths and their society, he is satirical about the sophistication of Eugenia, but to the extent that he regrets their incapacity to appreciate her, he adopts Eugenia's sophistication of tone in order to satirize the inadequacies of New England. The earlier statement that James's comedy is at the service of naturalness as against all that restricts or warps it does not mean that he necessarily prefers social simplicity to contrived social manners. Quite the contrary is often the case, and nowhere in his works more visibly than here. James as a pastoralist has no Theocritean faith in the completeness of bucolic culture. He is concerned, instead, with what we might call a Marvellian antithesis of art and nature. James conceives of these almost wholly in terms of social conduct and the

10 *Eur.*, p. 35.

way it does or does not reflect the real feelings of his characters.

The comedy inherent in this is that James's idealistic sense of human inclusiveness leads him to satirize nature for not including art to the same extent that he satirizes art for not being natural enough. Though the Wentworths may be called pastoral because of their habits and surroundings, they do not fulfil all that James would like to expect of such an existence. They are really less in touch with their own feelings and less free in expressing them than are their mannered and sophisticated European guests. Nor can their feelings be called simple or spontaneous when they are entangled in what James views as an oppressive belief that pleasure is always subservient to responsibility.

The Wentworths are ironically the descendants, we might conjecture, of the Puritans who in Hawthorne tore down the maypole at Merry Mount. New England Puritanism, which had submitted to the relaxing influences referred to in *Roderick Hudson*,[11] hovers about the novel in the person of the minister, Mr. Brand, with his evocations of seriousness and sincerity, and in the highly provocative references, about which more will be said, to church spires, church bells, and church-going. James makes a point of telling us on the first page that the time of the novel is 'some thirty years since,'[12] no doubt expecting his readers to know what this implies. All we can do is imagine the sort of world which James's readers could actually remember, but we can be helped in this by Emerson, who wrote in 1841, at about the time of the novel's action, a yearning and beautiful account of Puritan pastoralism in New England:

What a debt is ours to that old religion which, in the childhood of most of us, still dwelt like a sabbath morning in the country of New England, teaching privation, self-denial and sorrow! A man is born not for prosperity, but to suffer for the benefit of others, like the noble rock-maple which all around our village bleeds for the service of man. Not praise, not men's acceptance of our doing, but the spirit's holy errand through us absorbed the thought. How dignified was this! How all that is called talents and success, in our noisy capitals, becomes buzz and din before this man-worthiness! How our friendships and the complaisances we use, shame us

11 *R.H.*, p. 9.   12 *Eur.*, p. 1.

now! Shall we not quit our companions, as if they were thieves and pot-companions, and betake ourselves to some desert cliff of Mount Katahdin, some unvisited recess in Moosehead Lake, to bewail our innocency and to recover it, and with it the power to communicate again with the sharers of a more sacred idea?[13]

James takes a no less kindly view of piety and innocence, and in the plot of *The Europeans* he does what Emerson recommends: he allows for the casting out of a most elegant version of 'thieves and pot-companions.' An obvious distinction between the attitudes of Emerson and James is apparent, however, in the simple fact that James would never use the word 'complaisances' as pejoratively as Emerson does. More significantly, James, with a greater interest in personal drama than in general reflection about conduct, is thereby inclined, as Emerson is not, to the sardonic recognition that when innocence depends upon conscious self-denial it ceases to be very simple. When the state of innocence requires that we concern ourselves primarily with the benefit of others, the result, in James's view, can be the restriction of self-discovery and of the free play of expression. If the manners of the Europeans are a form of deception, then so is the simplicity of the New Englanders. Through his comedy James points to the deficiencies in both. While neither represents his conception of 'man-worthiness,' to borrow Emerson's term, the novel leaves no doubt that he finds artfulness, which can include the simple and the natural, more worthy than the natural and simple when it must exclude the artful. As always, his preference is for inclusiveness.

A tendency towards deception is a consequence both of New England pastoralism and of European manners as they exist in this novel. Thus, in addition to a direct confrontation of conflicting cultures, there is a deeper experience in *The Europeans* involving the struggle between different kinds of deception. The first, which is mostly reserved for the New Englanders, is a form of self-deception. A character like Charlotte, for example, will not admit even to herself that she is in love with Mr. Brand. This would involve caring too much for her

13 Ralph Waldo Emerson, 'The Method of Nature,' in *The Complete Works of Ralph Waldo Emerson*, ed. Edward Waldo Emerson (Boston, 1903), I, 220.

own prosperity, a neglect of her duty, in the words of Emerson, 'to suffer for the benefit of others.' The second kind of deception is defined most clearly by Eugenia's conduct. Far from involving self-denial, it is based upon a complicated sense of her own self-interest and of the sophisticated means necessary to express it attractively. Felix moderates between these two forms of deception. As James tells us several times, he is 'not at all serious', meaning that he is not given to oppressive reflection either about himself or about others, and that he can, as he does, express himself and his intentions openly and frankly. He represents as much of Europe, its refined Bohemianism, as the Wentworths can accept.

In accepting Felix, they must allow a modification in their philosophy of self-denial. Their deepest belief is in the responsibility to act so as not to disturb the expectations of the community. Personal sincerity, in their minds, is confirmed by public predictability, a notion pervasively American. Felix succeeds in modifying this prejudice in his relatives by encouraging Gertrude, and through her Mr. Brand and Charlotte, to act in obedience to her feelings and her honestly recognized self-interest. To accept Eugenia would be a further step in the development of the Wentworths towards a mature recognition not merely of the limitations of self-deception but also of the advantages and even the virtues of the kind of deception which she practices.

Her adoption of different roles and her capacity to say things which she knows she does not mean are attempts to take advantage of as many opportunities as possible. Behind the protection of her elaborate manners she can freely consult her own responses to these opportunities. Her deception of others is a way of being honest with herself. Though the Wentworths may agree that a person can be mistaken about her feelings, they cannot then go on to see that a person of imagination is capable of so many apparently contradictory emotions that she must develop an elaborate external manner as her only possible consistency. Under cover of artful social action, a variety of possibilities, both of her own feelings and of those she imagines in other people, can be tried out without the necessity of public self-justification. That is why a society which cannot absorb Eugenia is revealed as less creative than it might be, less able to take advantage of its potentialities. To locate a pun which is no worse than those usually allowed by the names in these novels, the 'worth' of such a society has 'went.' That does not mean that it is worthless, but only that in the relative simplicity of the life it is able to organize such a society is retarded, preserving both the charm and the inadequacies of its pristine existence.

The joke in the name of the Wentworths simplifies conditions which in the actual drama of the novel are more substantial and satisfying. James obviously admires the Wentworths, and he is far from being entirely committed to the virtues of Eugenia. She is simply more than these good but very limited people can handle. If James is making a sour commentary on New England it is less through the relationship between Eugenia and her relatives than through her relationship with Robert Acton. He is a man of travel, social sophistication, and considerable culture, so that he can be said to represent the society of the Wentworths at a high stage of conscious development. It follows, in the light of what has just been said, that he can almost accept Eugenia as part of his daily life. When he rejects her, it becomes apparent that the conditions by which this society holds itself together dictate that even if it could appreciate Eugenia it would not dare assimilate her.

The last line of the novel adequately expresses James's ironically tolerant and condescending view of the expulsion of his heroine. The paragraph leading up to it is occupied with descriptions of the happy marital futures. It is very much like those endings which James in 'The Art of Fiction' mockingly compares to the 'course of dessert and ices' at the end of a good dinner.[14] This paragraph indicates the extent to which *The Europeans* commends the frivolity it includes. But at the end is a sentence which complicates any merely sentimental aftertastes: '. . . and Robert Acton, after his mother died, married a particularly nice young girl.'[15] While there is a moderation on the final page between a number of possible biases, it is clear enough that the bias in favour of Eugenia has the last word. The irony in it is the kind addressed to readers who, it is assumed, are aware that the departure of Eugenia is a loss of something valuable.

14 *Partial Portraits*, p. 382.   15 *Eur.*, p. 209.

From the verbal jousting of the first scene to her evocation in the irony of the last line, she is the most imposing character in the novel. By his affection for her and his inducements to make us feel equally pleased, James gives dramatic life to more penetratingly ironic definitions of the European-American relationship than he has hitherto done. This makes the novel the reverse of 'empty' and 'thin,' and when James uses these terms, either he is not properly recognizing what he has accomplished or he is, in the expectation of greater work, avoiding an argument with his brother over a novel which is one of his shortest and least pretentious. Unfortunately, his self-deprecations are the probable cause for some persistently erroneous notions, particularly about the relative importance of the characters. Thus a recent critic chooses Felix as the central character and the 'observer' of the action.[16] If he were, the novel would be merely a confirmation, as we have seen, of Felix's gay and somewhat superficial view of experience. Aside from the fact that he neither observes nor is even told about most of Eugenia's meetings with Acton, it is apparent to any responsive reader that he simply compels less attention than his sister. Indeed, it is mostly because of her that we see not only his charm but also the limitations of his awareness and that of a society which can adopt him but cannot comprehend her.

I have been talking about the importance of character as measured against the thematic definitions of the novel. However, our actual awareness of character and action depends not upon their relevance to an extracted theme but upon our direct experience of the language that creates them. In *The Europeans* this experience is almost entirely comic, a fact conditioning anything we say about abstracted or generalized significance. The style of *The Europeans*, unlike that of the later novels, makes us feel perfectly relaxed in the presence of complicated possibilities. There are no technical obstructions in the writing to a self-assured participation in the serious entertainment of reading. Similarly, the ease and urbane grace of the comedy is a promise that understanding requires no special activity beyond a willingness of imagination and

16 Edwin T. Bowden, *The Themes of Henry James* (New Haven, 1956), p. 47.

appreciation. At no point does the style require excogitation upon the significance of its own grammar, and yet the modulation of tone gives us a sense of the emotional subtlety of character and meaning. The posture of the reader has that composure which includes the unself-conscious alertness of a man who expects and is accustomed to sophisticated discourse. The style, like the comedy, is addressed to those of high and assured cultivation, to readers free from any provinciality about specifically European or American aspects of what is presented. For all her theatrical foreignness, Eugenia does not bewilder us as she does Mr. Wentworth. We are made self-confident by the intimacy with which James addresses us, and his willingness to trust us with his jokes indicates that we are to share with him a view of the action which is above the particular prejudices of any of the characters, even Eugenia.

In the opening paragraph, for example, James has us subscribe to some of Eugenia's assumptions even while recognizing that they are so coloured by her personal manner as to appear necessarily peculiar to her relatives. It is not at once made known either that the city is Boston or that the woman looking at it from her hotel room is a European, so that while the basis for the comedy may be a European view of an American city, it comes into existence without recourse to these terms. The comedy and the values behind it are freed at once from any kind of parochial defensiveness:

A narrow grave-yard in the heart of a bustling, indifferent city, seen from the windows of a gloomy-looking inn, is at no time an object of enlivening suggestion; and the spectacle is not at its best when the mouldy tombstones and funereal umbrage have received the ineffectual refreshment of a dull, moist snow fall. If, while the air is thickened by this frosty drizzle, the calendar should happen to indicate that the blessed vernal season is already six weeks old, it will be admitted that no depressing influence is absent from the scene.[17]

James asks explicitly for our participation – 'it will be admitted' – in a fairly dreary view of an 'indifferent city.' The snow and the graveyard offer a prospect which we recognize as unfertile and unpromising, even before it takes on the

17 *Eur.*, p. 1.

qualities of an omen by being related to Eugenia's ambitious reasons for being where she is: 'this fact was keenly felt on a certain 12th of May, upwards of thirty years since, by a lady who stood looking out of one of the windows of the best hotel in the ancient city of Boston.' Though nothing has as yet been said about her being a European, the movement of the paragraph allows a satiric insinuation to fall upon the reference to 'the ancient city of Boston.' The joke is a matter of our noting in conjunction the allusion to 'the best hotel,' a building which only a few lines before is called a 'gloomy-looking inn.' The juxtaposition implies that the word 'best' would be used at all only by people who know no better, and we have already agreed to standards which call it 'gloomy.' By enjoying this little verbal joke, and it is not a very exciting one, we assent to criteria more worldly than those which might incline us to call the Tremont House 'best' in any sense, or the city of Boston, regardless of how Hawthorne felt, really 'ancient.' The fact that such words have validity for New Englanders is understandable but amusing.

The claim to cosmopolitan superiority involved in such a use of language is implicit throughout the opening paragraph. The style is fancy to the point of being sarcastically peri-phrastic: '. . . funereal umbrage [has] received the ineffectual refreshment of a dull, moist snow fall,' and the reference to the time of year, which a sentence later is precisely designated May 12, as being that period when 'the calendar should happen to indicate that the blessed vernal season is already six weeks old.' What can be James's assumptions about the reader when he writes in this way? The appeal is not merely to urbanity and cosmopolitanism. Here, again, is an instance in which James uses the convention that the novel is an entertainment to complicate our experience and to control it. In a word, his stylistic fanciness exists to amuse us, to give us an æsthetic pleasure. But when we agree to that we have agreed to some-thing of importance to the serious themes of the novel. James's style in this paragraph assumes an enjoyment in the decorative, an agreement with his readers that pretentious and extravagant language make the literal facts of reality, like the date, more exciting, more amusing, and, finally, more suggestive.

What has just been said is extremely significant, not only

for this novel but for an understanding of James as a novelist. James's style in *The Europeans* and the kinds of comedy it expresses are never opaque, but they can, as in this opening paragraph, be highly and obviously mannered. As a result we are led to a positive appreciation of mannered expression, particularly when, far from complicating matters, it gives them a manifest theatricality. On the basis of this, though there is much more evidence to be presented, it can be said that James would like us to react favourably not only to literary but to social manners, to artfulness in the expression of his characters as well as in his own style. In this sense, to like the novel is to like Eugenia, who is the dramatic embodiment of James's own predilection for the decorative and the flamboyant.

Indeed, James moves directly from the comic artificialities of the opening paragraph to an introduction of Felix and Eugenia in which their activities as well as the details of the scene are meant to allude to different forms of artfulness. While it is all left to inference, it is possible, at least in retrospect, to see the whole dramatic and social conflict of the novel represented in Eugenia's looking at the church spire across the way and thinking that it is 'the ugliest thing she had ever seen.'[18] She stands at the window in all her personal adornment gazing critically at the bare whiteness of the spire of a New England church. The theme of art as against simplicity and naturalness, complicated by having the latter of these thwarted by essentially religious scruple, is almost imperceptibly present in realistic description. It is given more vitally dramatic life, however, both in the personal style of the characters and in the literary style of the author.

As the scene develops, James makes us respond to the relationship between Felix and Gertrude in such a way that we inevitably arrive at a discrimination about their particular kinds of artfulness. We discover, in this, an essential difference between Felix and Eugenia, a recognition important to any consideration of the novel as something more than a simple pastoral. Once again, the weight of implication in no way disturbs the uncomplicated playfulness of the style or the casually achieved realism with which the scene is endowed. It is

18 *Eur.*, p. 3.

revealed that Felix is sitting at a desk, and while he keeps up 'a soft, gay-sounding humming and whistling,'[19] he is at work on pictorial designs and sketches. Eugenia, on the other hand, is pacing back and forth, now and again pinching her waist. When she is not looking unhappily at the street below she is in front of the mirror, making 'half-caressing, half-corrective' changes in 'the multifold braids of her hair.'[20] The contrast between Felix's activity and Eugenia's explains much about the parts they are to play in the dramatic organization of the entire novel. For one thing, her restlessness with their situation never disturbs his equanimity, either here or during the rest of their visit. A more significant difference, however, is in the use each of them makes of art. His is expended with self-confident pleasure in making pictures of the objects around them so that he can sell them for profit. By contrast, she is her own commodity. Her artfulness goes into decorating herself and, through social manner, into her conversations with other people. Though we appreciate this, we are also made aware of an attractive alternative to it in the less self-regarding practices of Felix.

Felix and Eugenia both tend towards what Mr. T. S. Eliot, in speaking of Othello, calls *bovarysme*, the capacity to dramatize the self by adopting an æsthetic rather than a moral attitude towards experience.[21] None the less, their different ways of doing this can have considerable moral significance. They both see the same view from the same window, but, unlike her, Felix reacts joyously to what it offers him and, in his drawings, sets about to recreate it. It is a mistake, which can lead to the most characteristic of misreadings, however, to decide that Eugenia's dissatisfaction is unattractive – 'this dreadful country' – merely because her brother takes all things as grist to his pleasure – 'this comical country,' he replies, 'this delightful country.'[22] On the basis of his willingness to respond creatively to the world outside him, it may seem that James is recommending Felix's point of view to the reader. To some extent this is true, but mostly for the reason that of all the objects around him he finds Eugenia one of the most delightful and

19 *Eur.*, p. 1.   20 *Eur.*, p. 2.
21 T. S. Eliot, *Selected Essays* (New York, 1950), p. 111.
22 *Eur.*, p. 6.

excitingly unpredictable. Because her artistry is used not only on her person but on her expression, on the way she talks, it can be said to be directed into herself before it is directed out upon the world. While her wit, like her general view of things, may be self-indulgent, it is less superficial than her brother's. Whatever she says shows an awareness of possibilities and complexities markedly absent in his conversation. The elaborateness of her manner is more praiseworthy from James's point of view than is Felix's gay frankness. Our recognition of this depends in part upon a sensitivity to style and comic manner, on our seeing that James's own literary expression in the novel has less of Felix's spontaneity of tone and more of Eugenia's obvious but urbane contrivance.

Felix, despite his deficiencies when compared with Eugenia, is, measured against the other characters, extremely intelligent and sensitive. Only by being so does he help us to understand and appreciate Eugenia. The pleasure he takes in her during the opening scenes is an indication of how James wants Eugenia to be taken by us. Felix is especially responsive to the manner of her expression rather than to its substance, thereby indicating that whatever Eugenia says, regardless of how serious it sounds, has in it the entertaining likelihood of being only a momentary self-dramatization. Everything she does is theatrical, and that includes the style of her speech. Her remarks indulge in some of the stagy sophistication and blasé exaggeration which have been noticed in James's own uses of language:

She turned away from the window at last, pressing her hand to her eyes. 'It's too horrible!' she exclaimed. 'I shall go back – I shall go back!' And she flung herself into a chair before the fire.

'Wait a little, dear child,' said the young man softly, sketching away at his little scraps of paper.

The lady put out her foot; it was very small, and there was an immense rosette on her slipper. She fixed her eyes for a while on this ornament, and then she looked at the glowing bed of anthracite coal in the grate. 'Did you ever see anything so hideous as that fire?' she demanded. 'Did you ever see anything so – so *affreux* as – as everything?' She spoke English with perfect purity; but she brought out this French epithet in a manner that indicated that she was accustomed to using French epithets.[23]

23 *Eur.*, p. 4.

Felix's calmness, as if he is used to such outbursts, the assurance that she is accustomed to French epithets, and the amusing way in which small things are comically enlarged – all these suggest that we are witness less to actual feelings of distaste than to a performance about it. Eugenia, 'who has a face full of intelligence,'[24] is not merely playing the clown. Instead, she is like a stage director who is at the same time playing a part; she is dramatically exploiting and, as it were, rehearsing some of her feelings. In the process her reactions to things that bother her become considerably more important than the objects themselves. She obviously enjoys being excessive about the world around her as well as exotic about herself when she tells Felix that 'it's the darkest day of my life – and you know what that means.'[25] To 'know what that means' requires that Felix and, by extension, the reader be intensely absorbed in Eugenia's life, as if she were a romantic stage heroine, someone whose experience is more than ordinarily glamorous and emotionally full. Her remarks literally insist that we feel this way, and it attests to James's brilliantly economical dramatic skill that in so few pages we agree to 'play along' with her as Felix has learned to do out of long acquaintance. It is intimated that our entertainment depends upon our believing in her character even though we may not literally believe in what she says. We are like Fielding's Patridge at the performance of *Hamlet*, with the important difference that we *choose* to be credulous in order to encourage the theatrical spectacle. James makes us laugh at the Baroness in this scene with the same admiration, and some of the vanity, which stimulates Clifford when he thinks 'it so comical that he should know – in spite of her figurative language – what she meant, and that she should mean what he knew, that he could hardly help laughing a little, although he tried hard.'[26]

The commendation of manners and artfulness in these first pages obviously helps determine our responses to the un-mannered Americans. James's intention that this should happen in a specific way and with particular implications is apparent from the number of parallels he devises between Gertrude Wentworth's introduction in Chapter II and Eugenia's in

24 *Eur.*, pp. 3–4.　　25 *Eur.*, p. 5.　　26 *Eur.*, p. 132.

Chapter I. The fact that the scene is in the country rather than in the city, that much is made of the purity and simplicity of natural surroundings, that Gertrude is simpler than Eugenia, and that the qualities she shares with her are largely nascent, indicate that she can be taken as a pastoral version of her European cousin. Like Eugenia, she is in a mood of rebelliousness when she is introduced, and her feelings find expression in a similar exasperation about church. The church spire across from the Tremont House, it will be recalled, 'threw [Eugenia] into a state of irritation quite out of proportion to any sensible motive.' She might be suspecting what Gertrude, in her present exasperation, feels very personally: that the atmosphere of moral seriousness represented by the physical evidence of Unitarian and Congregational churches is not congenial to flamboyant self-expression.

To Eugenia this was apparent in the simple, unadorned whiteness of the spire, while Gertrude recognizes it in yet another indication of the vacuum created by restraint upon personal enthusiasms: the quiet of her environment, where 'the intensely habitual stillness offered a submissive medium to the sound of a distant church bell.'[27] These, like other images of emptiness in the novel, give evidence of the restraints imposed upon individual desires and not, as in *The American*, of the opportunities for achieving them. A sense of this limitation makes both women 'restless', a word which James often applies to each. As their respective chapters open, each woman has the scene to herself. Charlotte, Gertrude's sister, is subsequently introduced here, just as Felix is introduced in the earlier scene, and the dialogue has almost the same implications. The meeting of the Wentworth sisters involves a conflict between Gertrude's rebelliousness and Charlotte's willing conformity. Similarly, the conversation between Eugenia and Felix revealed an essential difference between her temperamental dissatisfaction and his optimistic acquiescence. Charlotte is worried that Gertrude's refusal to go to church will disturb the habitual routine of the family, and Gertrude's response to this is like Eugenia's tolerantly superior treatment of her brother. Though Gertrude is not pretty, any more than Eugenia is, she shares with her a sense of personal style. Thus when

27 *Eur.*, p. 17.

Charlotte makes her entrance in a long, red India scarf, Gertrude naturally takes a certain mischievous pleasure in correcting her way of wearing it:

> Gertrude walked half round her, looking at the scarf, 'I don't think you wear it right,' she said.
> 'How should I wear it, dear?'
> 'I don't know; differently from that. You should draw it differently over your shoulders, round your elbows; you should look differently behind.'
> 'How should I look?' Charlotte inquired.
> 'I don't think I can tell you,' said Gertrude, plucking out the scarf a little behind. 'I could do it myself, but I don't think I can explain it.'
> Charlotte, by a movement of her elbows, corrected the laxity that had come from her companion's touch.
> 'Well, some day you must do it for me. It doesn't matter now. Indeed, I don't think it matters,' she added, 'how one looks behind.'
> 'I should say it mattered more,' said Gertrude. 'Then you don't know who may be observing you. You are not on your guard. You can't try to look pretty.'
> Charlotte received this declaration with extreme gravity. 'I don't think one should ever try to look pretty,' she rejoined earnestly.
> Her companion was silent. Then she said, 'Well, perhaps it's not of much use.'[28]

It may seem perverse to insist upon a similarity between a girl who is as prescriptive and melancholy as Charlotte and a man like Felix, who is 'almost never serious.' James does not make such a connection explicit, but it is implied in the dramatic organization of the novel. Charlotte represents in relation to her sister what Felix represents in relation to his – the notion that one should accept what life offers and make the best of it. The difference is that she sees life as offering responsibilities and he sees it as offering pleasures. She is a serious and dutiful version of him, and it is, therefore, not surprising that the Wentworths can understand him more easily than they can Eugenia. His manners, unlike Eugenia's, do not threaten radical changes in the world around them. He only intends to enjoy it more than they do, and to that extent this flatters their

28 *Eur.*, p. 20.

notion that their world is adequate even to the needs of a well-travelled and charming foreigner. He is a satisfied man and they are satisfied people. Gertrude and Eugenia are the only dissatisfied characters in the novel. As a result, they both give the impression to their relatives that they are not only' restless' but 'peculiar'. They appear 'peculiar' in a society whose standard of judgment is 'sincerity,' because they both seem to be engaging in deception.

The dramatic conflict in the novel is essentially between people who believe in manners and artfulness, which often pass for deception, and those who are suspicious of them. This is the basis for much of the comic dialogue. Deception and specific lies are a form of manners in so far as manners, to people who lack them, represent a disguise of what they consider 'real' feeling or the 'real' situation. The significance of *The Europeans* among the works of James is that in dealing with this subject it is more like the later than the early novels. Eugenia is closer to Madame de Vionnet of *The Ambassadors* than to the deceptive and mannered people who, in the novels up through *The Portrait of a Lady*, are nearly all villainous. In this novel James for the first time conceives of manners and deception as evidence not of social fixity or personal grotesqueness but of the desire to protect one's own inner freedom and to allow others the least difficulty and the least fear in fully expressing themselves. An indication that this view is exceptional in the early novels is the fact that just such confidence as James shows in Eugenia is what leads Isabel to think that Osmond offers her the greatest opportunity for what she calls 'free exploration'. Since the comedy in these novels has some of its ideological basis in James's satirization of 'fixity' as against various forms of freedom, it is surprising to find that in *The Europeans* his comedy commends exactly those things, manners and deception, which before were evidence of the attempt to limit freedom. Here they are the masks of freedom, its outer defences.

In the scene just discussed between Gertrude and Charlotte, there is a representative example, which is important to the meaning of the novel, of how deception leads to dramatic comedy. Although deception, like the manners of which it is a symptom, is usually associated in James with Europeans, it is

emphatically not an attribute of nationality here, despite the
invitation of the title to think of the matter uncritically. The
sharp difference between Europe and America is, in any case,
sufficiently blurred very early by recognizing a version of
Felix in Charlotte and of Eugenia in Gertrude. More important
still is the fact that the contrast which Eugenia's presence
apparently brings into the Wentworth household exists even
before she appears, though in a quieter way, in the difference
between Gertrude and Charlotte. This is true even to the
extent that Gertrude, when we first meet her, is engaged in
deceptiveness which, though less elaborate than any practiced
by Eugenia, carries essentially the same meaning. Just before
the talk about the proper way to wear a shawl, which can be
taken as a discussion of the morality of being artful, Gertrude
asks her sister to tell a lie to their father. Not wanting to go to
church on so beautiful a day, she asks Charlotte to 'say I have
a headache.' The exchange that follows is highly suggestive:
'"Would that be true?" said the elder lady, looking straight at
the pond again. "No, Charlotte," said the younger one
simply.'[29] A lie as conventional as this is really a form of artful
social decorum of which Eugenia herself makes frequent and
more interesting use. Both women use this kind of artfulness
to preserve their freedom of action and, simultaneously, to
pay respect to those who might be hurt or offended by it.
They take account of the value of the very conventions and
assumptions to which they refuse to be bound. Eugenia and
Gertrude are rebellious, but they are not revolutionary. The
difference between these two attitudes is seen in their resort
to deceptions, both to outright lies and to the social disguise
of manners, including flattery and stylized speech. Such lies
as the one Gertrude tells are, in effect, metaphors, and she hopes
that her auditors will not bother to take her too literally, that
they too will observe decorums by not insisting that she say
what she actually means. Gertrude takes a pleasure in saying
'things that puzzle [Charlotte] on purpose,'[30] an accomplishment requiring no great effort since for poor Charlotte all
statements are literal ones.

Charlotte's verbal world, which is representative of what
we can call the world of the Wentworths, is like the physical

world she willingly lives in: everything should be literally what it is and 'one should not try to look pretty.' The lack of ornament on the church spire is even more conspicuous in the Wentworth house. It is large, square, and handsome, seeming by virtue of its simplicity and unadorned whiteness to be nearly empty, unguarded and available to anyone who will walk in. The house represents the positive values of the artless and the unaffected. It stands open 'with the trustfulness of the golden age,'[31] so devoid of self-conscious decoration that it seems to call hospitably to everyone's desire for unaffected peace and solitude. Similarly, the character of the Wentworth family, sufficiently represented in Charlotte, has all of the attractiveness that comes from undefensive simplicity and modesty. Her kindness and self-sacrifice, particularly in her willingness to help Mr. Brand in his courtship of Gertrude, are the genuine expressions of a gentle and endearing nature.

Despite their many virtues, however, there is a consistent emphasis in James's dramatic comedy and in the tone of his own address upon the limitations of the Wentworths and their way of life. Their undisturbed tranquility involves an oppressive self-denial as a necessary price. Anyone who follows her natural desires, including that of not going to church on Sunday, is not meeting her payments. Nothing should be done merely for pleasure any more than for mere prettiness. James's attitude towards the Wentworths is admiring and his irony is always gentle, but he leaves no doubt about their restricted capacity for fullness of experience. Of the visit of Felix and Eugenia, for example, he observes that

The sudden eruption into the well-ordered consciousness of the Wentworths of an element not allowed for in its scheme of usual obligations, required a readjustment of that sense of responsibility which constituted its principal furniture.[32]

The description is of a world in which one does not disturb what has been accepted as the settled, indeed as the factual, reality of things. To do so means 'an extension of the field of possible mistakes.'[33] Gertrude, on the other hand, feels that girls ought naturally to want to look pretty if they are not, and that on a Sunday, 'when the sky is so blue,' it is natural to be a Sabbath breaker. The innocent lie which Charlotte is asked to tell complicates her sense of responsibility to her father, and it is evidence to her of something still more worrisome. In trying to act naturally Gertrude is so disruptive of the 'scheme of usual obligations' that, so far as Charlotte is concerned, she is acting unnaturally. Within this paradox lies the significance of the comedy in their conversation. It would follow logically from the Wentworths' view of life that Gertrude is deceiving herself. In her actions, as in her concept of dress, she is indicating that life is not necessarily what their scheme of existence has apparently proved it to be: serious, unpretentious, and bare. Art, for the New Englanders, is a betrayal of reality.

The implications of this as a comment on the New England ethos of the mid-nineteenth century will be referred to several times, but it would be a vulgarization of the dramatic actuality of the novel to discuss the matter in any prolonged general way. I am, in any case, less concerned with the idea than with its mode of existence in the work. When that is considered, it becomes apparent that the language and the dramatic action imply allegorical and topical meanings but do not impel them. They are held tightly within and constantly modified by the substantive life of the characters. Furthermore, the comedy through which we *experience* these meanings does not permit abstract generalization. The more the Wentworths are 'typed' as representative of New England in its primal aspect, the more loving and gentle is the comedy by which their attitude towards manners and artfulness is exposed. Personality is more important to James than what, in terms of the thematic schemes of the novel, can be called the 'right' attitudes. Thus, Mr. Wentworth is made more lovable by James's comedy than is Acton, who appreciates art and manners more than any of his fellow New Englanders. James's fondness for the old man's limitations is apparent throughout, but nowhere more charmingly than in the scene in which Felix commends the shape of Mr. Wentworth's head and asks to do a portrait of it. Mr. Wentworth replies with a delightfully solemn and characteristically suspicious denial of the necessity or morality of art:

Mr. Wentworth looked grave; he felt awkwardly, as if all the company had come in and found him standing before the looking-glass. 'The Lord made it,' he said. 'I don't think it is for man to make it over again.'[34]

This is an ingratiatingly home-spun reassertion of an attitude towards art and its tendency to meddle with nature which is an historical and literary characteristic of the Puritan sensibility.

Neither Gertrude, who immediately volunteers as a model for Felix, nor Eugenia, who is found gazing into a mirror both in the first and last scenes, recognizes any shame in trying, as James does himself, to 'make over' the facts of life. They are more loyal to opportunities than to obligations. Among other things this means that they both have an attitude towards their own pasts which seems irresponsible by the standards of their relatives and friends. Eugenia is willing to send what she calls a 'renunciation' to her husband in Europe, and Gertrude is anxious to renounce her obligations to act as if she were the victim of her previous attitudes. Both women want to undo what, to the satisfaction of others, has already been settled. In a small way they want to escape from their own histories. But if in this Gertrude reminds us of Claire de Cintré of *The American*, it is only to emphasize again how differently James in this subsequent novel is conceiving of manners. If Gertrude desires freedom from the past no less than Claire, she expects to find it not in the escape from manners but in the development and use of them. This is comically dramatized in her relationship with Mr. Brand, who is continually accusing her of not being 'true' to her past and to the assumptions which have always governed relationships within the Wentworth household. From this relatively light version of the problem of manners and sincerity, we can then go on to consider the greater complexities of it which are dramatized in the relationship between Eugenia and Acton.

The most ironic aspect of the situation between Gertrude and Mr. Brand is that he is himself the unknowing victim of the theories of responsibility which he preaches. He is the sad lover who, complaining for something which we know he

34 *Eur.*, p. 72.

does not really want, becomes the comic lover *manqué*. The portentous solicitude of his proposals makes it sound as if he were inviting Gertrude to share his fate instead of his life. It is by any standards a fairly boring prospect, since his fate is in his loyalty to the consistency of his ideas and his 'seriousness,' while Gertrude's, so he insists, is in her having at one time indicated an interest in him or, more importantly, in his 'thoughts'. Since his 'thoughts' are as true as they ever were, her growing indifference can only mean, so far as he is concerned, that Gertrude is not being herself.

The comedy of the situation is not lessened by the fact that her presumed peculiarity appeals to his sense of obligation and makes him even more than ordinarily assiduous. With his feelings smothered under layer upon layer of moral and intellectual garment, it is no wonder that it takes Felix to tell him that underneath it all he is in love not with Gertrude but with Charlotte. The point of the comedy is that Brand's conception of sincerity, as involving settled obligations to predetermined facts, makes him, all unwittingly, as insincere as he believes Gertrude to be. It is perfectly obvious that she is not the kind of wife he needs or could handle, and his persistence in believing so results in comic moments that are reminiscent of Mr. Elton's courtship of the heroine in Jane Austen's *Emma*:

'I didn't come to you this afternoon because you were not alone,' he began; 'because you were with a newer friend.'

'Felix? He is an old friend by this time.'

Mr. Brand looked at the ground for some moments. 'I thought I was prepared to hear you speak in that way.' he resumed. 'But I find it very painful.'

'I don't see what else I can say,' said Gertrude.

Mr. Brand walked beside her for a while in silence; Gertrude wished he would go away. 'He is certainly very accomplished. But I think I ought to advise you.'

'To advise me?'

'I think I know your nature.'

'I think you don't,' said Gertrude, with a soft laugh.

'You make yourself out worse than you are – to please him,' Mr. Brand said softly.

'Worse – to please him? What do you mean? 'said Gertrude, stopping.

Mr. Brand stopped also, and with the same soft straightforwardness, 'He doesn't care for the things you care for – for the great questions of life.'

Gertrude, with her eyes on his, shook her head. 'I don't care for the great questions of life. They are much beyond me.'

'There was a time when you didn't say that,' said Mr. Brand.

. . . 'You are trying, as I said just now, to lower yourself.'

'I am trying for once to be natural!' cried Gertrude passionately. 'I have been pretending, all my life; I have been dishonest; it is you who have made me so!'[35]

Mr. Brand can only stare, reminding her in doing so of the 'immense body of half-obliterated obligations'[36] with which she earlier associates his appearance. She may have new interests, but these do not for him cancel the old duties. For that reason her family is convinced that she will marry him. 'They think,' she tells Felix, 'I have obligations; and that I have encouraged him.'[37] The Americans in this novel have a more European addiction to the past than the Europeans do. For Gertrude to be true to her presumed obligations would mean that she would have to be true to a previous expression of herself which she has decided is now false. At the very point of self-discovery she is thought to be pretending. She seems to those who have known her to be most mannered when she is being most natural. In her response to the situation she becomes the one member of her family who can understand and admire the stratagems of Eugenia.

All the Wentworths and their circle, except Lizzie Acton, are charmed by Eugenia, though all at one time or another are defensively suspicious of her. Of the Wentworths themselves, only Gertrude, with a touching shyness of admiration, likes her not in spite of the fact that she has 'brought to the New World a copious provision of the element of costume'[38] but because of it. Eugenia's 'costume' is colourfully and comically represented in the furnishings by which she overburdens the little cottage – she calls it a chalet – which Mr. Wentworth lets her use. Her household arrangements, like her dress, are properties, as it were, for the theatrical expression of her personality through speech and social mannerism. While Charlotte seriously wonders if Eugenia is not simply a bad

35 *Eur.*, pp. 123–5.

37 *Eur.*, p. 116.

36 *Eur.*, p. 82.

38 *Eur.*, p. 59.

housekeeper and if she shouldn't offer to help clear away the 'superfluous draperies', Gertrude is reminded by them that she herself has been leading hitherto 'an existence singularly garish and devoid of festoons'.[39]

Part of the Baroness's 'drapery' is verbal, and it is through her style in speech that James gives us the experience of her charm and the significance of her art. This usually takes a form which Gertrude would be likely to appreciate, verbal deceptions and fibbing. Eugenia's purpose is not only to dramatize her exotic personality but also to stimulate any possible colour in the apparently bare lives of her relatives. It is not an easy job, and some of the best comedy in the novel occurs when she falls victim to her own audacity. On entering the severely white and angular frame-house of the Wentworths, for instance, she tells them that 'you have arranged your house – your beautiful house – in the – in the Dutch taste!' It is not remarkable that Mr. Wentworth detaches himself from this with the statement that 'the house is very old. General Washington once spent a week here.'[40] Critics of *The Europeans* tend towards a moralistic and provincial bias against Eugenia for remarks such as these, and this particular one has been called in Mr. Edwin Bowden's recent book 'a stammered inanity.'[41] Not even characters like Charlotte, who are satirized for their inability to recognize the social accomplishment of Eugenia's conversation, would be insensitive enough to call her inane or fail at least to suspect that there is a contrived richness of tone in her hesitations and repetitions.

The Wentworths usually receive her compliments the way they receive Felix's – in perfect silence. It is, for the most part, the silence of modesty, which makes them at many points amusingly endearing. It is also, however, an indication of their mistrust, and Charlotte, in particular, is anxious about the fact that Eugenia does not always mean what she says. Gertrude happily admits that, as a matter of fact, Eugenia usually means just the reverse of what she says – 'they should discover [the reason] when they knew her better.'[42] To Eugenia's compliment on her appearance she reacts with an immediate and trustfully vague faith in the virtue of flattering dishonesties:

39 *Eur.*, p. 60.   40 *Eur.*, p. 41.
41 Bowden, *Themes of Henry James*, p. 49.   42 *Eur.*, p. 64.

It was not the compliment that pleased her; she did not believe it; she thought herself very plain. She could hardly have told you the source of her satisfaction; it came from something in the way the Baroness spoke, and it was not diminished – it was rather deepened, oddly enough – by the young girl's disbelief.[43]

Gertrude's response illustrates another way in which James makes Eugenia the most imposing character in the novel. She is the only character about whom there is, as Gertrude still feels at the end, a 'mysterious impressiveness'.[44] If she were not the centre of attention, the theme of the novel would indeed be 'thin' and 'empty'. It would be concerned merely with Gertrude's success, despite the gentle and amusing incomprehension of her old New England family, in learning to be 'natural'. James makes our experience more significant than that by putting his emphasis on Eugenia and by showing how naturalness, far from being synonymous with simplicity, can exist most richly within the artfulness and deviousness of the grand manner. No one in the novel can finally comprehend her. She remains a mystery even for Felix. Because James does not allow her to remain a mystery for us, we are put in the position of necessarily passing a judgment on a community which is too simple to appreciate her full powers. This fact is missed by those critics of the novel, of whom Mr. Dupee and Mr. Leavis are notable exceptions, who find her merely a charmingly sinister woman hiding her crass intentions, a woman, as Mr. Osborn Andreas puts it, 'of a predatory nature'.[45] Part of the fullness of James's characterization of Eugenia is that it includes the possibility that she is merely predatory. He lets us entertain this notion by his indications of the difference between Eugenia and Felix.

While both of them are anxious to profit from the visit to the Wentworths, Felix, it is made clear, uses means which are conspicuously less censurable than hers. He is simply more honest about his intentions than she is, though this is largely because his whole capacity for experience is less highly developed. We have already noticed how James calls upon us in the very first scene to recognize a difference between Felix's

43 *Eur.*, p. 40.   44 *Eur.*, p. 202.
45 Osborn Andreas, *Henry James and the Expanding Horizon* (Seattle, 1948), p. 45.

artfulness and Eugenia's. His sketches are visible and specific, representing a cheerful and unself-conscious acceptance of the world outside him. When he visits the Wentworths he does portraits of the family, while it may be said that she continues to do 'portraits' of herself through her elaborate dress and the controlled theatricality of her expression. She is trying to sell herself even while she remains a mystery to her buyers, while Felix simply sells them flattering representations of themselves and of their surroundings, 'making, as he did, no secret of the fact that in guiding his steps to the Western world affectionate curiosity had gone hand in hand with a desire to better his condition.'[46] His more strictly social conduct is similarly open and scrupulous, particularly in his concern lest, in making love to Gertrude, he be guilty of 'a grievous breach of hospitality'.[47] Eugenia is dangerously close to being so in her dealings with Clifford, though he is so incapable of believing that a woman of thirty-three could still be romantic that he turns the portents of seduction into a boyish farce. Eugenia cannot do damage where she is so little understood, and Clifford, like the rest of his family, is preserved in his healthiness by the deficiencies in his imagination. Eugenia herself has, for the purposes of easy success, altogether too much of it.

Eugenia's preponderance of imagination is what makes any simple explanation of her motive or any conventional moralizations about it seem a vulgarly inadequate response to James's characterization. I said earlier that by virtue of Eugenia, *The Europeans* is more like the later than the early novels in its attitude towards social manners and personal style. This is of extreme importance to James's career, since it means that he began to experiment much earlier than is commonly assumed with a kind of character who could be, so to speak, the artist of her own experience. Like Kate Croy in *The Wings of the Dove*, Eugenia is endowed with a capacity for imagining almost as much as the novelist about the possibilities of her situation. Most simply, this means that she knows what she is doing and why she is doing it. Beyond that, she has the ability to see that in being a fortune hunter there are possibilities for self-dramatization and self-discovery which are as important as the fortune itself. Characters like Eugenia and Kate are too

46 *Eur.*, p. 101.   47 *Eur.*, p. 105.

reverent before the variety of their own personalities ever to be literalists about their own motives. In his affection for characters of this sort, James is making provision for the exercise of what he considered a great moral function of the novelist's art. This is the virtue, referred to earlier, of leaving characters free to explore and define their own natures, free of limitations imposed upon them by moral or social typing.

The Portrait of a Lady offers the best opportunity for a fuller discussion of this matter, but it may be remarked here that its relationship to comedy can be observed not only in James but in the best exemplifications of Restoration comedy of manners. The artfulness by means of which Congreve's Mirabell and Millamant restrain each other until, through the indirections of manners and courtship, each has had chance to disport the fullness of personality, the way in which their mannered playfulness brings them to full knowledge of one another before there is any movement towards direct possession, is a magnificent example of how created characters can be made to dramatize the best and most civilized artistry of their creators. James, like Congreve, not only dramatizes the concept of freedom within the relationships of his characters, but he also acts upon it as a principle of his own art. From what has been said about Eugenia in this novel, such a comparison to Congreve seems in order. This is particularly so if manners and their relationship to comedy are considered in a way best described by Mr. John Crowe Ransom in *The World's Body*:

The function of a code of manners is to make us capable of something better than the stupidity of an appetitive or economic life. High comedy, for example, is technically art, but substantially it is manners, and it has the agreeable function of displaying our familiar life relieved of its fundamental animality, filled, and dignified, through a technique which has in it nothing more esoteric than ceremonious intercourse.[48]

Eugenia exemplifies this notion more clearly than any of the similar characters who precede her, such as Christina Light, and as much as those who follow, like Myriam Rooth of *The Tragic Muse*. In all of them is that quality which James defines in *The American* when he remarks of Mrs. Tristram that

48 John Crowe Ransom, *The World's Body* (New York, 1938), p. 34.

She had a lively imagination, and she was capable, at certain times, of imagining the direct reverse of her most cherished beliefs, with a vividness more intense than that of conviction. She got tired of thinking aright; but there was no serious harm in it, as she got equally tired of thinking wrong. In the midst of her mysterious perversities she had admirable flashes of justice.[49]

Nowhere in *The Europeans* are there passages which are thus explicit in the definition of character. James's creation of a figure as fascinating as Eugenia, combined with his willingness to make her responsible for her own definition through wholly dramatic presentation, means that every detail in the novel takes on extraordinary vividness. We are made anxious to know all we can about Eugenia, to figure her out for ourselves, so that any description of place or of personal history stimulates us to more than ordinary imaginative effort. The result, as we have seen, is that the style can carry nuances and implications without any evidence of technical contrivance. In the sheer art of writing and dramatic insinuation this is the early James at his best.

In a like manner, Eugenia's personal style is so full of implication that it stimulates a high degree of speculation about the little James tells us of her past history. He succeeds in making us resemble those people at the theatre who are so entranced by the personal power in an actress's performance that they want to find some explanation for it in what little they know of her life off-stage. Eugenia's motive for visiting the Wentworths may well be the search for a fortune, but her motive for acting while there with such an expenditure of herself cannot be so easily explained. In fact, her own notion of what the word 'fortune' could mean is very vague, a result of her having a more imaginative awareness than Felix of what it could involve. He is a young man without a history, while Eugenia's history involves not only an embittering experience with the royal house of an impoverished European principality, but also, because she is a woman, a deeper consciousness of their mother's disgrace. After that lady's elopement with a European she was effectively exiled form the very society which Eugenia and Felix have now entered. In Boston, we are told, it had become 'the highest charity,' as regards Eugenia's mother, 'to think it well to forget her'.[50]

James gives no more than a page to these matters, but, for the reason I have suggested, they take on, like all the small details in the novel, the vitality that results from association with a woman whose exoticism encourages imaginative conjecture. Knowing about Eugenia's mother gives an added significance, for example, to her refusal to call upon families in Boston who have come to visit her little house. James makes no explicit connection between Eugenia's parental feeling and her actions, but this only increases the pleasure of seeing one on our own. It makes her comment to Acton, when she excuses herself from the visits, indicative of a great deal more than a desire to appear socially valuable: 'It is not inspiring. Wouldn't that serve as an excuse, in Boston? I am told they are very sincere; they don't tell fibs.'[51]

Such a remark suggests the possibility that Eugenia's social manner, far from being a cover for indifference and selfishness, is actually a way of being decorous about deeply felt experience. Taking this into account helps explain the nature of the comedy surrounding the reasons for her visit to the Wentworths. Some of it exposes her sentimental feelings about relatives and about being accepted by them, but, given what is suggested about her mother, it would be insensitive to take this as an invitation to cynicism. Rather, the comedy tends to accommodate us to the fact that Eugenia's high style is the instrument not of calculation but of rapidly changing and intense feeling. Any direct expression of feeling always embarrasses her. She is a little annoyed with Felix, therefore, when he reminds her, after she has made a supercilious remark about the reasons for their trip, that when originally planned:

'You said that it was the prompting of natural affection; and when I suggested some reasons against it you declared that the *voix du sang* should go before everything.'

'You remember all that?' asked the Baroness.

'Vividly! I was greatly moved by it.'

She was walking up and down the room, as she had done in the morning; she stopped in her walk and looked at her brother. She apparently was going to say something, but she checked herself and resumed her walk. Then, in a few moments, she said something different, which had the effect of an explanation of the suppression of her earlier thought. 'You will never be anything but a child, dear brother.'[52]

In the comedy of this exchange is evidence that Felix is not seriously trying to accuse Eugenia of deceitfulness. His claim to having been deeply moved is by way of comment on two different 'performances' and, by pointing to the contradiction between them, stimulating her to yet another. Knowing that she is a woman who is continually experimenting with the possibilities of her own feelings and motives, he is having fun with her, teasing her with a demand for consistency which he would not want her to satisfy. She has many parts, but she believes in all of them so effectively that she can ask before going to the Wentworths if they have 'nothing golden but their *ton*,' and proceed, on arrival, to beg their hospitality in a convincingly simple and sentimental speech:

'I came to look – to try – to ask,' she said. 'It seems to me I have done well. I am very tired; I want to rest.' There were tears in her eyes. The luminous interior, the gentle, tranquil people, the simple, serious life – the sense of these things pressed upon her with an overmastering force, and she felt herself yielding to one of the most genuine emotions she had ever known. 'I should like to stay here,' she said. 'Pray take me in.'
Though she was smiling, there were tears in her voice as well as in her eyes.[53]

James calls for particular attention to her tears by referring to them twice in so short a space, and this only emphasizes the fact that despite them there is never a loss of accomplished manner: 'she was smiling.' Her manner holds her personality together during the free movement of emotion and attitude going on inside her. It saves her from the sincere insincerity of Mr. Brand and from being too crudely summed up by the people with whom she deals. She never loses her poise because she honestly feels the emotions to which she gives theatrical expression.

The motives of such a character cannot be discussed as if we were sifting a pile of straw in order to find a needle. The pile is all needles. Her real motive for acting as she does is in the very confusion of her motive for being where she is. A guest of relatives who consider her mother a disgrace to the family, with every expectation of being divorced by a European princeling in order to satisfy political necessities which her status as a commoner make her unable to meet, and of an age in her life when her future must depend on a settled existence – these elements in her situation, along with her refusal to be indecorous enough to show emphatic concern for any one of them, make us willing to accept a variety of explanations for her conduct. James's own decorum in dealing with the facts of her life, his reluctance to put a particular stress here or there, succeeds as much as do her manners in giving us a properly mature awareness of Eugenia's character. James's own art is at the service of hers. She needs a rest, she wants acceptance within her family, she is looking for a rich husband, she is trying to seduce Clifford for whatever profit it will bring her. Given what we know of her, each of these things is a predictable consequence of her personality and history. She is mystifying and, like Gertrude, she is thought to be dishonest, because she must, to be honest with herself, keep all her motives at play and never give herself coarsely to one of them. If she is doing anything in particular, she is trying to find something about which to have a motive, an opportunity worth the concentration of her vitality. She finds this in Robert Acton, the one New Englander who seems to include the pastoral world in which he lives and the great world in which he has travelled, and from which Eugenia, and most of the art that decorates his wifeless home, have come.

The relationship between Eugenia and Acton is richer than any other in the novel and more revelatory of the central meanings. Both of them bring greater maturity, a wider experience, and more fully-developed feeling to their association than can any of the other romantic couples. They are aware of this, Eugenia feeling on first meeting that Acton is 'intrinsically, the most important person present'[54] and Acton enthusiastically telling himself that he 'deserved to enjoy a monopoly of her, for he was the person who had most adequately gauged her capacity for social intercourse.'[55] Feeling as he does, he has from the first a vague mistrust of her, caused by the speculation that so interesting a woman could not enjoy

54 *Eur.*, p. 45.   55 *Eur.*, p. 89.

living among the Wentworths. And the prolonging of her stay becomes for him 'a gracefully mystifying anomaly'.[56] Even while he is aware of possible dissimulations on her part, she is strongly convinced of his undeviating honesty. The peculiarity of his personality is that while he seems to be honest – 'one could trust him at any rate,' she thinks, 'round all the corners of the world'[57] – he proves strangely evasive and unreliable. The theme of deception and naturalness takes the curious turn of having Eugenia bothered by the unpredictability of Acton as much as Charlotte is by Gertrude's. He encourages her to assumptions, even to declarations, about which he then proceeds to do nothing. Her perplexities and the degree to which this forces her to expose her own feelings and expectations lead her to the most serious deceptions in which she engages. He is the one person to whom and about whom she tells outright lies: she tells him she has renounced her husband and she tells Felix that Acton has proposed to her and that she has refused him. The pathos of the relationship is that her confidence in his honesty takes no account of the instability in his self-awareness and his emotions. She thinks she is dealing with a man of the world, when in reality he is a man who is at home with his mother. The psychological necessities on both sides result in a tissue of deceptions which eventually, and almost without their knowing it, cuts them off from each other. James's dramatization of this and the comedy which results from it gives a final and most suggestive definition to the theme of naturalness and art.

Because Acton is considerably more complex than any of the Wentworths and cannot, therefore, be in any sense a comic foil to Eugenia, the comedy in the scenes between the two of them is often very quiet and subtle. He is in many ways thoroughly admirable, as the respect of the Wentworths would indicate, and, as Felix observes, he is the only person in their circle with no sense of 'oppression'. Yet from the very first Eugenia is confronted with almost constricting standards of public honesty, curiously combined with a perplexing personal deviousness. When he takes her to visit his invalided mother, he reveals these qualities in a particularly unprepossessing way. Eugenia, who is, as usual, trying to be especially pleasing, chooses to flatter Mrs. Acton with the remark that she has often heard about her from Robert, 'as such a son *must* talk of such a mother!' At this, Acton gazes at Eugenia 'in vivid consciousness that he had barely mentioned his mother to their brilliant guest', and she is caught for the first time in the sort of thing that Robert Acton considers a falsehood.

The Baroness turned her smile toward him, and she instantly felt that she had been observed to be fibbing. She had struck a false note. But who were these people to whom such fibbing was not pleasing? If they were annoyed, the Baroness was equally so; and after the exchange of a few civil inquiries and low-voiced responses she took leave of Mrs. Acton. She begged Robert not to come home with her; she would get into the carriage alone; she preferred that. This was imperious, and she thought he looked disappointed. While she stood before the door with him – the carriage was turning in the gravel-walk – this thought restored her serenity.

When she had given him her hand in farewell she looked at him a moment. 'I have almost decided to dispatch that paper,' she said.

He knew that she alluded to the document that she had called her renunciation; and he assisted her into the carriage without saying anything. But just before the vehicle began to move he said, 'Well, when you have in fact dispatched it, I hope you will let me know!'[58]

For a man who apparently objects to a bit of graceful flattery as a 'false note', his silence, when she is in effect offering herself to him, followed by vaguely encouraging suggestions, represents, in view of their earlier conversations about the 'renunciation', a certain amount of cunning. There is no reason, of course, why he should propose to Eugenia at all. The scene is to be taken mostly as an example of the way Acton, whatever his intentions, defensively experiments with the notion, thereby putting her in a position from which her pride can only be salvaged by further lies. Robert Acton is a tease, though to see this brings up more questions than it answers. We can only understand him by drawing very subtly placed inferences from certain of his gestures and statements.

These inferences do not make the word 'tease', with its essentially feminine connotations, at all inappropriate to this highly successful New England trader. If his teasing engages our compassion it is because, finally, he is teasing himself, trying to find out if he is capable of feeling as much for Eugenia as he believes he ought to feel. Once again, apparent deviousness can be taken as a form of sincerity, but Acton, unlike Eugenia, employs it because of a deficiency of emotional life rather than a richness of it. He is worried about not feeling enough at the same time that he is 'ashamed, for inscrutable reasons, of the vivacity of his emotion'.[59] His perplexity alternates, therefore, between doubts about himself and doubts about her. There is an intimation that he would like her to become his mistress, both when he invites her to Niagara and in the early exchange in which, after she has called him 'conventional', he remarks that 'there is one way in which the relation of a lady and a gentleman may always become natural'.[60] His remark, making a distinction between the natural and the conventional, is ironically relevant to the whole point of the novel – that the natural is more apt to flourish in artfulness than in the conventionalized simplicities of New England. It is extraordinarily characteristic of that society, as we find it in this novel, that it educates even its sophisticated members to feel that conventions, like marriage, are to be distinguished from expressions of natural feeling, which presumably can include romantic sexuality. One can the more readily see, in view of the implications of Acton's assertion, why, when his mother dies, he marries his nice young girl. There is a suggestion, even at the time of his invitation to Niagara, when his feelings are especially strong, that he is not capable of a mature romantic relationship with her even if he wants one. I quote the passage at length to indicate how James's own comments encourage the supposition that Acton's situation is more complicated than Joseph Warren Beach makes it out to be when he claims that the novel is so simple that Acton has nothing to perplex him beyond the question of Eugenia's honesty:[61]

From the first she had been personally fascinating; but the fascination now had become intellectual as well. He was constantly pondering her words and motions; they were as interesting as the factors in an algebraic problem. This is saying a good deal; for

59 *Eur.*, p. 88.   60 *Eur.*, p. 91.
61 Beach, *The Method of Henry James*, p. 223.

Acton was extremely fond of mathematics. He asked himself whether it could be that he was in love with her, and then hoped he was not; hoped it not so much for his own sake as for that of the amatory passion itself. If this was love, love had been overrated. Love was a poetic impulse, and his own state of feeling with regard to the Baroness was largely characterized by that eminently prosaic sentiment – curiosity. It was true, as Acton, with his quietly cogitative habit observed to himself, that curiosity, pushed to a given point, might become a romantic passion; and he certainly thought enough about this charming woman to make him restless and even a little melancholy. It puzzled and vexed him that he was not more ardent. . . . It was part of his curiosity to know why the deuce so susceptible a man was *not* in love with so charming a woman. If her various graces were, as I have said, the factors in an algebraic problem, the answer to this question was the indispensable unknown quantity. The pursuit of the unknown quantity was extremely absorbing; for the present it taxed all Acton's faculties.[62]

While he may dislike Eugenia's fibbing, the 'pursuit of the unknown quantity' in his relationship with her is not an attempt to determine whether she is a deceptive and lying woman. He gives her up not because she lies, but because, as James's reference to his fondness for mathematics might suggest, he is careful and cold, the victim of an emotional lassitude which even his calculations cannot explain. This is the 'unknown quantity,' the 'inscrutable reason,' and James's own adjectival vagueness can only encourage us to look for explanations in dramatic actions where neither he nor Acton directly controls what we see. The spectacle is of a man who contrives time after time to catch the woman he admires and thinks he loves in false positions, and who even then remains dissatisfied with his lingering affections for her. After the apparently conclusive lie which she tells him about Clifford's presence in her house at two in the morning – a 'closet scene' full of New England clumsiness – Acton still has only temporary relief from 'the discomfort of a charm of which his intelligence was impatient'.[63] When Eugenia sees him for the last time at his own house, he is discovered alone in the garden:

'. . . she is not honest, she is not honest,' he kept murmuring to himself. That is what he had been saying to the summer sky ten minutes before. Unfortunately, he was unable to say it finally, definitively; and now that he was near her it seemed to matter wonderfully little. 'She is a woman who will lie,' he had said to himself. Now, as he went along, he reminded himself of this observation; but it failed to frighten him as it had done before. He almost wished he could make her lie and then convict her of it, so that he might see how he should like it.[64]

After he has succeeded, by again suggesting the seriousness of his own intentions, in making her say that she has sent off her 'renunciation', 'he turned away; he wondered whether that would do for his lie'.[65] The mere fact that he can be sure that she is lying indicates that he has divined, with his fondness for calculation, that no woman as smart as Eugenia could be treated as he has treated her, and be expected to give up even a broken marriage for a reward as uncertain as the one he pretends to dangle in front of her.

If it were enough to discover that Eugenia lies, then he would by now have satisfied his scruples. But he continues to exercise his curiosity, to 'experiment' with her, as James repeatedly describes it, during their last meeting at the Wentworths. He first suggests directly that she is lying about her 'renunciation', and then proceeds to talk enigmatically about 'another marriage' which is to take place. Poor Eugenia suspects that he is speaking of his own rather than, what is actually the case, of Lizzie and Clifford. Her failure to guess that their engagement was in the offing actually does reveal, as Acton suspected it would, that Eugenia had some sort of design on Clifford. If nothing else she thought that she had at least opened his mind sufficiently to make Lizzie, whom Eugenia has always patronized to her brother, seem less desirable than he had originally thought. The subsequent conversation dramatizes the extremity of Acton's desire to cleanse his imagination of Eugenia's charms. It is a measure of how we are to feel about him and his society at this point that in response to his success Eugenia, who finally sees what is going on, emerges as almost heroically gracious. To her manners belongs the victory:

The Baroness threw back her head and smiled at her uncle; then turning, with an intenser radiance, to Robert Acton, 'I am

64 *Eur.*, pp. 178–9.   65 *Eur.*, p. 179.

certainly very stupid not to have thought of that,' she said. Acton
looked down at his boots, as if he thought he had perhaps reached
the limits of legitimate experimentation, and for the moment
Eugenia said nothing more. It had been, in fact, a sharp knock,
and she needed to recover herself. This was done, however, prompt-
ly enough. 'Where are the young people?' she asked.

'They are spending the evening with my mother.'

'Is not the thing very sudden?'

Acton looked up. 'Extremely sudden. There had been a tacit
understanding; but within a day or two Clifford appears to have
received some mysterious impulse to precipitate the affair.'

'The impulse,' said the Baroness, 'was the charms of your very
pretty sister.'

'But my sister's charms were an old story; he had always known
her.' Acton had begun to experiment again.

Here, however, it was evident the Baroness would not help him.

'Ah, one can't say! Clifford is very young; but he is a nice
boy.'

'He's a likeable sort of boy, and he will be a rich man.' This
was Acton's last experiment. Madame Munster turned away.[66]

In this conversation Acton treats Eugenia in a way that does
violence to those standards of conduct which, we have seen,
ideally govern the relationships between characters as much as
the relationship between them and their creator, the novelist.
He uses his imagination not to know her but to 'fix' her, to
be able once and for all to tag her as a dishonest women so that
he would not need to worry that she might be a great deal
more. Acton is by way of a warning to critics that James does
not particularly like this approach to a woman like Eugenia,
that if he does not commend the results of Acton's analytical
experimentation with her freedom he would not be likely to
approve those of, say, Mr. Joseph McG. Bottkol, when they
lead him to remark that Eugenia is 'a mere scheming adven-
turess'.[67] Acton has trapped Eugenia and he enjoys it. He will
no longer be threatened by the free exercise of her charms, and
he has, at the same time, given a moral justification to his
own emotional coldness. Here we find a weakened strain of
New England Puritanism indeed, not the denial of passion by
morality but the use of morality as an excuse for the inadequacy
of feeling. This is given emphasis, even to the point of comic

66 *Eur.*, pp. 205–6.   67 Bottkol, p. xix.

bravado, by surprisingly direct suggestions about Acton's inactive, to make an allowable pun, sexual power.

I call these implications surprising not simply because they are evidence against Mr. E. M. Forster's generally accepted remark that James is not much concerned with the 'carnality' of his characters.[68] On this point, Mr. Forster has been sufficiently answered by Mr. Geoffrey Tillotson.[69] My interest in the matter is that in Acton's characterization James boldly gives colour to what elsewhere are only vague suggestions about the sexual incapacity and even impotence of many of his male characters. James does not often seem to know that he is making these suggestions, so that even Newman appears, as Mr. Traschen[70] shows in his discussion of the early version of *The American*, to have a curious sexual passivity. As a result, there is a considerable public assumption that, for reasons having to do with his own life, James was not apt to see anything strange in the fact that his male characters were deficient in sexual emotion.

If that were true, then his portrait of Acton would be an act of courage which would seem to belie the confident humour with which James invests it. For all his travels and his self-assurance, Acton is shown to be not only prim but also a little prissy. Even his physical appearance, viewed in conjunction with his conduct at the end of the novel, takes on a relevance which it would not necessarily have by itself. He is said to have 'rather less than the usual stature and the usual weight – with a small quantity of dark hair and a small moustache'.[71] He is invariably seen with his hands in his pockets. This gesture of resignation is later given to Ralph Touchett, but here it is involved with Acton's sense that he need do nothing to justify himself. He is 'action' with the 'I' left out. It is nicely suggestive that only when he is with Eugenia is he ever said to take his hands out of his pockets. None the less, when he visits her house he always assumes a posture of extreme relaxation, stretched out in his chair, playing with one of her fans. His exaggerated relaxation

68 E. M. Forster, *Aspects of the Novel* (London, 1927), pp. 229–33.

69 Geoffrey Tillotson, *Criticism and the Nineteenth Century* (London, 1951), pp. 244–69.

70 T. Traschen, 'James's Revisions of the Love Affair in *The American*,' *N.E.Q.*, XXIX (March 1956), 43–62.

71 *Eur.*, p. 44.

is in part a refuge from native shyness, but his posture is customarily what hers might be – of a person expecting seduction rather than initiating it.

The focus of these suggestions is brought to considerable dramatic clarity and comic point when Eugenia pays her final visit to the Acton home. This is immediately before Acton's final 'experimentation' with her at the Wentworths. Eugenia first talks to his mother, who, with her son's capacity for quiet nastiness, has asked Eugenia to stay in America to entertain her son, but with the insinuation that she could never do so as lady of his house: 'You seem to me all so happy here – just as you are. . . . I wish you would stay,' she added, 'in your beautiful little house.'[72] After leaving her, Eugenia wanders in the garden and finds Robert, for whom her company would be 'so pleasant', lying on the ground 'motionless, flat on his back, with his hands clasped under his head':

'Excuse my ridiculous position,' he said.
'I have just now no sense of the ridiculous. But, in case you have, don't imagine I came to see you.'
'Take care,' rejoined Acton, 'how you put it into my head! I was thinking of you.'
'The occupation of extreme leisure!' said the Baroness. 'To think of a woman when you are in that position is no compliment.'[73]

Eugenia's trenchant wit is a foretaste of James's own when he tells us in the last sentence of the novel about the girl whom Acton did marry – 'after his mother's death.'

In summary, the comedy in the drama of personal experience is the ultimate source for the social and cultural satire achieved in this novel. This is so because Eugenia is the central figure both in the international theme and in the dramatizations of the theme of art and naturalness. These two themes are so closely connected that the first is only properly understood *through* the dramatization of the second. It has been made apparent that there are too many differences between the European characters, Felix and Eugenia, to allow us to take them together as representing 'Europe'. The same discriminations are required by the several New Englanders in the novel, as is evident in the case of Charlotte and Gertrude. All the

72 *Eur.*, p. 174.   73 *Eur.*, p. 176.

New England characters do, however, have one thing in common – they cannot comfortably include Eugenia either within their corporate or their individual lives. Acton, the one person who, by his own testimony, is most capable of appreciating her, becomes instead the exorcist for the little circle in which he lives. He is their champion in the social arena of worldliness, first discouraging her and then insulting her so cunningly that she cannot retaliate. Though he uses the weapons of sophisticated manners in doing so, he can tell himself that it is in the interest of a moral principle which his whole community would have him defend: Eugenia is not 'sincere'. By this evocation, Acton reveals that his worldliness is the mere outward trapping of a man who is essentially like his neighbours. They are more admirable than he because, finally, their public life is at least interchangeable with their private lives, and the first is never a contrived disguise for the inadequacies of the second. Acton's use of the Wentworth standard is a cover for what Mr. Forster would call an undeveloped heart and what is clearly an under-developed sexuality. By a self-deceiving deference to the shibboleth of sincerity, Acton, though at once a New England trader and a collector of *objets d'art*, misses what he himself admits is an 'opportunity'.

By letting the one person in this society who might have accepted Eugenia be the agent for rejecting her, James gives a most complex definition in this novel to European-American relationships: the so-called land of opportunity is afraid to take advantage of theatricality and the socially artful. Its inhabitants are charming, honest, and generous, but they are afraid of the exploration of character and experience represented by style and manner, by the social manifestations of art. Such an impression of their fear of opportunity must be modified by the fact that Gertrude's rebellion succeeds and that Mr. Wentworth consents to Felix as a son-in-law. But this is much less dramatically compelling, particularly when Felix's character begins in comparison with his sister's to seem more and more repetitious and superficial, than the fact that there can be no consent to Eugenia, to the attitudes towards life as artfulness which I have tried to define in talking about their impression of her as deceptive. She is rejected, however, less because she is deceptive than because Acton is incapable of ignoring this in preference to the fascination which she has for him. He cannot respond in a way which he himself often feels would be natural. Thereby, he is a more sophisticated version of Mr. Brand, who dared not recognize that he was in love with Charlotte. Here we see James allowing for very unexpected and subtle similarities between characters, forming them into social groups wholly through the identifications of one hidden psychological existence with another. And this fusion can occur despite many obvious ways in which characters may differ. In all that meets the eye, Acton has escaped from Mr. Brand's limitations; and unlike the unfilled bareness of the Wentworth house his house is so tastefully decorated that even to the experienced Eugenia it indicates not merely wealth but the will to use it for the pleasures of arts. It is therefore an especially pronounced comment on the persistence, the actual psychological inhesion, of New England Puritanism, that Acton above all others should be the means of her failure.

The Europeans is a more considerable achievement and a more exciting one to read to the extent that it turns the easy contrast of Europe and America around on itself, making the Europeans closer to the classic American opportunists than are their relatives from New England. After her momentary disenchantment on the day of her arrival in Boston, Eugenia sees evidence in the very landscape that America is in reality a New World and a land of promise. The pastoral atmosphere of the Wentworths, which she contrasts with the sculptured gables and Gothic churches of Europe, contributes as much to her expectations of good fortune as to Felix's. He 'always found images and promises in the western sky',[74] and when she is riding with Acton:

Sometimes for a couple of hours together, there were almost no houses; there were nothing but woods and rivers and lakes and horizons adorned with bright-looking mountains. It seemed to the Baroness very wild, as I have said, and very lovely; but the impression added something to that sense of enlargement of opportunity which had been born of her arrival in the New World.[75]

Eugenia has a keener sense of the land than the people who live in it, and in her recognition of its promise she is more like those who found it than those who settled there. If these

74 *Eur.*, p. 162.   75 *Eur.*, p. 92.

few lines of natural description remind us of Parkman,[76] perhaps it is because in his commemoration of La Salle he so often alludes to men like Daniel Greysolon du Lhut who, though they could qualify, like Eugenia, for the vanities of Versailles, chose instead to be pioneers, always for a specific profit, but always, too, for the reason suggested almost three centuries later in F. Scott Fitzgerald's evocation of 'the fresh green breast of the new world,' its offering to each of them of 'something commensurate to his capacity for wonder'.[77]

I mean to suggest by so apparently wild a comparison to Parkman that precisely because of her mixed motives and the social sophistry which she expends in the search of fortune in the New World, Eugenia offers a specifically *American* as well as a European comment on New England. She comes to America with all the expectations and fears of those who cross the ocean, 'cast loose,' as Irving describes it, 'from the secure anchorage of settled life, and sent adrift upon a doubtful world',[78] but after her experience here it is as if the land of promise were an illusion:

and now she felt the annoyance of a rather wearied swimmer who, on nearing shore, to land, finds a smooth straight wall of rock when he had counted upon a clean firm beach. Her power, in the American air, seemed to have lost its prehensile attributes; the smooth wall of rock was insurmountable. 'Surely, *je n'en suis pas la*,' she said to herself, 'that I let it make me uncomfortable that a Mr. Robert Acton shouldn't honor me with a visit!'[79]

The appeal in the language of this passage to our sensitivity about the myth of the American pioneer adventurer seems to me unmistakable. Because of it, and of all the experience in the novel of which it is a recapitulation, this so-called 'sketch', in which one critic can so far miss the point as to say that 'the reproof cast upon Europe is without shading',[80] succeeds in expressing a view of America, particularly of New England, which is more deeply and provocatively personal than any to be found in his novels before *The Bostonians*.

76 See Francis Parkman, *The Discovery of the Great West: La Salle*, ed William R. Taylor (New York, 1956), p. 202.
77 F. Scott Fitzgerald, *The Great Gatsby* (New York, 1925), pp. 217–18.
78 Washington Irving, *The Sketch Book* (Everyman ed.), p. 4.
79 *Eur.*, p. 155.
80 Cornelia Kelley, *Early Development of Henry James*, p. 263.

The Europeans, considered in its associations with James's career and the career of other American writers of the nineteenth century, allows us to feel that in James's mind the dismissing of Eugenia from America is the rejection of at least a kind of sophisticated art and manners. The Wentworths accept Felix, whose imagination is largely playful, but they cannot accept her. The complaint that America was a land without the high civilization necessary both to the writing of novels as well as to the proper appreciation of the novelist's art finds its first considerable voice in James Fenimore Cooper, who complains in his Preface to *Home as Found* that 'it would be indeed a desperate undertaking to think of making anything interesting in the way of a *Roman de Société* in this country'.[81] Hawthorne's equally discouraging view in his preface to *The Marble Faun* is quoted by James in his biography in 1879, the year after the publication of *The Europeans*, and evokes from him the now famous enumeration of 'the items of high civilization, as it exists in other countries, which are absent from the texture of American life, until it should become a wonder to know what was left'.[82] Even without the historical and literary context in which *The Europeans* came into existence, however, the configuration of its style with the dramatic action and with James's affection for Eugenia might lead us to extend the meanings of the novel into James's personal concern for the kind of literary art, as well as the social art, which even the most 'ancient' part of America would accept.

If *The Europeans* carries the implication of James's alienation from New England, it does so in a tone of affectionate amusement. His point of view might be described as that of a benevolent observer who feels that his exclusion from the scene he is watching is a necessary consequence of his own superior capacities. Much of the comedy bears out the implication that James conceived of New England as a place especially inhospitable to his own kind of art – the art of language and its more intricate uses. This emphasis on language is apparent in the somewhat crude satire by which the Wentworths are made linguistically ignorant, almost imbecilic. They are said not to know the meaning of such words as 'amateur', 'Bohemian',

81 James Fenimore Cooper, *Home as Found* (New York, 1860), p. vi.
82 *Hawthorne*, p. 42.

and 'morganatic', and they continue even at the end to be mystified by them. Clifford's verbal ineptitude seems more authentic than this when, in a passage already alluded to, he actually giggles with delight at finding that 'in spite of her figurative language'[83] he understands what Eugenia is saying. In addition, many explicit references are made to modes of speech, suggesting how the theme of manners and naturalness is inherent in the uses of language. Eugenia is viewed by the Wentworths as 'a kind of conversational mountebank, attired, intellectually, in gauze and spangles'.[84] While Felix 'understands often both what she said and what she did not say',[85] Mr. Wentworth worries because she speaks 'somehow a different language. There was something strange in her words.' 'Another kind of man, in his place,' he suspects, 'would accommodate himself to her tone'.[86] It is hard to imagine his being able to do so, especially in view of his discomfort during such an exchange as that which follows Felix's analysis of the artistic possibilities offered by Mr. Wentworth's face:

The Baroness rattled her fan, and gave her brilliant laugh. 'It is a risk to look so close!' she exclaimed. 'My uncle has some peccadilloes on his conscience.' Mr. Wentworth looked at her, painfully at a loss; and in so far as the signs of pure and abstinent life were visible in his face they were probably particularly manifest.

'You are a *beau vieillard*, my dear uncle,' said Madame Munster, smiling with her foreign eyes.

'I think you are paying me a compliment,' said the old man.[87]

Remarks such as this give Mr. Brand the idea that Eugenia ought to speak in French because 'it is quite the style that we have heard about, that we have read about – the style of conversation of Madame de Staël, of Madame Récamier'.[88] He might have added Madame de Sévigné, who once observed that she was often very far from being of her own opinion.[89]

---

83 *Eur.*, p. 132.   84 *Eur.*, p. 46.   85 *Eur.*, pp. 13–14.
86 *Eur.*, p. 70.   87 *Eur.*, p. 73.   88 *Eur.*, p. 67.
89 This statement by Madame de Sévigné is noticed by Elizabeth Hardwick, 'The American Woman as Snow Queen', *Commentary*, XII (December 1951), 546–50. Miss Hardwick makes an observation about American attitudes towards sex and love which is very relevant to what we find in *The Europeans:* 'Love can never be an art with us or even exceptionally artful, because we think it real only when it appears without human aid; it is rain from heaven, not the work of a clever imagination' (p. 549).

Indeed, her style of conversation convinces Clifford, as well as Charlotte, that 'everything she says is to be taken in the opposite way.'[90] On Eugenia's side, she cannot believe that the conversation she hears around her is as harmless as it pretends to be. There must, she feels, be a great deal that is not being said. 'You Americans have such odd ways,' she remarks to Acton, 'you never say anything outright; there seem to be so many things you can't talk about.'[91] Felix has any equally clear impression of American reticence. It leads him, in the scene in which he is painting his uncle's portrait, to make a mistake which results in a perfectly timed series of jokes:

'Clifford's situation is no laughing matter,' said Mr. Wentworth. 'It is very peculiar, as I suppose you have guessed.'
'Ah, you mean his love affair with his cousin?'
Mr. Wentworth stared, blushing a little. 'I mean his absence from college. He has been suspended. We have decided not to speak of it unless we are asked.'
'Suspended?' Felix repeated.
'He has been requested by the Harvard authorities to absent himself for six months. Meanwhile he is studying with Mr. Brand. We think Mr. Brand will help him; at least we hope so.'
'What befell him at college?' Felix asked. 'He was too fond of pleasure? Mr. Brand will not teach him any of those secrets!'
'He was too fond of something of which he should not have been fond. I suppose it is considered a pleasure.'
Fellix gave his light laugh. 'My dear uncle, is there any doubt about its being a pleasure? C'*est de son âge*, as they say in France.'
'I should have said rather it was the vice of later life – of disappointed old age.'
Felix glanced at his uncle, with his lifted eyebrows, and then, 'Of what are you speaking?' he demanded, smiling.
'Of the situation in which Clifford was found.'
'Ah, he was found – he was caught?'
'Necessarily, he was caught. He couldn't walk; he staggered.'
'Oh,' said Felix, 'he drinks!'[92]

Felix's idea of the natural in this conversation – 'C'est de son âge' – is close to that revealed by Eugenia in her rather jaded remarks about the relationship between Clifford and Lizzie. We can say that for Eugenia and Felix, as for the Romanized Americans in *Daisy Miller*, the concept of what is natural does not take a sufficiently imaginative account of the honestly childlike and simple. Their sense of the hidden complexities behind simplicity is no less mistaken than the Wentworths' suspicion that behind artfulness and deception is a self-acknowledged clarity of motive. The comedy of this novel results from the dramatic confrontation of these misconceptions, and it allows the reader a fairly dispassionate view of the *true* state of affairs on each side. None the less, the final impression is that while Eugenia yearns for a place amidst their simplicity, they are incapable of including her artfulness. To the extent that her artfulness is associated with the verbally imaginative and complicated, it is no wonder that at the end of the novel James's compassion and admiration are given more to Eugenia than to her American friends.

To have allowed us such a vitally discriminating view of his material even though it is admittedly of small proportion, to have accomplished this without disturbing the pleasing clarity of language and the lightness of comedy and without any limiting explicitness about the significance of the action is an achievement which makes *The Europeans* a novel of which James should have been prouder. It might be said that the most elaborate irony is not in the pages of the novel itself but in the circumstances which led him to deprecate it. Surely, when his brilliant and worldly brother wrote from Cambridge, Massachusetts, that *The Europeans* was 'thin' and 'empty', it must have occurred to Henry James that the theme of the novel is concerned with how the New England ethos, described in images of deceptively promising 'emptiness', could not contrive to make room for the sophisticated and the artful. This is ironic allegory more vengeful than any contrived by so generous a spirit as Henry James, Jr.

Confidence and Washington Square

I

To deal adequately with *Confidence* and *Washington Square* requires a brief recapitulation of certain features of James's development up to the date of their publication in 1879–80. The ideological basis for the comedy in the three novels already discussed involves a concept of 'free' and 'fixed' characters and of the dramatic oppositions between them. These terms apply not only to the social situations of the characters, to their relative freedom of self-definition within the nationality or social group of which they are members, but also to the relationship between James and the characters he creates, whether, for example, he 'fixes' them in some comically grotesque position for illustrative and comparative purposes, or treats them with that dramatic tentativeness reserved for the 'free spirits' who provide his novels with their leading interest. In *The Europeans*, the concept of 'fixed' and 'free' characters, rather than being the rationale for the comedy, becomes its object, so that what appears to be 'fixed' and mannered turns out to be most 'free' and natural. As a concomitant of this, James shows greater interest in the fact that the characters themselves feel compelled to limit or fix the freedom of one another. What begins in *Roderick Hudson* as a convenient principle of discrimination becomes in *The American* an allegorical system, only to give way in *The Europeans* to dramatic equivocation and ironic qualification about the ways in which fixity or freedom can be identified. Public evidence, in the latter novel, that a character is of a particular type, based on behaviour that reflects certain social allegiances, is radically reversed or qualified by private evidence derived from indications about his inner life. In *The Europeans* the so-called international theme as a system of observation is put wholly to dramatic uses. It provides means of identification which lead only to comic confusions among those characters who rely on them too heavily. Acton is a particularly rewarding example of the way in which personal psychology, far from being made to fit his role as a 'New Englander', radically redefines and vitalizes certain possible connotations of the term.

The Europeans achieves that 'interrelation between the conscious and the unconscious, between the social and the subjective' which Mr. Austin Warren finds only in the later James.[1] There is a deep concern in this novel with the very fact that 'subjective' life and 'social' life can be in a conspiracy with one another in the interests of disguising the unflattering implications of either one. And in the interval of a year between the publications of *The Europeans* and *Confidence*, James shows increasing interest in the way unconscious feeling and incipient awareness can be victimized by appeals to highly conscious social prejudice. Characters define one another in both *Daisy Miller* and 'An International Episode' by reference to visible social types and not by consultation with their intuitions about individual personality. The stories are ironic dramatizations of the pathos and inadequacy of this. In *Daisy Miller*, for example, Winterborne has lived abroad for so long, has so lost touch with the quality of girls from his own country, that he essentially adopts the standards of his Europeanized American friends. Daisy is typed as a vulgar American, and only when she is dead does he see that she is merely natural and innocent, though, as her given name implies, unnurtured. Mrs. Westgate of 'An International Episode' looks at social experience as if it existed entirely in terms of the Anglo-American contrast, her attitude being that 'when one goes to a foreign country one ought to enjoy the differences'.[2] As a result, she cannot see Lord Lambeth's love for her sister Bessie as anything more than an opportunity 'to frighten' some English aristocrats with the possibility of a marriage outside

1 Austin Warren, *Rage for Order* (Chicago, 1948), p. 161. My remarks about *The Ambassadors* at the end of this book, and about the late novels in the review mentioned below, suggest why I disagree with Mr. Warren. The interrelation he describes is not found as an accomplishment in any particular area of James's work, and demonstrably not in the late period. Rather, the often insurmountable difficulty for James of achieving this interrelation is everywhere apparent as the necessary condition of his special genius, even the compelling energy behind it. See my review of Frederick C. Crews, 'The Tragedy of Manners: Moral Drama in the Later Novels of Henry James', *The New England Quarterly*, XXX (March 1958), 123–7.

2 *Daisy Miller and An International Episode* (New York, 1892), p. 183.

their class. She, no less than Acton, likes to use other people's feelings to justify the limitations of her own, limitations revealed by her loyalty to the efficiency of wholly public classifications of people. In both stories the tendency of one character to 'fix' another according to assumptions about social or national types is no more adequate to a full awareness of character than it was in Acton's treatment of Eugenia. More than that, James makes it clear in the case of Winterborne, as well as Acton, that the use of abstract and publically warrantable standards of judgment is in reality a refuge from the confusion and insufficiency of their emotional lives. Conscious standards are shown to be a rationalization of unconscious feelings. In moving towards a greater interest in unconscious motivation, James gives a comic dramatization to the very process of defining character by other, more public means.

This development is accompanied by evidence of considerable reflection on the novelistic creation and use of characters. If such terminology for the definition of character as we find in *The American* is no longer satisfying, and if the reason for this is a growing awareness of psychological complexity, including the need of the characters themselves to believe in abstractions and typologies, then in what terms is character to be created and how are differences among them to be dramatized? To a writer who is concerned first and last with the morality of violating, for one's own limited profit, the integrity of another personality, the possibility of placing limits on the dramatic freedom of his characters by relating everything they do to psychological theory is as disturbing as the superficiality from which it is, conceivably, an escape. 'It is an easy step,' as Kenneth Murdock remarks, 'from the colonists' anxious self-analysis to Hawthorne's care "for the deeper psychology", which both Henry James and T. S. Eliot recognized',[3] and it is but a step further, it seems to me, to Emile Zola. In 1880, the year that marked the completion of both *Confidence* and *Washington Square*, and a year after James made his observation on Hawthorne's psychology, Zola insists that the novelist no less than the physiologist is engaged in a scientific experiment to determine the rules and nature of human behaviour. He entitles

3 Kenneth B. Murdock, *Literature & Theology in Colonial New England* (Cambridge, Mass., 1949), p. 197.

his essay 'Le Roman Expérimental', and begins with the assertion that 'il me suffira de remplacer le mot "médecin" par le mot "romancier"'[4] and simply to present the reader the text of Claude Bernard's *Introduction a l'étude de la médicine expéri-mental* written seventeen years earlier. The word 'experiment', we have seen, reverberates at the end of *The Europeans*; it abounds in the pages of *Confidence*, where it might be called a key term, and it is descriptive of Dr. Sloper's relationship with his daughter in *Washington Square*.

James had no fear of science as such, nor was he adverse to its application in the study of character, but while allowing this, he observes that 'Zola would apparently hold that it much more applies to *us*'.[5] In his review of Zola's *Nana*, another product of the year 1880, he regrets its 'air of tension and effort', a consequence of Zola's habit of carefully and scientifically measuring the relevance of all the data accumulated about his characters. Though this is done with the solemn expectation that it is in the interests of reality, the process has for James the opposite effect, and he asks if it is not also 'owing to the absence of a sense of humor that this last and most violent expression of the realistic faith is extraordinarily wanting in reality'.[6] James's attitude towards the scientific attempt to turn facts about human behaviour into theories about character is sufficiently revealed in his opinion that it cannot occur simultaneously with the comic sense, with what can be called the interested indifference by which character in action is left free from unremitting accountability.

His brother William is equally ironic about experimentation when discussing the German experimental psychologists – Weber, Fechner, Vierordt, and Wundt. Their method, he writes, 'taxes patience to the utmost, and could hardly have arisen in a country whose natives could be *bored*.'[7] William James's subsequent comments on this group might, with remarkable convenience, describe the activities of those calculating experimenters in romance, Acton in *The Europeans*, Bernard and Gordon in *Confidence*, and Townsend of *Washing-*

4 Emile Zola, *Le Roman Expérimental* (Paris, 1923), p. 2.
5 *Notes on Novelists*, p. 54.
6 Edel, *The Future of the Novel*, p. 95.
7 William James, *Principles of Psychology* (New York, 1890), I, 192.

ton Square. Along with Dr. Sloper, they all attempt to figure out the women with whom they are involved, and, having arrived by experiment at a theory of how they will react, they then proceed to take advantage of their knowledge. William James's *Principles of Psychology* appeared some ten years after the novels we are considering, and yet the applicability to them of his comments on experimental science is an indication that Henry James's preoccupation with ways of treating character is implicated in a diversified scientific-intellectual movement. We cannot but think of the victimized ladies of these novels when William James complains that with experimental psychologists

the Mind must submit to a regular *siege*, in which the minute advantages gained night and day by the forces that hem her in must sum themselves up at last in her overthrow. There is little of the grand style about these new prism, pendulum, and chrono-graph-philosophers. They mean business, not chivalry.[8]

His brother Henry is determinedly chivalrous in his treatment of characters who show some of that quality themselves, his animus being saved for the likes of Morris Townsend, who turn human relationships into what literally can be called a 'business'. Like John Stuart Mill in his criticism of Bentham, Henry James is opposed to the kind of analysis which can organize 'the merely *business* part of the social arrangement'.[9] Thus we find him energetically complying with those principles set down in 'The Lesson of Balzac', where he claims that in judging a novelist

It all comes back, in fine, to that respect for the liberty of the subject which I should be willing to name as *the* great sign of the painter of the first order. Such a witness to the human comedy fairly holds his breath for fear of arresting or diverting that natural license; the witness who begins to breathe so uneasily in presence of it that his respiration not only warns off the little prowling or playing creature he is supposed to be studying, but drowns, for our ears, the ingenuous sounds of the animal, as well as the general truthful hum of the human scene at large – this demonstrator has no sufficient warrant for his task.[10]

Just as, in the human experience of a novel, one character

8 *Ibid.*, I, 192–3.
9 John Stuart Mill, *Dissertations and Discussions* (London, 1859), I, 366.
10 *The Question of Our Speech*, pp. 100–1.

may 'arrest' the 'natural license' of another by regarding him merely as a specific social type, who is being 'peculiar' when he does not act according to its prescribed functions, so a novelist may do the same when he creates such grotesque representative figures as Mr. Barnaby Striker in *Roderick Hudson*. The extent to which he can be allowed dramatic life is totally dependent on his never exceeding his fixed and therefore comically entertaining grotesqueness. The same process can occur in a more complicated and morally serious way when a character's 'liberty' is confined by emphasis on a psychological oddity, as if James had tried to clarify everything about Acton by saying that he was impotent, or everything about Eugenia by her fear of age and her desire to revenge her mother. This kind of limitation on freedom can be a dramatic circumstance in a novel, as we shall see, wherein one character tries to analyse another and, as it were, to sum him up. It can also be a circumstance in the writing of the novel, so that the novelist uses character in the way recommended by Zola's essay. When this occurs, a character cannot be allowed to have what James regards as adequate 'natural license', which means, too, that a character is not allowed to define himself through the flow and tentativeness of dramatic action. James's desire for the dramatic rendering of experience has its moral foundation in this belief in the 'freedom' of his most important characters. Since he makes a point of divesting them of any obvious kinds of 'fixity' based on external features or upon static ones, such a nationality *in extremis*, he must create them almost wholly by revealing the inner workings of their characters. At this point he faces the danger, by over-explicitness, of 'killing the things he loves', as the saying goes from Oscar Wilde. This becomes more and more of a problem as his novels begin to probe the relationship between the face one shows to the world, the public rôle one assumes or is given, and the rhythm of unconscious life going on behind it. The danger, inherent in this problem, to James's whole view of his art and of morality is most apparent in *The Portrait of a Lady* where, as we shall presently see, even his most cherished value, the idea of individual freedom from social restriction, begins to look suspiciously like an abstract rationalization by which Isabel makes her fear of sex into an ideal of conduct.

The matters I have been discussing in a general way are given dramatic specificity in the two novels being considered in this chapter. Neither depends to any extent upon definition of characters by nationality or even by their subscription to James's ideal of 'freedom', and what little attention is given to social differentiation does not modify the impression that the characters in both novels are nakedly in touch with one another. They do not meet, like the characters in *The American*, in an intervening area where all of them have a status provided by their public identities. Rather, they proceed with a conscious directness to 'experiment' with one another's inmost feelings in order to discover some fixed and all-sufficient interpretation. The process itself is productive of comedy, since it leads, particularly in the case of Dr. Sloper, to the use of irony as a means of certifying the control of one character by another. But it is also the object of comedy when those characters who are subjected to experimentation consciously set out to befuddle the experimenter.

Confidence deserves to be discussed along with *Washington Square* precisely because it offers, by virtue of its relative inferiority, some usefully blatant illustrations of James's habitual concerns. The situations and the characters involved are reminiscent of all the earlier novels. The main characters are foreign to the countries in which they spend most of their time, and their romantic involvements have an admixture either of fortune-hunting or of a desire to escape marriage because of the suspicions of fortune-hunting. The plot is concerned, mainly, with the state of mind of Bernard Longueville regarding the motives of Angela Vivian and her mother, both of whom, largely for reasons of economy, live in various parts of Europe rather than in their native America. Soon after the novel begins, Bernard is called away from a stay in Siena by his friend Gordon Wright, a wealthy American dabbler in scientific experiments. Gordon has managed to fall in love at Baden-Baden, and he requires Bernard's opinion before he dares proceed with the romance. Bernard discovers that he himself had met the girl, Angela Vivian, sometime before, though very briefly, in Siena. He finds her enigmatic, and she becomes more so when, discovering that he is supposed to be evaluating her, she sets out to act as unlike herself as she possibly can. Bernard believes at first that she is a coquette, and then, observing certain actions of her mother, that she is a fortune-hunter.

He submits the results of his investigation to Gordon. Gordon has already been rejected once by Angela, and, apparently because of Bernard's estimation, he now returns to America. Restless and concerned lest he has done Angela an injustice, Bernard takes a trip to the East. About two years later, when he visits Gordon in New York, he finds him married to Blanche Evers, a flighty, flirtatious, and extraordinarily voluble young woman who was a companion of the Vivians during the stay at Baden-Baden. Bernard sees a great deal of Gordon and his wife until it is rumoured that he is having an affair with her. At this point he goes to California and thence to Europe. There, at the resort town of Blanquais-les-Galets, he meets Angela and her mother. He discovers that he is in love with her, and that what he had before thought strange in her conduct was really the modest intimation that she had fallen in love with him. Aware of the appearance of having betrayed Gordon for his own interests, he follows her to Paris, explains his earlier disservices, and they become engaged. By the way, he discovers that despite his advice Gordon had in fact proposed to Angela a second time at Baden-Baden and been turned down. This, and not Bernard's warning, led to Gordon's sudden departure for America.

At this point, Gordon comes to Paris with Blanche. They are accompanied by Captain Lovelock, one of Blanche's earlier beaus, and now a flunky with whom she carries on a public flirtation. Gordon, enraged at what he considers Bernard's disloyalty in proposing to Angela, determines to divorce Blanche and insists that Angela break her engagement to Bernard and marry him. Angela, recognizing that Gordon and Blanche are really in love with one another, decides to straighten matters out by agreeing to listen to Gordon's suit. Informing Bernard of her purpose, she sends him to London for two weeks, during which time, in a series of conversations that resemble modern psycho-therapy,[11] she makes Gordon

11 This point is made also by Leo B. Levy, 'Henry James's *Confidence* and the Development of the Idea of the Unconscious', *American Literature*, XXVIII (November, 1956), 356–77. Unlike Mr. Levy, however, I do not

recognize that he really loves Blanche. Meanwhile, Angela's mother convinces Blanche that she really loves Gordon. The novel ends happily for everyone, except for the inconsequential and clownish Captain Lovelock, who returns to his home in London.

While the story itself may sound tedious, it is not deficient in those situations which usually call forth James's dedicated interest. In outline, it is not less promising, for example, than *The Spoils of Poynton*, but we can recognize the relative superficiality of *Confidence* by observing that Angela offers as much, potentially, as the more fully articulated but very similar Fleda Vetch. Many of the situations and circumstances which in the earlier novels were explored with the purpose of concentrating and deepening our interest are here merely placed before us and either ignored or handled with an annoyingly smug weariness. It makes very little difference to the novel whether, for instance, the action takes place in one locality or another, and when the scene is placed in New York, it might just as well be in Paris or London, for all that is made of it, even as an appeal to the senses. There are attempts to signify that all the characters, except Captain Lovelock, are American, but these consist of allusions to 'simply the American pretty girl'[12] or to the 'moral consciousness of a little Boston woman',[13] and the matter is given absolutely no particularized or dramatized vitality. Nothing would have been lost by making all the characters English, as James, according to *The Notebooks*,[14] originally intended.

The futility which can be observed in the casual handling of place and nationality is equally apparent, and of more serious consequence, in the characterization. Angela, who is thought 'peculiar' even by her mother during the first half of the novel, becomes, without any intervening development, an agent of all-forgiving reason and good sense and, in the last half, finds

consider the novel a 'landmark in the history of James's long and rewarding study of human consciousness' (p. 358), partly because it is preceded by the more substantial *The Europeans*, in which the element of unconscious motivation is handled with greater tact and sensitivity.

12 *Confidence* (London, 1921), p. 24. Hereafter, this novel will be designated *Con.*

13 *Con.*, p. 69.

14 *The Notebooks of Henry James*, ed. F. O. Matthiessen and Kenneth B. Murdock (New York, 1947), pp. 3–7.

a solution to everybody's problems. Her mother, whose apparent force of character during the stay at Baden-Baden impresses the not so easily impressed Bernard, becomes in Paris little more than a sweet old thing. She once had 'views', she remarks, meaning that her attitudes were controlled by her ambitions, but now she has 'confidence' in the essential goodness of fate.[15] Such inattentiveness to the development of character is evidence of James's failure of interest in showing more than the not astonishing fact that human beings are a fairly unpredictable lot. Part of our impatience at the way characters change over a span of pages in which they are not even mentioned is caused by James's use of Bernard as a register for all of the action, much as he uses Rowland in *Roderick Hudson*. As a result, there is no dramatization of what happens to Angela or to Gordon while Bernard is travelling in the East, and when, at the end, he leaves Paris in order that Angela and her mother may engage in their therapeutic conversations with Gordon and Blanche, all the changes in attitude that are brought about are merely reported in letters which Angela sends him. To make matters worse, there is little evidence, as Mr. Edmund Wilson observes,[16] that James has bothered fully to comprehend the character of his hero. Everything around him is so insubstantial to begin with that none of his responses can be sharply delineated, and in a given situation the reader is free to decide either that he is sensitively generous or calculatingly self-interested. The novel invites the observation that an interest in the vagaries of unconscious motivation is not transformed into artistic achievement merely by giving us an account of them, any more than the recognition of contradictions in behaviour is a guarantee of a complex understanding of their causes.

If *Confidence* is so unsuccessful, if, as Mr. F. O. Matthiessen and Mr. Kenneth B. Murdock observe, it is 'probably the weakest of all his novels',[17] then it might be felt that there is nothing to be gained by bothering with it. It is not true, however, that a writer is revealed primarily in his best works. Like

15 *Con.*, p. 192.
16 Edmund Wilson, 'The Ambiguity of Henry James', in *The Question of Henry James*, p. 180.
17 *Notebooks*, p. xii.

many inferior novels by great novelists, *Confidence* makes available some of James's characteristic preoccupations with more obviousness and clarity than do his better efforts. The clumsiness and shallowness of treatment let the intentions show forth clearly and simply, and they are not dissimilar from those in the other early novels. Another reason for considering this novel with some care, one which is directly relevant to the subject of this study, is that it represents James's attempt to write a comedy of errors and intrigue in which, from beginning to end, he keeps what Constance Rourke calls 'the open sunny level'.[18] Miss Rourke's image is unintentionally suggestive of the novel's most conspicuous weaknesses. It is 'open and sunny' because the comedy casts no shades of complexity or depth of colour upon the action. It is light to the point of vapidity. It is so light that it does not comprehend the potential seriousness of its own subject-matter, so that the single important difference between the novel and the outline for it in *The Notebooks* is that James originally planned to have it end in a murder![19]

The subject matter is, as I have suggested, reminiscent of the novels already considered and suggestive of those which follow. A legitimate view of all the early novels is that, roughly speaking, they are about romantic ambition and its disappointments. Each of them shows in some aspect of plot how romantic feeling is distorted or even nullified by fortune-hunting or the suspicion of it. Recurrent motifs of this kind, however, provide a most uninteresting basis for a discussion of the deep preoccupations of James's imagination. Romantic love and financial opportunism are the pretexts, ideally, for the dramatization of other more engrossing kinds of human perplexity. In saying that *Confidence* gives a raw emphasis to matters which are found in all of the novels through *The Portrait of a Lady* and beyond, I am not thinking of similarities in the mere *donnée* of the action, but of ideas and intuitions which, habitually in James, attach themselves to it. A good example is in the terminology of the letter in which Gordon, describing his relationship with Angela Vivian, requests Bernard's help:

18 Rourke, *American Humor*, p. 255.
19 *Notebooks*, p. 6.

'I don't mean to say that this experiment itself has gone on very fast; but I am trying to push it forward. I haven't yet had time to test its success; but in this I want your help. You know we great physicists never make an experiment without an "assistant" – a humble individual who burns his fingers and stains his clothes in the cause of science, but whose interest in the problem is only indirect'.[20]

Gordon, who in fact spends most of his time dabbling in science, is being only slightly whimsical, and he is quite serious, as subsequent events reveal, in applying the term 'experiment' to his love affair. Much has already been said about Acton's having 'reached the limits of legitimate experimentation' in his attempt to confirm his worst suppositions about Eugenia. In *The American*, Newman is described at the outset as a 'born experimentalist',[21] and this habit conditions his love for Claire, though little is said about it, in that he regards marriage to her as an authentication of his immense financial success. When he fails, the Bellegardes tell him that their hearts were not in the engagement from the beginning: 'It was a bold experiment,' according to the Marquis.[22] Even his friends, Mrs. Tristram and Valentin, help him partly out of what they admit to be 'curiosity',[23] a term applied also to Acton's mathematical and romantic speculations. Though the terminology does not become importantly suggestive until *The Europeans*, it carries tentative implications in *Roderick Hudson*, where Rowland's interest in Roderick is, like Mrs. Tristram's curiosity about Newman, bred of a sense of personal inadequacy. When it appears that Roderick is to fail, Rowland writes to his cousin Cecilia that 'I certainly never pretended the thing was anything but an experiment; I promised nothing, I answered for nothing'.[24] And the earliest of the novels, *Watch and Ward*, has as its essential situation the attempt of a guardian-lover, Roger Lawrence, to educate an orphaned girl, Nora, and to turn her into a woman who will love him and to whom he may confidently propose marriage. (As the novel opens he is being rejected by a Miss Morton.) Roger's masculine inadequacy, to which James gives only a

20 *Con.*, p. 15.   21 *Am.*, p. 28.
22 *Am.*, p. 323.   23 *Am.*, p. 448.
24 *R.H.*, p. 266.

confused acknowledgment, expresses itself in fits of pique, and his relationship with Nora has many of the aspects, without any discernible comic intention, of Thomas Day's notorious educational experiments, not with one but with two adopted girls.[25]

More than any of the novels before it, *Confidence* is directly concerned with the element of 'experimentation' in human relationships, the calculated attempt by one character to test the intentions and capacities of another. *The Notebooks*, which begin with a plan for *Confidence*, give evidence that it was James's conscious intention to make 'experimentation' a major theme: 'I think it may be made very interesting here,' he writes, 'to mark the degree in which Stanmer [Bernard Longueville] – curious, imaginative, speculative, audacious, and yet conscientious, and believing quite in his own fair play – permits himself to *experiment* [James's italics] upon Bianca [Angela Vivian] – to endeavor to draw her out and make her, if possible, betray herself'.[26] Bernard is set to his task by Gordon, who, with his attachment to science and reason, wants 'to marry with my eyes open – I want to *know* my wife'.[27] In agreeing to help him, Bernard is only acting in a way characteristic of him, 'the restless and professionless mortal that we know, wandering in life from one vague experiment to another, constantly gratified and never satisfied'.[28] The failure of his 'experiment' is apparent less in his misinterpretation of Angela's feelings than of his own.

Given the circumstances at Baden-Baden, with Gordon trying to make a 'chemical analysis' of his love, assisted by a friend who, though amused and sceptical, still 'likes to feel his intelligence at play',[29] and all their efforts directed at a girl who is aware from the outset that, as she later tells Bernard, 'I had been handed over to you to be put under the microscope – like an insect with a pin stuck through it!'[30] – given these circumstances, all of the romantic recognitions in the second half of the novel are necessarily comic. When he gets round to marrying Blanche, Gordon admits that he had 'wanted to

<hr/>

25 See the excellent account of Thomas Day in V. S. Pritchett, *The Living Novel* (New York, 1947), pp. 38–49.

26 *Notebooks*, p. 4.   27 *Con.*, p. 33.
28 *Con.*, p. 143.   29 *Con.*, p. 90.
30 *Con.*, p. 195.

estimate scientifically the woman I should marry. I have altogether got over that, and I don't know how I ever came to talk such nonsense'.[31] But he has still to face the humiliation at the end of needing to be told by the very unscientific Angela that he actually does love his wife even though he doesn't know it.

Bernard, like Gordon, is eventually forced to recognize that he is motivated by feelings which do not submit to reason and calculation and for which these latter are merely ineffectual self-deceptions. When he recognizes that he loves Angela, it is patently not a consequence of the judicious considerations of a 'clever man'. The scene is at night on the beach at Blanquais:

Everyone had gone to listen to the operetta, the sound of whose contemporary gaiety came through the open, hot-looking windows in little thin quavers and catches. The ocean was rumbling just beneath; it made a ruder but richer music. Bernard stood looking at it a moment; then he went down the steps of the beach. The tide was rather low; he walked slowly down to the line of the breaking waves. The sea looked huge and black and simple; everything was vague in the unassisted darkness. Bernard stood there some time; there was nothing but the sound and the sharp fresh smell. Suddenly he put his hand to his heart; it was beating very fast. An immense conviction had come over him – abruptly, then and there – and for a moment he held his breath. It was like a word spoken in the darkness; he held his breath to listen. He was in love with Angela Vivian, and his love was a throbbing passion! He sat down on the stones where he stood – it filled him with a kind of awe.[32]

The evocation of an overpowering and elemental simplicity and of the 'immense conviction' of spontaneous and uncalculated feeling that comes as if from a voice in the night is an ironic, almost ridiculing commentary on all the calculation and measuring of emotion that has gone on previously. As a consequence, the romantic heightening in the style and in the circumstances of the scene very nearly mocks the feelings it invokes. It is possible to be reminded of Stephen Dedalus's walk on the beach in Joyce's *Portrait*, but if in the latter there is some question about possible ironies, there can be none in *Confidence*: Bernard is not even conceivably, like Dedalus,

31 *Con.*, p. 125.   32 *Con.*, pp. 169–70.

'near to the wild heart of life . . . alone and young and wilful and wildhearted'.[33] On the contrary, he is a man who 'greatly enjoys his own society',[34] 'a charming fellow, clever, urbane',[35] and so determinedly against submitting to the chances of life that when he happens to win at roulette he falls into a fit of depression because he 'had ceased to be his own master – he had given himself to something that was not himself'.[36] His language in objecting to gambling could serve perfectly to describe his reactions to the irrationality and unanalysable quality of love. Love comes to him the way his winnings do, without his willing it or calculating it, and by blind chance. For a time he tries to escape from love, just as he tries to get rid of his profits from roulette, sharing in this some of Gordon's distaste for the role of lover: '. . . to be fascinated is to be mystified,' Gordon remarks. 'Damn it, I like my liberty – I like my judgment!'[37] The romantic stories in *Confidence* do little more than show how silly it is to try to calculate one's own feelings and, that being the case, how even more fool-hardy even to attempt experimenting with the emotional life of someone else.

The novel takes a continuously light comic view of a series of events all of which prove that the controlled analysis of human action is made impossible by the stronger and un-calculated counter-assertion of unconscious and irrational feeling. This theme, it hardly need be said, is not original with James. It is worth remarking, however, that neither in his other works nor in the writings of those, like Hawthorne, who might have influenced him is the theme a subject, as here, for a sportive and trivial comedy of errors. Disparagement of systematic intellectual experimentation might have been found in much of James's reading in the Transcendentalists, and it is characteristically expressed in Emerson's assertion that 'a dream may let us deeper into the secret of nature than a hundred concerted experiments'.[38] Such statements are obviously so far from the spirit in which James handles the subject that no direct influence is conceivable. But such ideas were a part

33 James Joyce, *A Portrait of the Artist as a Young Man* (New York, 1928), p. 199.
34 *Con.*, p. 2.   35 *Con.*, p. 19.
36 *Con.*, p. 112.   37 *Con.*, p. 62.
38 Emerson, 'Nature', *C. Works*, I, 66–7.

of the intellectual heritage which was available to him and to William, whose ironic view of experimental psychology has already been noticed. Hawthorne is a particularly important case in point, and if there is something unattractive about those characters in James who are interested in mathematics, chemistry, and medicine, there is something thoroughly villainous about them in his predecessor. A typical instance is Dr. Rappaccini, about whom Professor Baglioni remarks that 'patients are interesting to him only as subjects for some new experiment'.[39] In the same volume, *Mosses from an Old Manse*, is the tragic story of Aylmer, 'a man of science, an eminent proficient in every branch of natural philosophy',[40] who experiments with the idea of making his wife perfect and, in succeeding, also kills her. Most conspicuous is the physician Chillingworth in *The Scarlet Letter*, made inhumanly cruel by 'devoting himself, for seven years, to the constant analysis of a heart full of torture'.[41] So far as James is concerned, 'the fine thing in Hawthorne,' to repeat the statement, 'is that he cared for the deeper psychology',[42] and this includes a perception of human vampirism such as James himself reveals in *The Sacred Fount*.

Confidence seems altogether too light-hearted and unimposing to belong with the works just mentioned. With *The Europeans*, however, it can be said to represent that moment in James when he himself became engaged, if not in the 'deeper psychology', then at least in the effort to make unconscious motivation a more consistently effective part of the actions he dramatizes. Obviously, he did not wait until 1880 to discover the unconscious or to acknowledge the vogue of experimentation. I am not tracing the growth of his thought, but only the attempts by which he tried to put certain parts of it into his fiction. While he was unquestionably aware, as anyone would be who read Shakespeare, that literature can dramatize the plight of characters who have not fathomed their own natures, it was not until *The Europeans* that the things he had to say required him to transpose his knowledge about

39 Hawthorne, 'Rappaccini's Daughter', in *Works*, II, 116.
40 Hawthorne, 'The Birthmark', in *Works*, II, 47.
41 Hawthorne, *The Scarlet Letter*, in *Works*, V, 205.
42 *Hawthorne*, p. 63.

unconscious motivation into art. In *Roderick Hudson* he was at pains to show young Roderick in the grip of a compulsion which he could not control. This is treated entirely, however, as a moral problem involving Roderick's fallacious and personally disastrous theories of determinism, and the dramatization takes account not of the psychology behind the theories but only of their public effects and obvious consequences.

It is significant that both *Roderick Hudson* and *The American* take an essentially melodramatic view of the unpredictable course of events: in the first there is a kind of 'demon' inside Roderick which neither Rowland nor James can do anything but observe, and in the second there is something demonic about Fate itself, so far as Newman is concerned. In neither case are we allowed to be any less shocked than the heroes. Their response to calamity is like Bernard's discovery that he is in love: '. . . it was like a word spoken in the darkness', an event which could not have been predicted on the basis of the way things seemed to be. In *Roderick Hudson* and *The American* the shock is expressed by melodrama in which James, foregoing his customarily satiric view of it, chooses to participate and by which he calls forth our compassion. The comedy which he does allow at the endings of these two novels is the sort which implicitly protests against the indifference and effrontery of the ordinary course of external nature, of things *outside* the characters. His irony at these points is 'a campaign, of a sort, on behalf of something better', as he remarks in one of the Prefaces.[43]

The difference between this and the treatment in *The Europeans* and *Confidence* of an unanticipated turn of events is apparent both in the parody of the love-struck Bernard on the beach and in the spoofing of romantic stage melodrama when Felix and Gertrude, in the final chapter of *The Europeans*, inform the shocked Mr. Wentworth of their intentions: 'Mr. Wentworth sat staring, with a light in his face that might have been flashed back from an iceberg'.[44] In both novels the unanticipated is pleasantly comic because it derives not from mysterious circumstances essentially outside the character, but from unconscious feelings which are at play in them and of which we, with James, are aware almost from the beginning.

The similarity between *The Europeans* and *Confidence* should

43 *The Art of the Novel*, p. 222.   44 *Eur.*, p. 191.

not obscure the fact that the first is much superior, and inherent in this is a matter of great importance to an understanding of the connection between comedy and characterization in James as a whole. The distinction I would make between the two novels is that *The Europeans* endows its characters not only with private but with what we can call public identities, while *Confidence* does only the first of these. A character has a public identity when he is given a place within some social grouping, which is made discernible by nationality, by characteristic mannerisms, or by shared assumptions and values. In *The Europeans*, James manages to give each of his characters a multiple identity. We cannot explain Acton's conduct, for example, by saying that he is sexually and emotionally immature without also saying that he is a product of New England Puritanism in its feebler stages. The result is that even while his unconscious motivations are exposed to us, he is allowed to maintain a public character which, like a shield, can deflect the potential cruelty of the ironic view we may take of his conduct.

James's ideal novelistic situation, best exemplified in *The Bostonians*, a novel of extraordinary psychological penetration even while it is a social satire, allows for a fusion in the characters of a hard outer consistency with a very complicated and often inconsistent emotional life underneath it. With these two elements in proper conjunction, James feels no reluctance about giving the most probing and revelatory emphasis to the comic delineation of personality. He would not, I suspect, indulge in the essentially Dickensian comedy of *The Bostonians* if Olive Chancellor's potential lesbianism did not exist within the public and very assailable context of the suffragette movement. Because it does, her character can bear the heaviest weight of James's irony and of our scrutiny without fragmenting into parts that could be tagged with one definition or another.

Confidence is a very weak novel because more than in any other the characters are deprived of the outer layers of resistance to James's probings and revelations. They are themselves made aware of this. They feel essentially defenceless in the face of their own experimental scrutiny. They lack that sense of freedom from the judgments of others which would accrue to them if they had anything like Eugenia's manner and the public status that goes with it. In no novel before *The Portrait of a Lady* is the word 'freedom' used so plaintively. The plot exists almost wholly to satisfy those contrivances and elaborate contradictory actions by which one character strives to demonstrate his freedom from the limiting definitions or theories imposed by another. They would all say with Angela, 'and then I don't like being deposited, like a parcel, or being watched, like a curious animal. I am too fond of my liberty'.[45] James's own natural reticence in dealing with the inner lives of his characters is such that their defenceless exposure in this novel to obliteratingly complete definition makes him shy of his customarily exuberant uses of comedy. To adopt William James's term when he describes a deficiency of experimental psychologists, Henry James's 'chivalry' is called forth by Angela's rather pathetic explanation to Bernard of her peculiar behaviour: 'I simply obeyed a natural impulse of self-defence – the impulse to evade the fierce light of criticism'.[46]

In response to this situation and to such characters as he has created, James's comedy is quite understandably less energetic and singularly less inventive than in almost any other work. This is especially true in the dialogue, a typical example of which is found early in the novel between Angela and Bernard. Before this occurs, James takes the understandable precaution of telling us at least a score of times that they are both 'clever':

'It is not what Wright says; it is what he does. That's the charm!' said Bernard.

His companion was silent for a moment. 'That's not usually a charm; good conduct is not thought pleasing'.

'It surely is not thought the reverse!' Bernard exclaimed.

'It doesn't rank – in the opinion of most people – among the things that make men agreeable'.

'It depends upon what you call agreeable'.

'Exactly so,' said Miss Vivian. 'It all depends upon that'.

'But the agreeable,' Bernard went on – 'it isn't, after all, fortunately, such a subtle idea. The world certainly is agreed to think that virtue is a beautiful thing'.

Miss Vivian dropped her eyes a moment, and then, looking up, 'Is it a charm?' she asked.

45 *Con.*, p. 87.   46 *Con.*, p. 196.

'For me there is no charm without it,' Bernard declared.

'I am afraid that for me there is,' said the young girl.

'You talk as if you had sounded the depths of vice!' he said, laughing. 'What do you know about other than virtuous charms?'

'I know, of course, nothing about vice; but I have known virtue when it was very tiresome'.

'Ah, then it was a poor affair. It was poor virtue. The best virtue is never tiresome'.

Miss Vivian looked at him a little with her fine discriminating eye.

'What a dreadful thing to have to think any virtue poor!'[47]

We know that close to the writing of this James had been reading Augier and Sardou,[48] and it might have been with their example in mind that he wrote a novel in which there are so many references to 'conversation' and such conversations as this. It is clearly intended to be witty and sharp, with its pattern of repetition, the brevity of assertion and retort, and the interpolated remark that Angela's eye has a 'fine discrimination'. The result, however, is disastrously banal and sophomoric: 'it depends upon what you call agreeable'. They are talking like people who have decided to be witty, who are doing their homework for a course in social conversation. Angela, who suspects that she is being experimented upon, deceives Bernard with the insinuation that she is not interested in virtue, and she is, thereby, actually experimenting with him and keeping him from making an adequate theory about her character. The conversation is a good example of the way the themes of the novel are given dramatic life. What is conspicuously missing is the kind of personal style which we find in the conversations of the other novels. The style of Eugenia, of Newman, of Mrs. Light, even, draws upon an accumulation of the certified experience of which they are the representative types. They speak for themselves, but they have the authority of all the associations of a culture or of a social and even theatrical convention within which they are made to exist. Characters without public density of some sort are for James impossible subjects for comedy, which is to say that they cannot absorb the completeness and the urgency of his interest.

47 *Con.*, pp. 46–7.   48 *Letters*, I, 60.

II

That characters can be given a public solidity without the evocation of their place within a traditionally mannered society or even within a nationality is apparent in *Washington Square*. While he was writing it for the *Cornhill Magazine*, James was highly conscious of the fact that by using only American characters, and by setting the scene of their actions almost wholly in the still developing city of New York, he was deprived of certain resources which he had found useful in the novels before *Confidence*. He complains to Howells that it is a 'poorish story – the writing of which made me feel acutely the want of "paraphernalia." '[49] His feeling is expressed more generally in the same letter, when he argues against Howells' contention that an American novelist is as well provided for in his native country as is his English or French counterpart:

> I sympathize even less with your protest against the idea that it takes an old civilization to set a novelist in motion – a proposition that seems to me so true as to be a truism. It is on manners, customs, usages, habits, forms, upon all things matured and established, that a novelist lives – they are the very stuff his work is made of; and in saying that in the absence of those 'dreary and worn-out paraphernalia' which I enumerate as being wanting in American society, 'we have simply the whole of human life left,' you beg (to my sense) the question. I should say we had just so much less of it as these same 'paraphernalia' represent, and I think they represent an enormous quantity of it.[50]

The last sentence might serve to confirm the point of the allegory in *The Europeans* by which, in my reading of the novel, the exclusion of Eugenia from the Wentworths' is a dramatic image of the incapacity of the New England ethos to include highly civilized artistic expression. But Eugenia was more than 'manners, customs, usages, forms,' and in citing these as necessary requirements of the novelist, the 'very stuff his work is made of', James is somewhat sentimentalizing his case. Eugenia was, above all, a theatrical person, and to the conventions not merely of the theatre but of what we might call our mythic imagination, a novelist can always appeal for a body of customs and assumptions which are relevant even to the most undeveloped society. This is too often forgotten, particularly by the literary branch of the Southern Agrarians, while from all sides there is the repeated assertion, grim and vague, that great novels depend upon a society in which tradition is a living thing. While this may be true, it should not be construed to mean, as it usually is, that the society itself has to be traditional. A group of backwoodsmen from every corner of the country can gather together and give quite a lively image of 'manners' and 'form'. They can share innumerable 'customs, usages, habits' which depend entirely upon an intuitive theatrical sense. By this I mean that everybody somewhere along the line develops in his imagination a picture of typical or even mythic figures – the 'bad' woman with a heart of gold, the clever city man and the shrewd farmer. Literary tradition is as much a matter of a writer's almost unconscious sense of these as it is of his conscious imitation of other works. James in particular has a very intuitive sense of theatricality and of the conventional typologies. The very outrageousness in his naming of characters, such as Henrietta Stackpole and Fanny Assingham, is a way of catering to our desire *not* to believe in the living reality of fictional characters. It is central to my argument that James is almost always anxious to assure himself that a character is not a person, but that he is much larger than any person could be. Only by being so can he absorb the fullest analysis and the toughest, most wild-swinging efforts of James's comedy.

In terms of what has just been said, it is possible to see how *Washington Square* can be a novel in which there is great substantiality of character and extremely effective comedy without any recourse to the sort of 'old civilization' referred to in James's letter. To put it briefly, *Washington Square* is in its basic situation a melodramatic fairy-tale, complete with characters who have archetypes in everyone's most rudimentary literary experience and imagination. There is no need to have read Balzac's *Eugénie Grandet* to be aware of literary analogues if we consult our memories of Cruel Father, Motherless Daughter, Handsome Lover, and Fairy God-Mother, in this case an aunt. James's transposition of these elements from the Old to the New World makes them stand out with even sharper and larger clarity. He himself indicates an awareness of the value of such a procedure when, referring to his first conception of *The American*, he recalls:

I doubtless even then felt that the conception of Paris as the consecrated scene of rash infatuations and bold bad treacheries belongs, in the Anglo-Saxon imagination, to the infancy of art. The right renovation of any such theme as that would place it in Boston or at Cleveland, at Hartford or at Utica – give it some local connection in which we had not already had so much of it.[51]

James effectively accomplishes this 'renovation' in *Washington Square*, giving it that strength and thickness of surface upon which he can expend the full force of his imagination. This is a case, much like *The Europeans*, where the public status of the characters permits James the greatest freedom in going to work on their private identities. The difference between the two novels is that the public status of characters in *Washington Square* depends not at all on their social place or nationality, and is wholly a matter of their similarity to stock characters in stage melodrama and the fairy tale.

James compels our attention precisely because his dramatization of character and situation modifies and even reverses the suppositions which their public and conventionalized reputations encourage. This is why a recognition of James's comedy, invariably overlooked in the mole-like search for buried philosophical treasure, is indispensable to any understanding of his achievement. In an extended use of the terms, 'comedy' and 'dramatization' become almost interchangeable in James: both describe the vital art of turning the anticipated into the unexpected response. These novels do not allow us to presume that certain actions, such as the exploitation of a sweet-natured but awkward young woman, carry with them a predetermined moral attitude. Given this as a subject-matter, a novel can be pleasantly comic or severely depressing or what the author will, depending entirely on the evocations of his language. Not to acknowledge this in a reading of *Washington Square* is to fall into an account of it as controvertible as Mr. Jacques Barzun's, first printed in 1943 in an otherwise valuable essay, 'Henry James, Melodramatist'. His opinion of the novel is reaffirmed by a very recent reprinting of his article in *The*

51 *The Art of the Novel*, p. 24.

Energies of Art, and I make such an issue of it only because Mr. Barzun *seems* to be saying exactly what I have said about the situation and characters in the novel:

The wickedness of being cold, of deliberately sacrificing others to one's lusts, of taking advantage of another through legal or social or emotional privilege, obsesses James. *Washington Square* is an unparalleled example, in which Dr. Sloper's remark to his daughter, 'You will do what you like,' is as terrifying as the crack of a whip. And its force is derived from the essentially melodramatic situation of a motherless daughter victimised by a subservient aunt and a selfish father – a being for whom the melodramatic epithet of 'fiend in human form' is no longer sayable but still just.[52]

The opening sentence comes close to saying what this chapter has perhaps repeated too often, that James is acutely conscious of 'experimentation' in human relationships, and the rest of the statements give an impression of *Washington Square* not unlike the one which I have briefly sketched. None the less, it should be apparent from my general argument that I would find Mr. Barzun's account seriously misleading. Mr. Barzun sees what James is saying, but he gives no indication that he has experienced the way in which it is said. While it is true that James is obsessed with the idea of one human being taking emotional advantage of another, it is not true that he is obsessed with the 'wickedness' of this. There is no 'wickedness' in any of the novels I am discussing, with the exception of *The American*, which presents one of the few instances in James of characters about whom it is possible to be morally unequivocal. In considering James's preoccupation with relationships in which one character victimizes another, it is well to remember that very often, even in the extreme case of Osmond, the victimizer is also something of a victim.

We are made most aware of this when trying to find the source of some of James's comic sense. To notice the comedy in James is to participate in a highly impersonal and morally sophisticated rendering of experience. In narrating *The Bostonians*, for instance, he is too urbanely civilized to neglect the possibilities for comedy even in situations as melodramatically evil as those Mr. Barzun describes. What follows from this is

52 *The Question of Henry James*, p. 265. Reprinted in Jacques Barzun, *The Energies of Art* (New York, 1956), p. 233.

a modification of the inexpensive moral judgments that melodrama customarily invites. James's conception of evil is closer
to Shakespeare than to Webster, a writer who could only
conceive of it melodramatically. It seems to me unlikely that
Mr. Barzun could have responded to James's scrupulous weigh-
ing of emotional involvement and still be able to observe that
for Dr. Sloper 'the melodramatic epithet of "fiend in human
form" is no longer sayable but still just.' If it is no longer
'sayable', then it cannot be 'just', now or ever, and it is specifically such humane creations as the moral atmosphere of James's
novels that have made such epithets not only unsayable but
meaningless.

The issue may be rephrased by saying that the comedy to
which we are asked to respond in the novel and the nature of
the judgments on conduct which is implied in it, put us in a
mood which can only be called contemplative. How indeed
does it happen that a man as brilliant and witty as Dr. Sloper,
with whose appreciations James himself is associated for the
first half of the novel, can become by the end so brutal and
uncomprehending? To take him throughout simply as a
melodramatic figure is to ignore the fact that before the
terrible scene on the Alps his ironic observation of experience
is, with some slight modification, James's own. James encourages us to feel this by giving a consistently melodramatic
view of Dr. Sloper only to the foolishly romantic Mrs. Penniman. 'She has got such an artificial mind',[53] as Mrs. Almond
very rightly puts it. What James calls her 'foolish indirectness
and obliquity of character'[54] is the subject of some of Dr.
Sloper's comic abuse. This takes the form, when he accuses
her of giving Townsend the run of the house, of his *pretending*
to be fiendish, sarcastically exaggerating her silly impressions
of him and playing, with an ironic contempt, upon her coarse
sensationalism:

She was tasting the sweets of concealment; she had taken up the
line of mystery. 'She would be enchanted to be able to prove to
herself that she is persecuted,' said the Doctor; and when at last he
questioned her, he was sure she would contrive to extract from his

53 *Washington Square* (London, 1921), p. 39. Hereafter, this novel will be
designated *Wash.*
54 *Wash.*, p. 9.

words a pretext for this belief. 'Be so good as to let me know what is going on in the house,' he said to her, in a tone which, under the circumstances, he himself deemed genial.

'Going on, Austin?' Mrs. Penniman exclaimed. 'Why I am sure I don't know. I believe that last night the old gray cat had kittens.'

'At her age?' said the Doctor. 'The idea is startling – almost shocking. Be so good as to see that they are all drowned. But what else has happened?'

'Ah, the dear little kittens!' cried Mrs. Penniman. 'I wouldn't have them drowned for the world!'

Her brother puffed his cigar a few moments in silence. 'Your sympathy with kittens, Lavinia,' he presently resumed, 'arises from a feline element in your own character'.

'Cats are very graceful, and very clean', said Mrs. Penniman, smiling.

'And very stealthy. You are the embodiment both of grace and of neatness; but you are wanting in frankness'.

'You certainly are not, dear brother'.

'I don't pretend to be graceful, though I try to be neat. Why haven't you let me know that Mr. Morris Townsend is coming to the house four times a week?'[55]

The comedy in this passage is in the tradition of literary anti-feminism, of the situation in which the reasonable and assertive male intentionally sets out to shock the giddy imaginations of the women who surround him. The scenes between Fielding's Squire Western and his sister are funny partly for this reason. Sloper is exasperated, like the Squire, by being constantly in a household full of women but having no wife, so that none of his sense of their inferiority is softened or made more tolerable by romantic feeling. This is particularly true in Sloper's case, since the premature death of his beautiful wife is an irremediable sorrow, and 'save when he fell in love with Catherine Harrington, he had never been dazzled, indeed, by any feminine characteristics whatever'.[56] A man of this sort, who has at the same time generously tolerated the company of Aunt Lavinia long after her usefulness has ended, is not likely to feel put upon by a litter of kittens, and we can take what he says about them less seriously than she does. The contrast in their patterns of speech, with her humourless and literal responses and his witty habit of picking up her language and turning it sarcastically against her, suggests that Dr Sloper's only alternatives are to address her as he does, with the enjoyment of using her as as an object of wit, or to address her not at all.

James is actually more sarcastic than Sloper about Lavinia's habit of melodramatization. There is a recurrent snigger in his references to her as a 'woman of imagination', and in derisive explanations of her conduct, such as the fact that 'she was very fond of kissing people's foreheads; it was an involuntary expression of sympathy with the intellectual part'.[57] The satire in her characterization has an important consequence: it means that her view of Catherine's situation absorbs most of its potential melodrama and projects it comically:

She had a vision of this ceremony [a marriage of Catherine and Townsend] being performed in some subterranean chapel – subterranean chapels in New York were not frequent, but Mrs. Penniman's imagination was not chilled by trifles – and of the guilty couple – she liked to think of poor Catherine and her suitor as the guilty couple – being shuffled away in a fast-whirling vehicle to some obscure lodging in the suburbs, where she would pay them (in a thick veil) clandestine visits; where they would endure a period of romantic privation; and where ultimately, after she should have been their earthly providence, their intercessor, their advocate, and their medium of communication with the world, they would be reconciled to her brother in an artistic tableau, in which she herself would be somehow the central figure.[58]

Because of such comedy as this, directed against melodramatic feeling about Catherine's plight, the actual melodramatic horror of the scene in the Alps, the turning-point in the movement of the novel, has a thoroughly brutal impact. We know on the basis of what precedes it that if comedy could legitimately afford any relief to the experience, James would have been aware of it. There is no hint of parody, however, even though the scene is full of stock sensationalism: it is set among 'hard-featured rocks and glowing sky,' and before he actually deserts her by hurrying on ahead, Dr. Sloper, looking at Catherine with 'eyes that had kept the light of the flashing snow summits', asks, 'should you like to be left in such a place as this, to starve?'[59] Because Dr. Sloper has enough of James's

57 *Wash.*, p. 150.   58 *Wash.*, p. 99.   59 *Wash.*, p. 156.

own humorous awareness of fraudulently romantic self-expression, his own intensities at this moment seem to arise from a compelling emotional necessity. The scene marks the point in the novel where Dr. Sloper's way of expressing himself about Catherine begins to diverge most radically from James's. By tracing the progress of that divergence we see how James's identification with Sloper's ironic manner in the first half of the novel gives way to a criticism of it. This will serve to indicate something about James's own feelings at this point in his career about the proper comic use of the characters whose destinies he controls.

Dr. Sloper represents that half of James which is interested in the 'fixed' externality of people, in their type, as I have been calling it, and the nature of his irony is an indication of this. Sloper is, indeed, like Zola's novelist in that, as James tells us, he has, as physician, 'passed his life in estimating people (it was part of the medical trade), and in nineteen cases out of twenty he was right'.[60] 'I am helped,' he tells Mrs. Montgomery, 'by a habit I have of dividing people into classes, into types'.[61] This habit applies very specifically to Catherine: he suspects from the first that she is 'commonplace' and when she 'had become a young lady grown he regarded the matter as settled'.[62] Here, as in most matters, he is right, and the novel does nothing to convince us until after the trip to Europe that Catherine is not stolid, tedious, and dully sweet. In this, James and Sloper are in essential agreement. Naturally, James's sentiments cannot ever appear to be exactly the same as the Doctor's. As the narrator he can, first of all, make sympathetic statements about Catherine which her father can only indirectly reveal through his actions and conversation, while, so far as adversely critical remarks are concerned, we naturally feel that they are less cruel said behind her back, as it were, by James, than to her face by her father. But these matters are simply a part of the necessary difference between the kinds of personal revelation possible to the author, and those that can be made by a character in a novel which is omnisciently narrated.

Taking this into account, it is still evident that the comedy in James's introductory remarks about Catherine has the tone of Sloper's irony. Our approval of James's tone necessarily

60 *Wash.*, p. 81.   61 *Wash.*, p. 90.   62 *Wash.*, p. 11.

disposes us, though with slight trepidation, to admire the
Doctor's. A good indication that James intends this is in his
juxtaposition of his own and Dr. Sloper's comments on
Catherine's dress. Every reader of the novel will remember the
scene at Mrs. Almond's dance when Sloper finds himself face
to face with his daughter and, after seeing that her red satin
gown is both too expensive and too mature for a women her
age, greets her with the question, 'Is it possible that this
magnificent person is my child?'[63] His irony in the subsequent
conversation is extremely unkind, especially as used on so
helpless and uncomprehending a target, and yet it has its
source in the same attitude towards Catherine which we find
some pages earlier in James's own account of her taste in clothing:

When it had been duly impressed upon her that she was a young
lady – it was a good while before she could believe it – she suddenly
developed a lively taste for dress: a lively taste is quite the expression
to use. I feel as if I ought to write it very small, her judgment in
this matter was by no means infallible; it was liable to confusions
and embarrassments. Her great indulgence of it was really the
desire of a rather inarticulate nature to manifest itself; she sought to
be eloquent in her garments, and to make up for her diffidence of
speech by the fine frankness of costume. But if she expressed herself
in her clothes, it is certain that people were not to blame for not
thinking her a witty person.[64]

The passage indulges in a touch of unironic compassion, but
so does Dr. Sloper on many occasions, as when, at another
party of Mrs. Almond's, her embarrassment at being seen by
her father in conversation with Townsend is so obvious that
'the doctor felt, indeed, so sorry for her that he turned away,
to spare her the sense of being watched'.[65] Generally, however,
James's comedy in the early chapters is like Dr. Sloper's: that
of a highly witty man who would refuse to be intimidated, by
sentimental reasons, from enjoying the comic possibilities of
Catherine's deportment. Indeed, before her affair with Townsend becomes passionate enough to reveal the hidden depths of
her character, she offers little else to an agile mind than a
subject for ironic pleasantries. Otherwise, the vocabulary for

63 *Wash.*, p. 24.   64 *Wash.*, pp. 13–14.
65 *Wash.*, p. 57.

one's reaction exhausts itself with the remark that after all 'she's a very harmless young woman.'

Dr. Sloper uses her for his own entertainment in the way James uses characters whom he comically 'fixes' in order that his jibes will never seem to do an injustice to the human potentiality for improvement. 'Decidedly,' he observes to himself, 'my daughter is not brilliant'.[66] Sloper's irony is a way of testing his conclusions by seeing just how passive and unresponsive she is, and he is so certain that he has her figured out that if she does resist it is not an indication of her promise but merely a 'surprise', which entertains him the more. The word 'entertainment' is used by every character in the novel and by Sloper himself to describe his treatment of his daughter. And even after he has decided that she is capable of determined opposition to him, he remarks to Mrs. Almond that 'I wanted to see if she really would stick. But, good Lord, one's curiosity is satisfied! I see she is capable of it, and now she can let go'.[67] He cannot conceive of her acting out of a private motive of which he is unaware. So far as he is concerned, she can only have a kind of public function, in the sense that he is her audience and everything she does is of necessity designed not for her needs but for his expectations. She exists for his pleasure or she does not exist at all. The threat of disowning her in the Alps is a confirmation of what I am suggesting: a Catherine whose feelings he can no longer take ironically would indeed not be the same Catherine who is his daughter.

There is an extraordinary pathos in the scene in the Alps, however, which tinges all of Slopers' ironies and cruelties. He doesn't dare believe in the potentialities of his daughter. His capacity for love has been destroyed by the failure of all the other potentialities he believed in – the death of a wife he adored in giving birth to Catherine, and the death of his son at the age of three, 'a boy of extraordinary promise'.[68] The irony of his fate is more injurious than any he concocts, when, in the very process of losing the last of his family, he begins to sense potentialities in her for which he had given up hope. If she is not superficial, if she really does 'matter', as James would say, then he is fated to be deprived of her by the logic of his whole life, and his wit is a way of assuring himself that

66 *Wash.*, p. 38.　　67 *Wash.*, p. 175.　　68 *Wash.*, p. 4.

while everything worth while may be taken by death, Catherine, at least, will not be lost by anyone's falling in love, with her. If his judgments had the arrogance of imperturbable self-sufficiency, and if his ironic cruelties derived from an assured independence of the need to be loved, then he would hardly have to call on Morris Townsend's aunt to be told, 'Don't let her marry him!'[69] The comfort he derives from this is not that he is right about Townsend, but that he is right about Catherine; that he need not fear that he has failed to see in her more than a disinterested man might.

His need to view her as he does and the nature of his attention, once he has decided that she is commonplace, is deftly indicated in the fact that we first see him addressing her about her clothing, and later, even after the effects upon her of her passion, finding her 'about as intelligent as the bundle of shawls'.[70] He can only comprehend the surface of her character because he wants to believe that the rest of it is a settled matter. To express this in terms which indicate the nature of Sloper's similarity to James, we can say that he chooses to depend upon her 'fixity', just as James depends on the character of the Bellegardes, on any of his 'fools and fixed constituencies', on Catherine herself, for that matter, for almost half the novel. The difference between Sloper and James is that Sloper will not permit himself to see the possibilities of Catherine's 'freedom', her capacity for defying any theories which he may have about her. He does not allow her a chance to dramatize the as yet unrealized qualities of her nature.

James's ironic voice and Sloper's are never, to repeat, exactly the same because in the latter there is always a taint of direct cruelty, but they begin to separate entirely at about the point when Catherine and her father leave for Europe. The change occurs not because Catherine becomes more pitiable but because she becomes less so. She becomes interesting. This is seldom noticed in criticism of the novel, which prefers to focus on her as a pathetic cipher, explaining, usually with some of the patronizing charity of Miss Mary McCarthy, that 'in James there is a delicate tenderness toward Catherine that is the courtesy extended to all inanimate and inarticulate creatures' and that to mistreat her is a 'crass insensitiveness on

69 *Wash.*, p. 94.   70 *Wash.*, p. 153.

man's part to life of a lower order'.[71] This account, however plausible, yet requires the answer that when Catherine is essentially lifeless she is subjected to James's very nimble wit. It is as if he were trying to coerce her into life. Somehow, the circumstances of her birth, involving the death of her mother and the subsequent bitterness of her father, combined with her own frightened quiescence, give one the somewhat poetic impression that she is a child still-born. When she becomes, in fact, a woman, there is a distinctly noticeable change in James's tone. On her return from Europe, even Mrs. Penniman notices a difference: that her appearance has improved, 'she looked rather handsome',[72] and that there is a disturbing authority, especially for Aunt Lavinia, in her manner and speech. Catherine's way of addressing her aunt gives James an opportunity for some delightfully malicious pleasure:

> Mrs. Penniman was not used, in any discussion, to seeing the war carried into her own country – possibly because the enemy generally had doubts of finding subsistence there. To her own consciousness, the flowery fields of her reason had rarely been ravaged by a hostile force. It was perhaps on this account that in defending them she was majestic rather than agile.[73]

James's comic appetite, it should be clear from this, has not flagged at this point in the novel. All its energy is simply directed away from Catherine. By loving Townsend, she has achieved, as James beautifully phrases it, 'the clairvoyance of her passion'.[74] This is what gives her the confidence to judge Aunt Lavinia 'finally and without appeal', to feel 'absolved' of the duty to justify her intentions to her father, now that she values herself enough to recognize a note of contempt in his voice, and to speak even to Townsend with impressive personal power when he plans a trip to New Orleans without her:

> 'When persons are going to be married they oughtn't to think so much about business. You shouldn't think about cotton; you should think about me. You can go to New Orleans some other time – there will always be plenty of cotton. It isn't the moment to choose – we have waited too long already'.[75]

71 Mary McCarthy, *Sights and Spectacles* (New York, 1956), p. 124.
72 *Wash.*, p. 165.   73 *Ibid.*
74 *Wash.*, p. 202.   75 *Wash.*, p. 189.

Having had no object for her love until the age of twenty, save her father, and having been unable to express even that except through shy evasions in her dealings with him, Catherine finds in Townsend someone who makes her feel worthy of giving love and of demanding it. When this happens her father's irony, despite the rightness of his diagnoses, becomes unworthy of both of them. He is unwilling to see that the reason for her passivity in Europe is not her childish modesty or her customary unassertiveness, but evidence, instead, of romantic preoccupation, of what James calls her 'undiverted heart'.[76] His wit becomes a mockery of her for even pretending, as he sees it, that she is a woman in love. As he passes her window on the day of Townsend's final departure, 'he stopped a moment on the bottom of the white steps, and gravely, with an air of exaggerated courtesy, lifted his hat to her.'[77] He does not know that Townsend has left her, but, even worse, perhaps, he simply assumes that to her the masculine gestures of formal deference are of necessity a caricature. When he does know that the affair is finished, though he is for ever in the ironic position – this man who prides himself on being 'always right' – of not knowing how it ended, he has a final moment of revengeful 'entertainment' in asking Catherine:

'How does he take his dismissal?'
'I don't know!' said Catherine, less ingeniously than she had hitherto spoken.
'You mean you don't care? You are rather cruel, after encouraging him and playing with him for so long!'
The Doctor had his revenge, after all.[78]

Dr. Sloper's irony at the beginning of the novel was that of a disappointed but brilliantly witty man dealing with the pathetic and clumsy simplicity of his daughter. His irony involved the imposition of worldly knowledge upon a person who acted in almost total ignorance of it. By the end, his irony is that of a man who can deal with complications in his daughter's experience and her unpredicted emotional growth only by maintaining a view of them which is cruelly and sarcastically simple.

His brilliance of mind functions almost wholly along the

76 *Wash.*, p. 163.   77 *Wash.*, p. 194.   78 *Wash.*, p. 209.

lines of Zola's novelist, who might as well be an experimental physician. He admits to 'dividing people into classes, into types', and he assures Mrs. Montgomery that 'I may easily be mistaken about your brother as an individual, but his type is written on his whole person'.[79] Again, he reveals an interesting habit of speaking of the exteriors of the people he is analysing, and his sureness about Townsend is really not an intuition about his personality so much as a conclusion based on a knowledge of environment. That is the point, perhaps, of the title of the novel and most certainly of the descriptions in it of New York. Although for Mr. Dupee these passages provide 'an atmosphere and no more',[80] they actually serve the important function of making us recognize the fantastic development of a great city in which everyone is both literally and metaphorically moving uptown. In view of this no young man of any worth could possibly be impoverished or out of a position. James's descriptions of the city, along with his characterization of Townsend's successful cousin Arthur, who is marrying Sloper's niece and planning to move every three or four years 'because the city's growing so quick – you've got to keep up with it',[81] effectively suggest to us, even before it is confirmed, that Townsend is a ne'er-do-well. Sloper himself married an heiress and moved into what was then the embodiment of 'the last results of architectural science'[82] in Washington Square, but he was also at the time a successful physician. He can see clearly into the character of Morris Townsend because he knows how such a man might respond to the social and economic environment of New York; Sloper has been a combination, as it were, of Morris Townsend, the fortune-hunter, and Arthur Townsend, the energetic man of affairs. To be right about Morris requires exactly the talent of which Sloper boasts: a knowledge of types and of their response to external circumstance.

Thus his mind works well enough on all the world which surrounds Catherine, and we admire his perceptions of her place in it just so long as that world seems more substantial than anything going on inside her. In the environment of polite New York society, she is the type of ordinary, soft, and

79 *Wash.*, p. 90.   80 Dupee, *Henry James*, p. 63.
81 *Wash.*, p. 28.   82 *Wash.*, p. 16.

simple-minded girl and, having so decided, he perceives her in her external relationships with considerable intelligence and wit. But while he sees all round her he never bothers to take another look inside. For that reason, James, who at the beginning was himself addicted to a view of Catherine which lent itself to social comedy, disengages his view from Sloper's just as soon as Catherine reveals the movements of inner life. She becomes a 'free' character for James and remains a 'fixed' one for her father.

All of his passion, when she stays true to Townsend even after the trip to Europe, is expended not in an analysis of her feeling but in elaborate colorations of the situation. He can even suggest that she hopes he will die:

'Your engagement will have one delightful effect upon you; it will make you extremely impatient for that event'.
Catherine stood staring, and the Doctor enjoyed the point he had made. It came to Catherine with the force – or rather with the vague impressiveness – of a logical axiom which it was not her province to controvert; and yet, though it was a scientific truth, she felt wholly unable to accept it.[83]

Sloper's wit in these remarks is that of a man who is not addressing himself to a person he knows but to a situation in which he contrives to place her. Roughly, it is the sort of comedy we found in *The American*, when Madame de Belle-garde speaks to Newman as if she were engaging in a theatrical skit designed to show how great ladies deal with visiting barbarians. Her talk is not meant to take his individuality into account any more than Sloper's has any possible relevance to Catherine as a particular human being. When he talks to her in this way he is dealing with her once again as a 'type', assuming that a girl in her situation would wish her father dead. James's achievement in the characterization of Dr. Sloper has its most brilliant manifestation when, in such speeches as these, we discover that the Doctor's sensibility has become, at least tangentially, like Aunt Lavinia's. She is predominantly the person who creates situations without regard for the fact that, given the people with whom she is dealing, the situations are absurd. Just as Sloper's irony becomes

83 *Wash.*, p. 119.

brutal as the novel nears its crisis, so her silliness becomes vicious, notably in her insinuation that the Doctor murdered his wife and son and will also kill Catherine:

'Whatever you have done, stop doing it; that's all I wish'.
'Don't you wish also by chance to murder your child?' Mrs. Penniman inquired.
'On the contrary, I wish to make her live and be happy'.
'You will kill her; she passed a dreadful night'.
'She won't die of one dreadful night, nor of a dozen. Remember that I am a distinguished physician'.
Mrs. Penniman hesitated a moment. Then she risked her retort. 'Your being a distinguished physician has not prevented you from already losing *two members* of your family!'
She had risked it, but her brother gave her such a terribly incisive look – a look so like a surgeon's lancet – that she was frightened at her courage. And he answered her, in words that corresponded to the look: 'It may not prevent me, either, from losing the society of still another'.[84]

The control of tone in the Doctor's very impressive re-joinder effectively suggests his superiority to Lavinia in intellectual and temperamental energy. He becomes increasing-ly like her, however, in that his language indicates a bias against obvious reality and in favour of its most outrageous possibili-ties. Since his habits of mind will not allow him to understand Catherine, all he can do is speculate about the theoretical possibilities of her situation in the abstract. In doing so he, no less than Lavinia, creates rôles for her which she is simply not large enough to fill, though he speaks to her as if she were. In this lies the explanation for the cumulative brutality in the comic dialogue.

We can say, in conclusion, that it is best not to think of this novel as a melodrama, but to observe that in response to the experience which it includes Dr. Sloper becomes a melo-dramatist and James does not. The development of his character is from scientist to melodramatist. *Washington Square* is a masterpiece if for no other reason than its making us *feel* the closeness of these two ways of manipulating life. The scientific attitude, with its presumptions about the predictability of a course of events, necessarily leads to melodrama when human

84 *Wash.*, p. 124.

beings refuse to imitate the logical hypotheses which are imposed upon them. Thus, *Washington Square* recapitulates the connection, noticed in every novel we have considered, between melodramatic expression and the discovery of the unpredictable.

Melodrama is the voice of the scientific mind when its theories have been defied by facts, when it is raised in a very illogical protest against the freedom of what it had assumed it had fixed. To apply this proposition to such various novels as *The American* and *Washington Square* requires only that its terms be given a legitimate latitude. In doing so it can be said that scientific logic and what is often called specifically American innocence can be almost synonymous. There is little difference between a belief in the inevitability of progress and a faith in the efficacy of scientific experiment. In Faulkner, the greatest American novelist to follow James, there is indeed a kind of fusion in the figure of Thomas Sutpen, from *Absalom, Absalom!*, of Christopher Newman, the innocent, and Dr. Sloper, the scientist. Sutpen's trouble is

that innocence which believed that the ingredients of morality were like the ingredients of pie or cake and once you had measured them and balanced them and mixed them and put them into the oven it was all finished and nothing but pie or cake could come out.[85]

Simply because he believed in the necessary virtue of logic and of a 'design' for living in which other people could be used, Sutpen calls forth the outraged response of those whose own private needs he violates. To this he can only respond with a plaintive and still innocent bewilderment about what he calls 'a maelstrom of unpredictable and unreasoning human beings'.[86] *Absalom, Absalom!* is a novel which absorbs and evaluates a highly melodramatic content, and just as Sutpen, the calculating man, deserves to be associated with the exorbitantly emotional Rosa Coldfield,[87] so Sloper belongs in a class not merely with Lavinia but with Mrs. Light of *Roderick Hudson*. They are an improbable combination only superficially;

85 William Faulkner, *Absalom, Absalom!* (New York, 1936), p. 263.
86 *Ibid.*, p. 275.
87 See my essay, '"Strange Gods" in Jefferson, Mississippi', *William Faulkner: Two Decades of Criticism*, ed. Frederick J. Hoffman and Olga W. Vickery (Michigan State Press, 1951), pp. 217–43.

essentially they really do belong together. Each calculates the future and tries to control the fate of a daughter, and each reacts in the sáme way when the daughter refuses her assignment.

Washington Square differs from *Roderick Hudson* and *The American*, however, in that its melodrama is significant more to the psychological than to the moral life of its characters. Melodramatic style in the speeches of Dr. Sloper is not satirized, as it is in Mrs. Light, nor is it to be commended, as in the case of Newman, where it is a complaint that freedom to determine one's destiny is itself in the grip of historically dignified powers of restriction and emotional impoverishment. In *Washington Square*, in *Confidence*, and in the proposal scene of *The Europeans*, melodrama directs our attention towards psychological complications in those characters whose reactions create it. The vocabulary of science and experimentation which is found in each of these novels places the problem of unpredictability not in Fate or in history but within the human personality and the self-delusions it contrives.

To see this is to care more for the problem of Dr. Sloper than for the chance to call him a fiend or a villain. As I pointed out at the beginning, all the circumstances of the novel are in the convention of a melodramatic fairy-tale. But the novel itself is a literary achievement in so far as it exceeds the expectations initially aroused by its given circumstances. Sloper is corrupted precisely because he believes in them with an accelerating desperation. In escaping from this, James is detached from the Doctor's ever-heightening ironic tone, and he leaves him at last to the ineffectual torment of his own sense of humour. Thus, in its dramatic development, *Washington Square* confirms the very nature of its own literary achievement; it shows us the melodramatic direction which was open to it but which James declined. Once again, the experience dramatized within the novel is a version of James's own artistic experience in writing it, particularly as this relates to the creation and uses of character. This becomes even more apparent in the last and greatest of the early novels, *The Portrait of a Lady*.

V

The Portrait of a Lady

T HERE is general agreement that the novels of James from *Roderick Hudson* to *Washington Square* are the work of apprenticeship for the writing of *The Portrait of a Lady*. Most of the themes and all of the characters in this novel exist in less subtle form in the earlier works. Isabel, in the first half, is a composite of Mary Garland, Gertrude Wentworth, Daisy Miller, and Bessie Alden of 'An International Episode,' and, in the second half, of Angela Vivian, the heroine of *Confidence*, and Claire de Cintré. The character of Osmond has very tentative roots in Rowland Mallet, but more substantially in Dr. Sloper. Even the quality of his wit resembles the doctor's, particularly when he is contending with his sister, the Countess Gemini, a later Aunt Lavinia who has actually had the experience of her romantic imaginings, while his relationship with Pansy has aspects of Sloper's relationship with Catherine. The deception of Isabel by Madame Merle and Osmond has earlier versions, all of which concern love and marriage, in the deceptions carried out by the Lights, the Cintrés, and Townsend, and in what seems to be the deceptiveness of Eugenia and Longueville. This is only a sampling of a very extensive and fairly obvious pattern of recurrences which, of itself, is of little importance. What matters is that James's creative energy is apparently stimulated by kinds of experience which are remarkably consistent over a number of years and throughout the whole of his early fiction. As a consequence, it is possible, as we have seen, to find a close connection between the dramatic action of these novels and James's own situation as it is revealed in the various modes of his literary expression. Roughly speaking, all these novels are about the difficulties which arise from the inadequacy of one character's judgment of another; about the efforts, mostly through various kinds of deception, by which some characters try to deflect the judgments of others, and about the failures of judgment on the part of a character because of his commendable qualities of trust and spontaneity. The circumstances in each novel are in the realm of epistemology, but the dramatic rendering of them is in the nature of entertainment.

In the comedy we can witness James's effort to find a way of rendering experience which suggests a judgment on it but which in no way diminishes its claim upon our imagination, upon that attention which, he felt, no writer could anticipate in his audience except in 'the simpler, the very simplest forms'.[1] A novelist, he observes in the Preface to *The Portrait of a Lady*, is under 'a special obligation to be amusing'[2] because 'he is entitled to nothing, he is bound to admit, that can come to him, from the reader, as a result of the latter's part of any act of reflexion or discrimination.'[3] By the minor characters, on whom he tends to expend most of his comedy, only the simpler forms of attention can be said to be stimulated. Yet with such characters as Isabel Archer he is unquestionably appealing to fairly complicated acts of intelligence and judgment. Thus, when he uses the word 'amusing' he must have in mind those qualities in fiction, including comedy, which actually tend to complicate our responses. We can designate these qualities with the word 'entertainment', and say that the entertainment which a novel provides is what prevents us from seeing in the action merely an opportunity for the exercise of moral approval or disapproval. If the novelist is 'amusing', if he beguiles the reader with his inventiveness, then he succeeds in making us suspend those coarse moral definitions which, according to James's stricture, he might otherwise anticipate. Comedy, amusement, the whole concept of entertainment, one might say of fiction, is, as James sees it, a way of keeping an imaginary human action, and the characters in it whom he admires, free from the 'vague moral epithets' which, according to his adverse criticism of Froude, can be made to stand in lieu of 'real psychological facts'.[4]

James's notion of a psychological fact is not what a present-day reader's would probably be. As he uses the term 'psychology', it refers to any observed element in a character's personal history, however disreputable, which, by its appeal to our

1 *The Art of the Novel*, p. 54.
2 *Ibid.*, p. 57.   3 *Ibid.*, p. 54.
4 Unsigned review of James Anthony Froude's *Short Studies on Great Subjects*, *The Nation*, V (October 31, 1867), 351.

imagination and compassion, prevents us from being morally dismissive. It is obvious that such an appeal is especially provided for in the writing of fiction. It is equally clear that one's susceptibilities to fiction depend upon a willingness to be deceived, to play a game without constantly thinking that a score will be tallied at the end.

The reader of James's novels is amused by the spectacle before him much as are the heroes and heroines inside the novel, so that their innocence is to some extent imitated by ours. Isabel is James's heroine partly because, like the other Americans in the early novels who visit Europe, she allows herself to be 'entertained', to be taken in, as it were, in a way not unlike Rowland, Roderick, Newman, and Daisy Miller. While in the early part of the novel she tends to judge theoretically, she is almost never guilty, unlike Henrietta, of using 'moral epithets'. Even when the culpability of Madame Merle begins to emerge, Isabel 'asked herself, with an almost childlike horror of the supposition, whether to this intimate friend of several years the great historical epithet of *wicked* were to be applied. She knew the idea only by the Bible and other literary works.'[5] When she does learn the truth about Madame Merle, she forgoes the epithet for the 'real psychological fact', disappointing Countess Gemini's urgent appeal to 'be a little wicked, feel a little wicked,'[6] with an expression of pity for the blight of Madame Merle's maternal affection in the loss of Pansy.

The pathos of her situation is that she responds to things with all the generosity which James encourages in his reader and which he himself demonstrates, but that she does so in a wholly untutored and idealizing way. When Osmond gives her a fairly honest account of himself, suggesting many of his more obnoxious limitations, James reveals that 'this would have been a rather dry account of Mr. Osmond's career if Isabel had fully believed it; but her imagination supplied the human element which she was sure had not been wanting'.[7] Her 'mere errors of feeling' have been sufficient to make her tremble, and 'the chance of inflicting a sensible injury upon another person, presented only as a contingency, caused her at

5 *The Portrait of a Lady* (Boston, 1882), p. 455. Hereafter, the novel will be designated *Por*.

6 *Por.*, p. 480.   7 *Por.*, p. 232.

moments to hold her breath'.[8] Isabel's scrupulousness is by way of a pastoral imitation of James's. It is exercised without the advantage of his knowledge and experience. Indeed, his knowledge allows him to be brutal without shame, because the injuries he inflicts with his satire are in defence of those like Isabel who bear his emblems but are unarmed.

James has a keen and ready eye for 'fools', for all those who are insensitive or irreverent towards idealistic aspiration. One effect of his habit of amusing us with them is to protect his favourites. However self-indulgent Roderick might be, he is less so than the foolish and contemptible Mrs. Light, for example, just as the social awkwardness of Newman assumes, by contrast with the often preposterous formality of the Bellegardes, a refreshing and sometimes pleasantly amusing vitality. Yet, as we saw from attention to James's metaphors in *The American*, we are not allowed to respond to the Bellegardes with simple and unequivocal disapproval. While we may always be suspicious of them, they are rendered for a good half of the novel both glamorous and entertaining by the excessiveness of the language which is used to describe them. The comic metaphors serve to imply a moral judgment, but they do so in such a witty and hyperbolic manner that the moral implications tend to be absorbed into and diminished by our amusement. Our judgments cannot be abstract and are held in check until we accumulate the verifications provided by the subsequent action.

This method of presentation is one of the means by which James makes the act of reading and response an imitation of the action, within the novel, by which the hero or heroine is enamoured and deceived. *The Europeans* may be taken, in fact, to show how much is missed when, like Acton, Mr Wentworth, or Queen Victoria, we decide that we are not amused, thereby excluding from our lives that extravagant and entertaining artfulness of manner which may have its source in attitudes towards life which we judge immoral. Similarly, the stultification of response, this time to affection and love, is important to the theme of *Washington Square*, where it is inherent in the comedy provided by Dr. Sloper's wit. The novel is largely concerned with the injuriousness in human

8 *Por.*, p. 42.

affairs of an irony that expresses an unimaginative self-assurance about the inclusiveness of one's own judgments. In each of these novels the nature of the comedy reveals James's anxiety lest the characters he values most be judged by the reader too coarsely, too harshly, or too epithetically.

Of all the early novels, *The Portrait of a Lady* offers the fullest expression, both in the relationships among its characters and in the features of its style and composition, of the drama and comedy of judgment. The major artistic problem of the early novels is, at the same time, their subject: the relationship between judgment and pleasure, between knowledge and entertainment, between the limitations or fixities which awareness imposes upon our experience of the world and the freedom of response and aspiration which innocence allows. Isabel Archer, more than any character in James, is an embodiment of these problems, and it is through her that *The Portrait of a Lady* dramatizes a fictional version of them. Since they are also James's problems as a novelist, in his relationship to his reader and to his characters, Isabel's career can be viewed as an enactment of the very concerns which James feels in the process of creating her. Isabel's ambition is James's achievement, and the position she desires from which to see life most knowledgeably and compassionately is, by the testimony of the novel itself, the one which James has attained.

By making Isabel Archer susceptible to his own desire to take an abundantly large and imaginative view of human experience, James involves her in the quest for that personal condition to which all his favourite characters aspire, the condition of freedom. The term 'freedom' is very recurrent and important both in James's fiction and in his essays. It defines an ideal to which such characters as Isabel are dedicated, and the condition within which the great practitioners of James's art have laboured. When he speaks of the world as the subject of the novelist's attention, it is often in language noticeably similar to Isabel's when she is theorizing about her repeated ambition to take 'a large human view of her opportunities and obligations',[9] and to the language of others, like Ralph and James, the narrator, who find in her aspirations an incentive to imaginative free-play of their own. In his letter

9 *Por.*, p. 195.

to the Deerfield Summer School in 1889, for example, replying to an invitation to discuss the art of the novel, James gives some advice to the students which has a familiar ring. His letter is an appeal for freedom of observation, for putting aside all meanness and limitation of view. It might well remind us of Ralph's idea of giving Isabel, through a fortune, the freedom to take full advantage of her desire 'to begin by getting a general impression of life':[10]

'Oh, do something from your point of view; an ounce of example is worth a ton of generalities; do something with the great art and the great form; do something with life. You each have an impression colored by your individual conditions; make that into a picture, a picture framed by your own personal wisdom, your glimpse of the American world. The field is vast for freedom, for study, for observation, for satire, for truth. . . . I have only two little words for the matter remotely approaching to rule or doctrine; one is life and the other freedom. Tell the ladies and gentlemen, the ingenious inquirers, to consider life directly and closely, and not to be put off with mean and puerile falsities, and be conscientious about it. It is infinitely large, various and comprehensive. Every sort of mind will find what it looks for in it, whereby the novel becomes truly multifarious and illustrative. That is what I mean by liberty; give it its head and let it range. If it is in a bad way, and the English novel is, I think, nothing but absolute freedom can refresh it and restore its self-respect.'[11]

Assertions which tell us that Isabel has 'an immense curiosity about life',[12] or that, as against Osmond, she pleads 'the cause of freedom',[13] or other uses of words like 'freedom', 'liberty', and 'knowledge' are so frequent in this novel that there is no need to collect them here. That Isabel has faith in exactly those ideals which James wants to see represented in the art of the novel is apparent from the fact that his vocabulary when talking about fiction is identical with that used to describe Isabel's ambitions and hopes. The similarity which can be inferred from this between Isabel's attitude towards experience as she sets out on her career and the novelist's attitude in his writing and

10 *Por.*, p. 45.

11 'The Great Form' (a letter to the Deerfield Summer School dated Summer, 1889), in *The Future of the Novel*, ed. Leon Edel, p. 29.

12 *Por.*, p. 28.   13 *Por.*, p. 377.

observation is extremely important to any understanding of Isabel's place in *The Portrait of a Lady* and of James's place in it as her creator.

To begin with, the qualities of 'absolute freedom' and comprehensiveness, which are recommended in the letter to Deerfield, are exactly what Isabel thinks she is finding when she falls in love first with Madame Merle and then with Gilbert Osmond. Part of her love for Osmond derives from her capacity to divine in him those 'histories within histories', as they are called in the revision,[14] which are a guarantee against vulgar judgments or a concern for the opinions of others. And though she has reservations about Madame Merle, she discovers in her a person who 'appeared to have, in her experience, a touchstone for everything'.[15] She is sure that Madame Merle will be able to judge fairly of Henrietta, and this leads her to the admiring conclusion that

'that is the supreme good fortune: to be in a better position for appreciating people than they are for appreciating you'. And she added that this, when one considered it, was simply the essence of the aristocratic situation. In this light, if in none other, one should aim at the aristocratic situation.[16]

The 'aristocratic' is, for her, an 'ideal' situation because it promises exemption from the restraints which generally hamper appreciation and because it provides the deepening experience which permits confidence and security of judgment. The advantages which Isabel has in mind are essentially those which James regarded as most desirable for a novelist. There is some likeness, as a matter of fact, between Isabel's 'supreme good fortune' and James's notion of the fine central intelligence. Long before he discusses the idea in his Preface, and over ten years before he wrote *The Portrait of a Lady*, he expressed the essential meaning of the concept of central intelligence in terms which, again, are like those ascribed in the novel to Isabel's ideal:

In every human imbroglio, be it of a comic or a tragic nature, it is good to think of an observer standing aloof, the critic, the idle

14 *The Portrait of a Lady* (London, 1921), I, 352. Subsequent references to this edition will be to *Por*. rev.

15 *Por*., p. 165.   16 *Por*., pp. 165-6.

commentator of it all, taking notes, as we may say, in the interest of truth.[17]

It is clear that Isabel is not such an observer as James here imagines, and it is precisely in the nature of her unhappiness and her betrayal that she never achieves the 'situation' she admires. The similarity between James, the novelist in the novel, with his enviable position for observation, and Isabel, the heroine who tries to achieve it, explains why James is so lovingly sympathetic about her girlish eagerness at the beginning and about her failure at the end. With so congenial a subject, and one with such relevance to his intellectual autobiography, it is the more remarkable that he is able to maintain, though not with perfect consistency, the poise of the 'observer standing aloof'.

The style through which James expresses his role as the observer and narrator in *The Portrait of a Lady* is an indication of his security, of the achieved aristocracy of his position. This is particularly apparent in the quality of the comedy, where there is represented that ideally civilized view of experience which Isabel desires and which she fails to detect in Ralph. James's style has the characteristics, put into language, which identify Ralph as the most admirably intelligent character in the novel. He has, we are told, an inclination to 'jocosity and irony',[18] a phrase which James significantly changes in the revision to 'adventure and irony'.[19] The latter words aptly describe the nature of the comedy in this novel – it is used to champion the cause of speculativeness and imagination and to expose the various seductions to which it may fall prey. James's tone, and, by his leave, Ralph's, is affectionate and encouraging, but it is also superior; it is tolerant, but it is above all self-confident. By the moderation of voice in the narrated style, particularly in the first half when Isabel is being introduced, James constrains us to habits of response and understanding that make us sympathetic observers of Isabel's career and partisans of the values to which she subscribes.

While James's voice at the opening is not identical with Ralph's, it expresses an equally amused and undefensive

17 Review, [George Eliot's] *The Spanish Gypsy: A Poem*, *North American Review*, CVII (October 1868), 633.
18 *Por.*, p. 30.   19 *Por.* rev., I, 43.

urbanity of mind. For a good half of the passage with which the novel begins, the tone has a quality which is characteristic of certain observable features of English conversation. There is a noticeable habit of verbal exaggeration, by which relatively small things assume extraordinary proportions, accompanied by extremely imposing discriminations about them. The total effect is close to the mock epic. The first paragraph sounds as if James were sifting the afternoon into exquisite little pieces, giving the whole description a kind of elegant prissiness:

Under certain circumstances there are few hours in life more agreeable than the hour dedicated to the ceremony known as afternoon tea. There are circumstances in which, whether you partake of the tea or not – some people of course never do – the situation is in itself delightful. These that I have in mind in beginning to unfold this simple history offered an admirable setting to an innocent pastime. The implements of the little feast had been disposed upon the lawn of an old English country-house, in what I should call the perfect middle of a splendid summer afternoon. Part of the afternoon had waned, but much of it was left, and what was left was of the finest and rarest quality. Real dusk would not arrive for many hours; but the flood of summer light had begun to ebb, the air had grown mellow, the shadows were long upon the smooth, dense turf. They lengthened slowly, however, and the scene expressed that sense of leisure still to come which is perhaps the chief source of one's enjoyment of such a scene at such an hour. From five o'clock to eight is on certain occasions a little enternity; but on such an occasion as this the interval could be only an eternity of pleasure.[20]

The diction, none of which was altered in the revision, has a fastidious pomposity – 'ceremony known as afternoon tea', 'some people of course never do' – and we are to imagine this use of language not as part of an impersonal narration, but as a fairly personal address – note the use of 'I' – from someone striking a very individual social posture. The fastidiousness and the pomposity are harmlessly and, therefore, the more amusingly expended upon an event which is by no means less delightful than he claims. But his eager discriminations, the minute measurement of the remnants of the afternoon, the repetitions of words like 'such' and 'certain', give an excessive and correspondingly satiric note to the ritualized feelings that are at the

20 *Por.*, p. 1.

same time being commended. James assumes a definable role in this passage. He sounds like an overly impressed American who has 'gone' English, who is more English than the English. None the less, the voice teases itself, as of a man who does take delight in English habits, but with such amused and self-assured adaptability that he can exaggerate and gently spoof them.

To be aware of the stylistic accomplishment here, we need only recall for a moment certain passages in *The American*. The comparison is a natural one, not only because both novels involve the experiences in Europe of relatively untutored Americans, but also because both novels are concerned here and there with exploiting the comedy inherent in the confrontation of two cultures. In her first conversation with Newman, Madame de Bellegarde expresses her sense of opposition in a way which makes her own culture both civilized and humorously inquisitive, and transforms Newman's into one which is peculiar to the point of anthropological curiosity ('I have seen several Americans'[21]). Her wit reveals a high cultivation and a considerable intelligence, but we are left to think that both of these are at the service of provincial assumptions about Paris and America. It takes considerable daring and confidence on James's part to allow such licence to the expression of an attractively entertaining and satiric view of the hero and his background. It is part of the weakness of *The American*, however, that ultimately James is not daring enough in his characterization of Newman, that he idealizes him, sometimes ridiculously, and that his own satiric wit is used on occasion obtrusively in Newman's favour. There is a crudity of tone, as at the engagement party, whenever James feels the need to come to his hero's defence. As a result, a comic contrast between Newman's values and those of the French, which is often given an effectively complex dramatic rendering, is turned into satiric diatribe in behalf of the hero.

The passage, discussed on pages 47 to 49, in which James describes Newman at the Bellegardes' party has a stridency of invective which is as far from the aloofness of James's ideal commentator, or from Isabel's aristocratically perceptive observer, as the early novels ever get. The revisions in no way moderate the tone, even though they were made long after the

21 *Am.*, p. 169.

writing of *The Portrait of a Lady*. The conclusion is obvious:
at no time could the character of Newman or his perplexities
engage the kind of refined and cultivated attention which
James gives to Isabel Archer. Her social relationships involve
for him attitudes and awarenesses that are deeply entangled in
his feelings about his own relationship to the fictional world
he creates. In *The American*, Newman's difficulties in French
society signify little more than aspects of the European-American contrast about which his feelings were substantially simpler.
They do not, as do the personal difficulties of Isabel, serve as the
condition for dramatizing the psychological and moral, one is
tempted to repeat the epistemological, problems which attend
relationships among people who, except for Henrietta, have
consciously escaped from any confinement within the European-American definition. Nowhere in the early novels, except
intermittently in *The Europeans*, is James as aloof as he is here
from prejudices about American and European manners. And
in *The Portrait* more than in any of his other works, he reveals
a capacity to be comically invigorating by playing upon and
then disappointing our expectations about cultural differences.

If James's style creates an atmosphere in which there is a
liberal opportunity for the most unprovincial kinds of feeling
and attitude, the style of social discourse among the characters
in the opening scene does no less. Indeed, if there is any question
of James's highly sophisticated comic intention in his opening
description, it is soon dispelled by the dramatic action which
immediately follows. Far from being conscious of an 'eternity
of pleasure', two of the people actually taking part in the
'ceremony known as afternoon tea', Ralph and Lord Warburton, are instead aware of its agreeable tedium. More than
that, the host and the owner of what James calls 'the peculiarly
English picture' is a 'shrewd American banker' drinking out
of an unusually large cup, while he listens to the desultory talk
of his son and his neighbour. The talk among the gentlemen
establishes a condition for social discourse which blends easily
into the witty virtuosity of James's introduction:

'Warburton's tone is worse than mine [Ralph said]; he pretends to
be bored; I am not in the least bored; I find life only too interesting.'

'Ah, *too* interesting [his father remarked]; you shouldn't allow it
to be that, you know!'

'I am never bored when I come here', said Lord Warburton. 'One gets such uncommonly good talk'.

'Is that another sort of joke?' asked the old man. 'You have no excuse for being bored anywhere. When I was your age, I had never heard of such a thing.'

'You must have developed very late'.[22]

The boredom of the young men is not a very serious matter. Like everything else in the scene it is treated as a joke, so that Mr. Touchett, not without amusement himself, complains that 'you young men have too many jokes'.[23] They joke about Ralph's health, his ugliness, and Mr. Touchett's illness, about Warburton's politics, and, when old Touchett remarks that conditions are 'getting more serious' in the world, about seriousness itself: 'The increasing seriousness of things,' Ralph remarks, 'that is the great opportunity of jokes'.[24] All of the jokes reveal a high degree of self-assurance on the part of the characters, as in Warburton's remark on Mr. Touchett's 'development', and, even more, a considerable confidence within the group in the intelligence and essential good-will of one another.

It can be said, then, that the social relationship among the characters at tea is not unlike the presumed relationship between James and his reader: we are all men of the world without being in the least tired of the fun offered by talking even about our boredom. The importance of the resemblance between James's tone and that of the gentlemen at tea is not merely that they are both comic in about the same ways. More significant, is that just when the social environment of the novel, the 'color of its air',[25] to use James's phrase, comes into being as a discriminating and sophisticated one, Isabel Archer, with all her impetuosity and youthfully theoretical eagerness, is brought into the scene.

The dramatic situation can be most naturally described in a question: how are people of this sort, James the narrator as well as those at tea, who talk as they do and who have a sense of the hovering ridiculousness even of Ralph's fatal illness, how are they to respond to the entrance of a bright-eyed American girl who can carry on conversations which are often embarras-

22 *Por.*, p. 6.   23 *Por.*, p. 7.   24 *Ibid.*
25 See 'The Lesson of Balzac', *The Question of Our Speech*, pp. 79–87.

singly pretentious? With its manifestation of social and intellectual standards that are a measure for evaluating things through
most of the action, the extremely moderated comic tone of the
opening is also the instrument, for a good half of the novel,
by which James characterizes Isabel and through which Ralph
expresses his love for her. It is vitally important to see this if
we are to recognize that some of Isabel's seductively phrased
self-analysis is not to be taken at face value, and if we are to
understand why James's characterization of her is often intentionally elusive. The chivalrousness and intelligence in his
treatment of Isabel is apparent in the genially critical comedy
of the voice at the opening and throughout the novel up to
the point of her marriage. This is the sort of comedy which
James admired in the 'expressive and sympathetic smile' of
Alphonse Daudet, 'the smile,' he wrote in 1883, 'of the artist,
the sceptic, the man of the world'.[26] By means of such comedy,
both James and Ralph can express an amused and mature
tolerance of the heroine's vagaries. And in James's style, the
reader can actually *feel* that 'respect for the liberty of the
subject', in this case of Isabel, which he calls in 'The Lesson of
Balzac' – '*the* great sign of the painter of the first order'.[27]

There are two ways in which Isabel is endowed with the
'freedom' which James respected so unreservedly. The first
is by the practical generosity of James, as her creator, and of
the Touchetts, as her benefactors; the second, by the generosity
of spirit which breathes through James's style and through the
social life of Gardencourt. It is characteristic of James to absolve
his favourites from ordinary limitations. They are usually
rich, more than normally intelligent, morally superior, and
socially appealing. Isabel is all these things, except that at first
she lacks the wealth and the kind of companionship by which
her virtues can be adequately stimulated. By the various provi-
sions which the Touchetts make for Isabel, James secures all
the necessary practical conditions for her 'freedom'. This is
particularly true of the fortune which Ralph arranges for the
specific reason, as he tells his father, that 'she wishes to be free,
and your bequest will make her free'.[28] But more importantly,

the Touchetts, like James himself, allow Isabel the full bent of her self-dramatizing tendencies. Each of them has a self-confident tolerance which assures Isabel that she can express herself without fear of being called to a restricting account of motive or consistency. Even Mrs. Touchett, with her somewhat unimaginative, conventional reaction to Isabel's rejection of Warburton, admits to being charmed by Isabel's independence. When Ralph is curious about what his mother plans to 'do' with her, she replies that Isabel is not, after all, 'a yard of calico. I shall do absolutely nothing with her, and she herself will do everything that she chooses'.[29] In this remark, as in the general conversational tone among the Touchetts, there is a characteristic toughness of mind, which, curiously enough, reveals itself in the nature of their kindness. Their generosity is invariably indirect, not only when Ralph manages to give Isabel a fortune through the will of his father, but also when Mrs. Touchett lets her feel that she is paying her own expenses on the trip to Europe. Not only the fact but also the manner of their generosity is meant to free Isabel from restrictive obligation. The witty toughness of their talk with one another exempts everyone from the intimidations, the limitations of response that can result from assertions of praise or kindness that are too direct. Isabel's friendship with Mrs. Touchett begins when she greets her with 'you must be our crazy Aunt Lydia',[30] and Mr. Touchett's conversations with Ralph involve considerable humour, some of it rather rough, about his son's illness: 'Oh no, he's not clumsy,' he assures Lord Warburton in the presence of Ralph, 'considering that he's an invalid himself. He's a very good nurse – for a sick nurse. I call him my sick nurse because he's sick himself'.[31] Secret generosity, the disguise of love by joking – these are the ways of Ralph, his father, and, to an extent, his mother, for letting others escape the embarrassments of obligation.

    The liberation of personality which is encouraged by the social atmosphere of Gardencourt is implicit in the comedy which permeates the dialogue. In this way the ideal of 'freedom' is given dramatic and stylistic existence. We can, to repeat, actually hear and feel what it is like. This is especially true in those scenes in which Ralph and Isabel deal with the pheno-

29. *Por.*, p. 36.   30 *Por.*, p. 20.   31 *Por.*, p. 5.

menon of Henrietta Stackpole, a woman who is not only
'serious' but undeviatingly fixed in her opinions. A fair sample
of the kind of discourse which Isabel thought sufficiently
intelligent before she came to Gardencourt is offered by any
one of Henrietta's remarks after she arrives there herself.
Within the atmosphere of Gardencourt she becomes a comic
figure even for Isabel. The urbane amplitude of mind which
she encounters in Ralph drives her to ever stronger assertions
of a parochial Americanism. Given the high values attached
in the novel to urbanity of judgment, Henrietta is an eccentric,
almost, were it not for her redeeming perceptiveness, one of
James's comic grotesques. As James himself puts it in the revision, she is 'the all-judging one'.[32] 'Persons, in her view,'
Ralph thinks at one point, 'were simple and homogeneous
organisms'.[33] It is natural that such a person should become the
comic foil to Ralph, whose attitude is summed up in his advice
to Isabel: 'Judge people as critics, and you will condemn them
all'.[34] Much of the broadest comedy in the first half of the novel
derives from the conversations between Ralph and Henrietta
and the contrast between his supple and extemporizing mind
and her attempts to confine him within the limits of her
doctrinaire and superficial categories:

'I don't suppose that you are going to undertake to persuade me
that *you* are an American,' she said.
'To please you, I will be an Englishman, I will be a Turk!'
'Well, if you can change about that way, you are very welcome,'
Miss Stackpole rejoined.[35]

Her misconceptions of Ralph include an inability to understand the mildly ironic joking that plays through all his conversation, and at one point she even accuses him to Isabel of
having insulted her with the imputation that she had proposed
to him. It is indicative of James's talent for inventing comic
parallels to the more portentous elements in his stories that
Isabel should tell Ralph about this misunderstanding. She
thereby becomes involved in a joking attitude towards the
subject of marriage proposals and of European attitudes towards
women just two chapters before her rejection of Warburton,

32 *Por.* rev., I, 358.   33 *Por.*, p. 80.
34 *Por.*, p. 218.   35 *Por.*, p. 71.

when these same matters will provoke her to confused and painful self-scrutiny:

> Ralph stared. 'Has she complained of me?'
> 'She told me she thinks there is something very low in the tone of Europeans towards women'.
> 'Does she call me a European?'
> 'One of the worst. She told me you said to her something that an American never would have said. But she didn't repeat it'.
> Ralph treated himself to a burst of resounding laughter.[36]

Isabel's capacity to take a large view of Henrietta's eccentricity, to acknowledge her silliness and yet remain affectionately loyal to her, is due not simply to the sharper awareness of social and intellectual qualities which comes from her contacts with Ralph and his friends. Rather, it results from the *manner* in which Ralph prods her into this awareness. The scene in which this is most charmingly dramatized indicates two very important things about the quality of literary expression in the novel whenever Isabel is being shown in a critical light. The first of these is the way James permits Ralph to exercise a comic playfulness, a capacity to avoid all obvious pedagogical seriousness, thereby allowing Isabel to come painlessly and with only pleasurable embarrassment to a recognition of her own absurdities. The second is James's ability to 'take care' of his heroine without resorting to the blatancies and idealizations which have been noted in *The American*. The tone allows for that 'adventure and irony' in response to Isabel which is both for Ralph and James the guarantee of a sceptical idealism. When she discusses Henrietta with Ralph her sentimental view of her friend's nationality is expressed in language reminiscent of Henrietta's own verbal habits:

> 'Well,' said Isabel, smiling, 'I am afraid it is because she is rather vulgar that I like her'.
> 'She would be flattered by your reason!'
> 'If I should tell her, I would not express it in that way. I should say it is because there is something of the "people" in her'.
> 'What do you know about the people? and what does she, for that matter?'
> 'She knows a great deal, and I know enough to feel that she is a

36 *Por.*, p. 78.

kind of emanation of the great democracy – of the continent, the country, the nation. I don't say that she sums it up, that would be too much to ask of her. But she suggests it; she reminds me of it.'

'You like her then for patriotic reasons. I am afraid it is on those very grounds that I object to her'.

'Ah,' said Isabel, with a kind of joyous sigh, 'I like so many things! If a thing strikes me in a certain way, I like it. I don't want to boast, but I suppose I am rather versatile. I like people to be totally different from Henrietta – in the style of Lord Warburton's sisters, for instance. So long as I look at the Misses Molyneux, they seem to me to answer a kind of ideal. Then Henrietta presents herself, and I am immensely struck with her; not so much for herself as what stands behind her.'

'Ah, you mean the back view of her', Ralph suggested.

'What she says is true,' his cousin answered; 'you will never be serious. I like the great country stretching away beyond the rivers and across the prairies, blooming and smiling and spreading, till it stops at the blue Pacific! A strong, sweet, fresh odour seems to rise from it, and Henrietta – excuse my simile – has something of that odour in her garments.'

Isabel blushed a little as she concluded this speech, and the blush, together with the momentary ardour she had thrown into it, was so becoming to her that Ralph stood smiling at her for a moment after she had ceased speaking.

'I am not sure the Pacific is blue,' he said; 'but you are a woman of imagination. Henrietta, however, is fragrant – Henrietta is decidedly fragrant'.[37]

The civilized sweetness of Ralph's temperament and the loving gentleness of his pleasure in her artless enthusiasm is never more ingratiatingly dramatized than here, and the passage ought to be kept in mind when, in Rome, we see Isabel as the wife and hostess of Gilbert Osmond: 'She was dressed in black velvet; she looked brilliant and noble'.[38] There, she is representing her husband; here she is expressing herself. In this exchange, she learns to see the absurdity of her speech without anyone needing to remark it. In the revision, however, James makes a point of having her description of Henrietta and America carry even more of a comic burden. For the statement that Henrietta 'reminds' her of the continent, James substitutes the line 'she vividly figures it'; for Isabel's statement that she likes what 'stands behind' Henrietta, he later provides the phrase 'masses behind'.[39] Both changes allow Ralph's remark about 'the back view of her' to become exorbitantly funny. The possibility of a human being representing something or someone else, which bears, as I suggest, on what happens eventually to Isabel, and which will be discussed later at some length, is here the object of comic ridicule. Henrietta becomes in Isabel's description a grotesquely literal representation of the size and smell of the whole American continent.

Needless to say, the comedy is to serious purpose. This calls quite explicitly for definition, however, when Isabel repeats to Ralph the erroneous charge so often made by Henrietta: 'You will never be serious.' The ultimate sadness of her situation is that while she sees in Ralph a capacity for appreciation not unlike that which makes her fall in love with Osmond, she cannot recognize in the humour with which he expresses it the guarantee that, with him, her own tastes and predelictions will not be insidiously stifled. She chooses Osmond, and after three years of marriage comes to the discovery that 'he took himself so seriously; it was something appalling'.[40] Her failure is in her incapacity to see the significance of comedy. No wonder that she mistakes in Osmond the virtues that belong to Ralph. The similarity created between the two men is another instance of James's capacity to evoke the complexity of moral choice by showing the correspondences between the admirable and the corrupt. A measure of his genius is his ability to prove dramatically that no personal characteristic is of itself necessarily good or evil except within the structure of a particular personality. Osmond is made into Ralph Touchett *in extremis*, and Isabel may remark that

Ralph had something of this same quality, this appearance of thinking that life was a matter of connoisseurship; but in Ralph it was an anomaly, a kind of humorous excrescence, whereas in Mr. Osmond it was the key-note, and everything was in harmony with it.[41]

'Everything was in harmony with it' – in that phrase, carrying implications of a systematic measuring and 'placing' of

39 *Por.*, rev., I, 130.   40 *Por.*, p. 376.   41 *Por.*, p. 229.

experience, is the secret of the essential difference between Ralph's connoisseurship and Osmond's. Ralph may be a connoisseur, but his expression of this has a comicality which suggests the reverse of a desire to make everything harmonious with the prejudices of his own taste. As against Osmond's insistent reduction of Isabel's individuality to the service of his egoism, there is the always liberating humour of Ralph. He allows her the fullest liberty of expression, imposing nothing upon her but the smiles and the wit of which her own blushes, even before he speaks, admit the necessity and the justice.

II

The ambience which is provided for Isabel at the beginning of the novel is a perfect achievement of James's theories about the sort of existence which a novelist ought to allow his heroines. As her creator, he gives Isabel a kind of freedom which Balzac provides for Madame Marneffe and Thackeray denies his Becky Sharp. James himself best explains the significance of this in 'The Lesson of Balzac'. The passage shows once more his dedication to a terminology about character which I have put to considerable use:

'Balzac aime sa Valérie,' says Taine, in his great essay – so much the finest thing ever written on our author – speaking of the way in which the awful little Madame Marneffe of *Les Parents Pauvres* is drawn, and of the long rope, for her acting herself out, that her creator's participation in her reality assures her. He has been contrasting her, as it happens, with Thackeray's Becky Sharp or rather with Thackeray's attitude toward Becky, and the marked jealousy of her freedom that Thackeray exhibits from the first. I remember reading at the time of the publication of Taine's study – though it was long, long ago – a phrase in an English review of the volume which seemed to my limited perception, even in extreme youth, to deserve the highest prize ever bestowed on critical stupidity undisguised. If Balzac loved his Valérie, said this commentator, that only showed Balzac's extraordinary taste; the truth being really, throughout, that it was just through this love of each seized identity, and of the sharpest and liveliest identities most, that Madame Marneffe's creator was able to marshal his array at all. The love, as we call it, the joy in their communicated and exhibited movement, in their standing on their feet and going of themselves and acting out their characters, was what rendered possible the saturation [with his ideas] I speak of; what supplied him, through the inevitable gaps of his preparation and the crevices of his prison, his long prison of labor, a short cut to the knowledge he required. It was by loving them – as the terms of his subject and the nuggets of his mine – that he knew them; it was not by knowing them that he loved.[42]

Balzac, he continues, protected his heroine 'in the interest of her special genius and freedom', and he contrasts this with what he calls Thackeray's 'moral eagerness', his desire, 'to make sure, first of all, of your moral judgment.'

The relevance of these ideas to the presentation of character in James's early novels is obvious enough. James's problem, briefly, is to avoid sacrificing the complexity or richness of character in the interest of moral edification or the representation of abstract qualities. This is a particularly crucial matter, since as a novelist James is also anxious to avoid subverting the emblematic qualities of his characters by overly strenuous psychological definition of motive. Complexity for him resides in action motivated by the most intense moral consciousness, and this often has little to do with what we now consider psychological motivation. Since James's judgments of such action are expressed largely through the comedy, the problem of the evaluation of character and its 'exposure' is, very often, one of comic tone. While this is a matter of literary technique, it has its source in James's own personal morality. For that reason the problem of judgment becomes, as we have seen, not only a dramatic circumstance within the action of the novel, but also the observable condition in the style through which the action is given life. Dr. Sloper of *Washington Square* reveals what it means to use comedy not as an expression of tenderness but of an undeviating and arrogant judgment. His comedy is full of sarcasm, and it is significant that James in an early essay on Turgenev expresses the opinion that the ultimate novelist should be 'purged' of just that quality.[43] Though Turgenev could occasionally 'forswear his irony and become frankly sympathetic',[44] he could do so only in his

42 *The Question of Our Speech*, pp. 96–7.
43 *French Poets and Novelists*, p. 320.   44 *Ibid.*, pp. 286–7.

conceptions of women, and his besetting limitation was that
his ironic temper led him to the excess of seeing all human
aspiration with a ruthless pessimism. James used the word
'irony' at the time of the essay on Turgenev, 1874, as a synonym
for 'sarcasm', and it indicated what he took to be a notion in
Turgenev's novels that there was something conclusively vain
in human effort.

Quite another sort of irony, observable in the passages just
discussed from *The Portrait of a Lady*, provides the means by
which James and such humorously minded heroes as Ralph
avoid being 'sarcastic'. The comedy in this novel, as it comes
from the Touchetts in the opening chapters and from James's
narration, allows Isabel unencumbered liberty of expression
and theoretical aspiration. Both from sickly and ugly Ralph
and from his dying father the presumption is in favour of the
brighter side of things. It is clear from the exchange between
Ralph and Isabel about Henrietta, for instance, that some of
the comedy in the novel is meant to show the extreme youthfulness and intellectual immaturity of the heroine. Far from
being sarcastic about these, however, the comedy tends to
make us take pleasure in them.

Ralph, Mr. Touchett, Warburton, and Madame Merle are
people of great verbal exactness, so much so that their wit
depends on twisting whatever is conventionally phrased into a
joke. One consequence, created by the maturely intelligent
social life in the novel, is that some of Isabel's conversation
sounds like that of a young girl imitating what she mistakenly
believes to be intellectually sophisticated talk. This is most
endearingly evident when she addresses remarks such as ,'Oh,
I do hope they will make a revolution! I should delight in
seeing a revolution',[45] to an auditor who is as kindly and
graciously playful as Mr. Touchett. Though he tells her that
he has heard her 'take such opposite views',[46] he does not hold
her to any strict accountability for them. And neither does
James, a fact which can explain the difficulty and the peculiarity
of this novel.

James's insistence on Isabel's 'freedom' from accountability
even to herself for the resolution and explanation of vague,
often contradictory statements extends to those parts of the

45 *Por.*, p. 61. 46 *Ibid.*

novel in which he characterizes her by his own, often symbolic-
ally suggestive descriptions. To take an instance often discussed,
we are told that in Albany she likes to read alone in a room
which she chooses for its atmosphere of mysterious melancholy
and which is secured from the outside street by a bolted door
whose sidelights have been filled with green paper. 'But she
had no wish to look out,' James continues, 'for this would
have interfered with her theory that there was a strange, unseen
place on the other side – a place which became, to the child's
imagination, according to its different moods, a region of
delight or of terror'.[47] The peculiarity and inventiveness of
detail encourage inferences that Isabel is displaying something
more than the usual pleasures of a child in picturesque and
remote parts of a house. The passage demands attention and
determines the focus of many readers because it seems to provide a key, if one is looking at the scene in terms of the completed action of the novel, to the eventual difficulties of the
heroine. 'Isabel's history is prefigured,' writes Mr. Quentin
Anderson, 'in the image of her speculation before the locked
door of the "office" in Albany'.[48] The locked room is an image,
he claims, of Isabel's 'self-absorption,' and it is only Osmond's
proposal, ironically enough, which 'makes possible the opening
of a long closed door'.[49]

The notion that Isabel is self-absorbed involves the kind
of denominated judgment which the whole tone of her
characterization warns us against, and quite explicitly at one
point when the matter is affectionately disposed of with the
remark that 'you could have made her blush, any day in the
year, by telling her that she was selfish',[50] or, as the revision has
it, 'a rank egoist'.[51] There are few of us, however, faced with
the obliquity of this novel who have not at one time or other
agreed with Mr. Anderson's reading of this passage and with
his ascription of its significance to the novel as a whole. In
disagreeing with him, I am concerned not with what we may
imagine about a character like Isabel but rather with the
fact that the quality of expression in the novel informs us that

47 *Por.*, p. 19.
48 Quentin Anderson, *The American Henry James* (New Brunswick, 1957),
p. 44.
49 *Ibid.*, p. 187.   50 *Por.*, p. 44.
51 *Por.* rev., I, 63.

we may imagine many things but that we are not to believe all of them. The image of the room in Albany does lend itself to translation into a 'portrait' of Isabel which is what Mr. Anderson says it is, but it could also give a very different one. Either can be sustained by the novel as a whole. Why read the passage as indicating self-absorption or the tendency to see 'delight' and 'terror' as exclusive alternatives? We could as easily read it, both in view of later action and in its immediate context, as suggesting Isabel's capacity, even in a place as un-stimulating as Albany, to imagine experience of a more heightened and colourful kind than her actual situation warrants. Given the kind of expression to which the novel as a whole is dedicated, we cannot translate the implications of this passage into a characterizing term that 'fixes' Isabel Archer. She admits, as a matter of fact, to being 'absorbed in myself'.[52] This admission is merely an experimental and moralistic self-deprecation, however, and it derives from aspects of her character which are important to James's conception of the over-all meanings of the novel. He alludes to these when he tells us that 'she was always planning out her own develop-ment, desiring her own perfection, observing her own pro-gress'.[53] She has a novelist's interest in herself, though, as Mr. Richard Chase observes, it is that of a novelist more romantic than James.[54] To say this is to describe a *process* in her thinking. This is an important task in a novel which is everywhere concerned with kinds of consciousness, and it brings us closer to its dramatic centre than do terms, like 'self-absorbed', which are predicated upon the assumption that we are dealing with a character already formed rather than in the process of forming herself.

Isabel is continually making statements about herself which are, if we ignore the social atmosphere of the novel, as tempt-ing to the reader who is seeking explanations as is the locked door in Albany. The style and plausibility of her remarks often sound, indeed, like authentic summations, such as a commentator might make upon a character. A good example,

52 *Por.*, p. 194.
53 *Por.*, p. 44.
54 Richard Chase, *The American Novel and Its Tradition* (Garden City, 1957), pp. 134-5.

which incidentally has the same burden as the passage on
Albany, is her conversation with Ralph about 'experience':

'You want to see life, as the young men say'.
'I don't think I want to see it as the young men want to see it;
but I do want to look about me'.
'You want to drain the cup of experience'.
'No, I don't wish to touch the cup of experience. It's a poisoned
drink! I only want to see for myself'.
'You want to see, but not to feel,' said Ralph.
'I don't think that if one is a sentient being, one can make the
distinction,' Isabel returned.[55]

The peculiarity of this passage, and of many like it, is, to
repeat, that the vocabulary is like a novelist's in his presentation
of a character or like a literary critic's when he is discussing
one. The difference is that a literary critic or a novelist, unless
he were assuming a dramatic rôle, would not be allowed to
talk as carelessly and vaguely as Isabel does. The drift of her
remarks leads understandably to Ralph's assertion that she
wants 'to see, but not to feel,' and yet she is allowed simply to
pull out from under this with her reply that such a thing is
impossible. One can, of course, work out what she has in mind:
she can feel something about what she sees without taking a
more active participation in it. But the product of our interpretation is less to the point than the quality of her language,
which makes any interpretation slightly untrustworthy. It is
in keeping with the intentions of the novel as a dramatic form
to leave Isabel's terms as vague as they are, and to see in their
elusiveness, rather than in the meanings we can derive by
translating them into quite other terms, a revelation of her
character. Thus, on the basis of her remarks to Ralph we could
say *not* that she is a girl who wants to see life and is afraid of
directly experiencing it, but that she is a girl whose attempts
to explain her position result in a fuzzy use of language. We
can say further that the position itself could be taken as a
rationalization for a confusion of impulses, a confusion which
is apparent both in her conduct in Albany and in her way of
talking about herself.
It will be crucial to the final appraisal which is to be given

55 *Por.*, p. 130.

the novel in this chapter, that the inferences about Isabel's psychological peculiarity which we can draw from such passages as those I have been discussing are not allowed in the total structure to make us at all cynical about her vocabulary of 'freedom'. We cannot, without changing the rhythm and direction of the novel, decide that her general love of liberty is really a fear of the realities of particular experience. James does give us, however, a very tentative suggestion about Isabel which, if developed in conjunction with all that is fully achieved, would have, for me at least, made the novel a greater work than it is. I refer to the implication that there can be no such thing as the 'freedom' which Isabel wants and which Ralph and James want for her, simply for the reason that regardless of opportunity in the world outside, there are in everyone the flaws, the fears, the neuroses that fix and confine and stifle.

In admitting the defects of his heroine, and in suggesting others, James manages to put us in a state of mind in which we agree that they are mostly the function of age and inexperience. He warns us quite explicitly about the vulgarity of using 'scientific criticism' on a girl who is so unformed and so promising:

Altogether, with her meagre knowledge, her inflated ideals, her confidence at once innocent and dogmatic, her temper at once exacting and indulgent, her mixture of curiosity and fastidiousness, of vivacity and indifference, her desire to look well and to be if possible even better; her determination to see, to try, to know; her combination of the delicate, desultory, flame-like spirit and the eager and personal young girl; she would be an easy victim of scientific criticism, if she were not to awaken on the reader's part an impulse more tender and more purely expectant.[56]

This exhortation is full of very strong feeling. The abrupt and overlapping changes of tone indicate James's anxious desire to convince the reader that for all the oddities he may see in Isabel, he is to love her the more and to engage the less in any attempt to sum her up. Balzac *aime sa Valérie* and James his Isabel. Part of the 'freedom' we allow her is the use of her abstract and self-aggrandizing vocabulary, the very pre-

56 *Por.*, p. 43.

tentiousness of which is, in part, what makes us 'tender and more purely expectant.'

James's contrivance in allowing Isabel to act without any specification of motive is particularly provocative because the novel is concerned throughout with the possibilities of marriage – with Isabel's acceptance or rejection of certain qualities represented in her suitors and with her reasons for doing so. Considering this, we come upon the connection between the quality of some of the social satire in the novel and the permissiveness in James's relationship to his heroine.

Briefly, he prefers to make her choice of a husband a sign of her superiority to customary social values rather than indicative of deeply psychological motive. Any possibility of directing social satire against Isabel for her rejection of an English lord is explicitly declined by James, and, indeed, very directly purged from the reader's mind. Throughout Chapter XII, where he dramatizes Isabel's difficulties over Warburton's proposal, he eschews the kind of satire which derives its standards from what he calls 'the more quickly-judging half of mankind.'[57] He is referring to qualities in the responses of all his readers which are conditioned by what are presumably the social 'facts of life'. Isabel herself gives an instance of these when she admits that Warburton's proposal represents a 'magnificent "chance"',[58] and throughout the chapter James goes to considerable effort to include the attitudes of the 'judging' world. He does so, however, only in the process of telling us of their inadequacy and in warning the reader that if he adopts them he cannot possibly understand Isabel's problem or her decision. All he would be able to do is to view her satirically. Having told us at the beginning that Isabel anticipates the proposal, James observes that 'it may appear to some readers that the young lady was both precipitate and unduly fastidious, but the latter of these facts, if the charge be true, may serve to exonerate her from the discredit of the former'.[59]

This is followed by an equally disciplinary assault on the reader who might view Isabel's problem from the generally accepted social assumption that an orphaned American girl in need of a fortune must be in want of an English lord. 'At the risk of making the reader smile, it must be said that there had

57 *Por.*, p. 88.   58 *Por.* rev., I, 137.   59 *Por.*, p. 87.

been moments when the intimation that she was admired by a "personage" struck her as an aggression which she would rather have been spared'.[60] Not content with issuing these warnings nor with the fact that in the scene on the lake between Ralph and Henrietta he has already indicated a capacity, when he thinks it appropriate, to dramatize the comic and satiric possibilities of a young lady's presumptions about European proposals of marriage, James is so concerned that we may treat his heroine's uncertainty from the narrow view of social advantage that he resorts to what he himself regarded as a Trollopean misdemeanour. He violates the historical tone of the novel and 'winks at us and reminds us that he is telling us an arbitrary thing'[61]:

Smile not, however, I venture to repeat, at this simple young woman from Albany, who debated whether she should accept an English peer before he had offered himself, and who was disposed to believe that on the whole she could do better. She was a person of great good faith, and if there was a great deal of folly in her wisdom, those who judge her severely may have the satisfaction of finding that, later, she became consistently wise only at the cost of an amount of folly which will constitute almost a direct appeal to charity.[62]

It is plain enough from James's remark on Trollope, and from the regard he expresses in the Prefaces for the benefits of suspense in a wholly dramatic rendering of experience, that James writes as he does in this passage because he is writing under a compulsion. He writes in a manner not most pleasing to his art, an example of which is illustrated in the style, with its implications of comic detachment, that we find in the opening chapter. Here, in Chapter XII, it is as if our view of his heroine was seriously threatened by the intrusions of standards totally unlike those created in the first paragraph of the novel, as if the impositions of a 'vulgar world' might overwhelm the author's customarily ironic and urbane voice. He is not ironic himself, and he warns us against being so, against the 'smile'. The significance of this is obvious once it is recognized that the 'smile' is only a symptom of something to which he is even more opposed: the judgments of what are referred to throughout the chapter as the 'public at large', the 'multitude', the 'more quickly judging half of mankind', as these things are

60 *Ibid.*   61 *Partial Portraits*, p. 117.   62 *Por.*, p. 88.

possibly exemplified in us. James is trying to protect Isabel from a certain kind of irony simply by telling us that if we choose to smile at her it is because we fail to see that her response to Warburton's proposal is more complicated than are our customary social preconceptions about the opportunity she is offered. Lord Warburton himself is aware that his proposal to a girl who has neither beauty nor wealth and whom he has seen for no more than twenty odd hours is not the kind of action that 'justifies a man to the multitude'.[63] Being who he is, however, he can quite easily dismiss such thoughts from his mind. It is not so easy for Isabel, and her difficulties in disentangling her feelings from what other people might think of them attests to how far she is, at this point, from the ideal of the 'aristocratic situation'. Her perplexity leads her even to the making of statements which she does not mean, so that at one point she tells Warburton that she cannot believe that his proposal is serious:

These words of Isabel's were not perfectly sincere, for she had no doubt whatever that he was serious. They were simply a tribute to the fact, of which she was perfectly aware, that those he himself had just uttered would have excited surprise on the part of the public at large.[64]

James's admiration for Isabel expends itself most enthusiastically upon her attempts to get away from the need to 'pay tribute' to the public at large. It is because she finds herself paying such a tribute, even in discussing, much less deciding upon Warburton's proposal, that she rejects him. Mr. F. R. Leavis remarks that her refusal 'doesn't strike us as the least capricious',[65] and he stresses the importance of the 'lapse' in taste when Warburton, in Chapter VII, asks Mrs. Touchett if Isabel might stay up alone with the gentlemen. According to Mr. Leavis, Warburton's conduct 'brings to a concrete point for us the rightness of her decision against him'.[66] But since the 'lapse', if it is one, is brought to our attention by Mrs. Touchett, it is at least arguable that we are not to place as much emphasis on it as Mr. Leavis does, particularly when we

63 *Ibid.*   64 *Por.*, p. 89.
65 F. R. Leavis, *The Great Tradition* (London, 1948), p. 148.
66 *Ibid.*, p. 149.

consider that Mrs. Touchett's objections to Isabel's visit to London bring forth comment from James that

Like many ladies of her country who have lived a long time in Europe, she had completely lost her native tact on such points, and in her reaction, not in itself deplorable, against the liberty allowed to young persons beyond the seas, had fallen into gratuitous and exaggerated scruples.[67]

I am not primarily interested in correcting Mr. Leavis's reading of this particular passage, which has been widely accepted. Rather, my purpose here, as in the discussion of Mr. Quentin Anderson's interpretation of the scene in Albany, is to show in a particular instance that an explanation of Isabel's conduct or of a character like Warburton cannot safely be made in terms that are as objective and specific as those which usually satisfy James's critics. Upon this matter depends one's entire understanding of Isabel's conduct and of what James is saying in his presentation of her. She herself is confused about her reasons for doing things, because at this stage in the novel she is intimidated, despite her talk about 'freedom', by constricting social customs which seem to make her reticence publicly absurd. As a result, the chapter represents her attempts to find now one and now another explanation for her intuition that she cannot marry him. All her reasons add up to one thing: she cannot marry him because by every consideration which has meaning in the social world from which she comes and in the society which, by marriage to Warburton, she would enter, it appears absolutely logical that she should.

Warburton offers her something that neither Caspar, nor Osmond, nor Ralph could offer; he is the one man in her life who belongs to a discernably organized society. It is just that which she rejects in declining his offer of marriage – conventionalized society and all that it implies about 'system' in human effort and conduct. This seems to be what is meant by having her allude to his 'system' in close conjuction with a reference to him as a 'social magnate'.[68] It is therefore relevant to her choice that he is the only person in the novel, except for the innocuous Bantling, who is not an expatriate, and that he is also the only person who, manifesting a belief in public action, is seriously political. That he is interested in politics at all,

67 *Por.*, p. 119.   68 *Por.*, p. 87.

rather than the nature of his political liberalism, is what explains the otherwise peculiar emphasis on politics in Isabel's mind when she considers his proposal. To put it perhaps too emphatically, it might be said that Isabel's rejection of him is a repudiation of constituted society in the interests of an idealism of the self and of its sufficiency. In so far as it can be defined by her aspirations and her actions, 'freedom' for Isabel means that she need feel responsible only to the good opinion she can have of herself and not to the judgments of anyone else.

The significance of Isabel's detachment from social 'system', in the sense of her independence from its prejudices and suppositions, bears heavily upon the brilliant achievement in this novel as it involves James's autobiographical sympathy with her. The road to her ruin is paved with James's good intentions as well as her own. 'Her general disposition,' expressed in her interview with Warburton, is 'to elude any obligation to take a restricted view'.[69] In like manner, James's 'disposition' in the dramatization of her career is to be completely above any of the restrictions imposed by conventional social prejudice or national provinciality. This expresses itself at the beginning of the novel in the charming civility of tone which is intended to breed us, as it were, to the point where we will regard other experiences in the novel with attitudes equally civilized. Along with this, the comic rendering of the crudities of Henrietta on the subjects of England, America, and marriage have the effect of suppressing any response to Isabel's actions which depend upon a suspicion that she is equally crude. We are to regard her choices as evolving from an almost Platonic idealism about human possibility. At the point in the novel where this idealism is offered what seems like a fairly satisfactory social realization, James becomes uncertain of the dependability of his reader. The delicate poise of his comedy is forsworn, and he appeals directly to us not to 'smile' at Isabel. The reason for his anxiety lest we find her conduct eccentrically amusing is clear enough: Isabel is expressing in her *actions*, as well as by her vocabulary, those very values of independence from social confinement which provide the basis for James's own ironic superiority of tone in his style.

69 *Por.*, p. 92.

III

Each of the early novels has revealed a considerable auto-biographical tendency, seldom apparent in the external action but distinctly implied in the qualities of literary expression, particularly in the comedy. It can be said in general that the comedy in these novels is always a reflection of James's commitment to the ideal of individual freedom. In using the word 'freedom' so often, he has in mind something more complicated than the condition of being able to act entirely as one sees fit. When Ralph, discussing Isabel's inheritance with his father, remarks that 'your bequest will make her free',[70] he gives an indication of the significance of freedom by saying that he wants to make Isabel rich because she has a great deal of 'imagination': 'People [are] rich when they are able to gratify their imagination'.[71] The extremely high demands which James puts upon the word 'imagination' are apparent in this and in all the early fiction, and his discriminating awareness of its significance is everywhere observable, notably in the revisions, where he is especially careful in his use of the word. F. O. Matthiessen has noticed, for example, that in the revision of *The Portrait of a Lady*, even so admired a figure as War-burton is denied Ralph's original commendation as a 'man of imagination' and is instead referred to as 'a man of a good deal of charming taste'.[72] Matthiessen is somewhat mistaken, however, in deciding that the word is used to designate an ability to judge things properly. Rather, it has to do with a capacity that often flouts good judgment, and it refers, generally, to reverently eager expectations, which Warburton lacks, about the unplumbed opportunities that life offers. Thus, even the individuality of Warburton's radicalism is a reaction *within* the social system of which, for Isabel's taste, he is too conspicuously a part. 'Imagination' in James is always connected with a conception of the future and with a desire to achieve more than the rewards which could be had if one accepted what organized society considers pre-eminently valuable.

Ralph, through a gift of money, tries to give Isabel the

70 *Por.*, p. 160.　　　　71 *Por.*, p. 159.
72 See F. O. Matthiessen, *Henry James, The Major Phase* (New York, 1944), p. 156.

power to act upon her imaginations of freedom. He hopes that her imagination might range so freely that she need not bother to consult customary restrictions on possibility and need not fear the intimidation of other people's opinion. Money puts her beyond the need to respond conventionally to such opportunities as Warburton offers. But with the design of making her capacity for freedom not contingent merely upon wealth, James lets her reject Warburton long before her inheritance. His stylistic manœuvering so conditions us to the act that we are not likely to join the 'more quickly judging half of mankind' in deciding that as a poor girl she ought to have accepted him. Therein we see the essential Americanism of this novel – how much it affirms her aspirations against what it shows to be ordinary social expectation. The attitudes towards experience here are very similar to those we found in *Roderick Hudson*. If Ralph is 'an apostle of freedom',[73] then so is Rowland Mallet, who has his Roderick just as Ralph his Isabel, and if Mr. Striker is a kind of 'fool', who is at the same time fairly right about things, then so is Henrietta. In James's first novel as in this, the essential conflict is between 'fixed' and 'free' characters. The conflict is relatively simple in *Roderick Hudson* in that it depends upon James's categorization of the minor characters and of their relationship with the major ones. This cannot be said of *The Portrait of a Lady*, written, astonishingly, only five years later. The theme it shares with the novels that precede it has become by then so extremely complicated by James's developing attitudes that he temporarily leaves it for the new directions apparent in *The Bostonians*.

These complications are apparent in yet another manifestation of that defensiveness about his heroine which we have been considering. In his attempt to preserve the integrity of her Quixotic imaginings he shows us how each of them has an extreme and comic version, the excesses of which she manages to escape. Isabel's opinions are, more often than not, theoretical, and they develop less from responses to specific things than as conceptions of how one ought to respond, derived from observations of the kind of person she imagines she would like to be. On her arrival in England she talks in a way similar to what we later find in Henrietta Stackpole, and

73 *Por.*, p. 404.

she has an equally touristic attitude towards England and Europe. Henrietta remarks, soon after arrival at Gardencourt, that she intends to describe Ralph in one of her articles because 'there is a great need just now for the alienated American, and your cousin is a beautiful specimen'.[74] Isabel's pained superiority to this should not make us forget that not twenty pages earlier she herself had spoken to Ralph about '"specimens"; it was a word that played a considerable part in her vocabulary; she had given him to understand that she wished to see English society illustrated by figures'.[75] The change in Isabel is to be ascribed to a temporary and, again, theoretical change of allegiances from the point of view of an earlier friend, Henrietta, to that of a later one, Mrs. Touchett.

The technique of characterization by which James reveals similarities between Isabel and characters who seem otherwise quite unlike her has gone unnoticed. This has happened largely because criticism has paid too little attention to the surface of Isabel's conversation, and too much to what is wrongly assumed to be its depth, as if it were a dramatic paraphrase of what James himself 'means'. The point, more often, is that the opinions she spouts are merely trial balloons which she has borrowed from others for purposes of investigating the misty reaches of her own mind. As a result, her conversation has about it the ring of parody. With the reference to 'her aunt' left out, for example, even those well acquainted with the novel might ascribe the following speech to Henrietta rather than to Isabel:

'Now what is your point of view?' she asked her aunt. 'When you criticize everything here, you should have a point of view. Yours doesn't seem to be American – you thought everything over there so disagreeable. When I criticize, I have mine; it's thoroughly American!'

'My dear young lady,' said Mrs. Touchett, 'there are as many points of view in the world as there are people of sense. You may say that doesn't make them very numerous! American? Never in the world; that's shockingly narrow. My point of view, thank God, is personal!'

Isabel thought this a better answer than she admitted; it was a tolerable description of her own manner of judging.[76]

74 *Por.*, p. 73.   75 *Por.*, p. 54.   76 *Por.*, pp. 49–50.

The substance of this conversation concerns the making of criticisms and judgments without having as a standard some official or institutional commitment such as America. Concern with the making of judgments that are at once personal and beyond provincial loyalties is the central circumstance behind the style and tone of the novel and the determining factor for the dramatic situations in which Isabel finds herself. In the interests of becoming a better 'judge', Isabel unhesitatingly, if silently, gives up an old vocabulary in this conversation for a new one. By this characteristic act, she leaves Henrietta alone to absorb James's satire on provincial Americanism. Being at the centre of the action, Isabel is surrounded, so to speak, by the various people whose attitudes she has at one time adopted, momentarily bringing one or another to the centre with her, but only to send him back to the periphery, there to represent through the rest of the novel a fixity of attitude from which she herself has escaped. The only important exception to this is Ralph, whose wholeness of perception becomes hers only through experience. It is not available, as are the more limited perspectives of Henrietta, Mrs. Touchett, Madame Merle, or Osmond, through the self-conscious selection of a social manner.

This is not to say that there is any falsity in Isabel's various imaginations of herself. Indeed, there is a high consistency in the evolution of her point of view and its consequences in the choices she makes. Her progress from one kind of discourse to another is measured by a straight line on which she may be thought to move as far as she can away from any attitude which seems to her constricted by external circumstances such as nationality or social convention. Isabel is able to justify what Henrietta calls her 'change' by telling her friend how the actual conditions of her life, with or without the various personal influences to which she submits, would dispose her to a natural independence of institutional points of view:

'I can do what I choose – I belong quite to the independent class. I have neither father nor mother; I am poor; I am of a serious disposition and not pretty. I therefore am not bound to be timid and conventional'.[77]

77 *Por.*, p. 140.

One gets a sense of the peculiarity of this novel, within the tradition of English fiction which deals with ambitious orphans, by thinking of Isabel as an Emersonian Becky Sharp. Her particular situation frees her from allegiance to social hierarchy, but the advantage she sees in this has nothing to do with the freedom to act indiscriminately in the pursuit of wealth and social position. Quite the contrary, she wants a sort of enlightenment, a spiritual and by no means discernible grandeur. To her mind, as to that of James's most conspicuous orphan, Hyacinth Robinson of *The Princess Casamassima*, the ideal of an 'aristocratic situation' has ultimately nothing to do with class. It is a matter of being in a position to appreciate more and to see more than the members of any particular class, even the aristocracy, are allowed. Isabel has no trouble finding more evidences of what she considers 'aristocracy' in Madame Merle than in Lord Warburton. Yet, from the beginning, she suspects that even Madame Merle is less admirable than she might be simply because she cares too much for the world's opinion and approval. They have their first disagreement, in fact, over the older woman's belief that 'we are each of us made up of a cluster of appurtenances.' Isabel, with all the overstatement of a young person in a moment of frustrated loyalty to a beloved and presumably wiser adult, grandly responds:

'I think just the other way. I don't know whether I succeed in expressing myself, but I know that nothing else expresses me. Nothing that belongs to me is any measure of me; on the contrary it's a limit, a barrier, and a perfectly arbitrary one. Certainly the clothes which, as you say, I choose to wear, don't express me; and heaven forbid they should! To begin with it's not my choice that I wear them; they are imposed upon me by society'.[78]

If Isabel would be a Thoreau, she does not find a Canadian woodsman's congeniality in Madame Merle's immediate reply: 'Should you prefer to go without them?' Later, to Madame Merle's warning that people will draw conclusions if she goes alone to the house of a handsome bachelor like Osmond, she reacts with the thought: 'What cared Isabel Archer for the vulgar judgments of obscure people'.[79] By ignoring such judgments when she finally accepts Osmond's proposal of marriage, she is, according to her statement to Henrietta,

78 *Por.*, p. 176.   79 *Por.*, p. 275.

being perfectly natural. She belongs, as she says, 'quite to the independent class', meaning that she belongs to no class at all in the commonly accepted meaning of the term.

It is a fact easily ignored that Isabel's marriage to Osmond is precisely the most predictable and consistent thing that could happen to her even if she did not have the fortune which attracts him and which allows her the flattering sense that she is at last giving something instead of taking it. In her conception of him and, indeed, in all that seems to us apparent in his situation, he is a man without social identity. That is why she loves him. She assures Caspar Goodwood that she is 'marrying a nonentity',[80] readily agrees with Mrs. Touchett that he has no money, no name, no importance, and tells Ralph that, unlike Lord Warburton, Osmond has

'no property, no title, no honours, no houses, nor lands, nor position, nor reputation, nor brilliant belongings of any sort. It is the total absence of these things that pleases me. Mr. Osmond is simply a man – he is not a proprietor'.[81]

She exults in the fact that he is 'a specimen apart',[82] and with a brilliant daring James even allows him to lay claim to the Jamesian virtue of renouncing practical social ambitions and advantages. In permitting this, James indicates in yet another way how Isabel's imagination responds to those very conditions of life to which his own is romantically but less sentimentally drawn. Osmond tells her that his life has affirmed 'not my natural indifference – I had none. But my studied, my wilful renunciation'.[83] So great is the appeal of his separateness, of his 'originality', by which she means his exclusiveness of any socially observed types, that she cannot heed even his own explicitness when he tells her before the marriage: 'No, I am not conventional. I am convention itself'.[84] It is remarkable how little he actually deceives her about the fact that his life is a matter of forms, of calculated attitudes. She is totally absorbed in the heroism of her choice. Osmond has so polished his aloofness that she sees in its a reflection of her own idealized aspirations. She hopes the marriage will lead to 'the high places of happiness from which the world would seem to lie below

80 *Por.*, p. 289.   81 *Por.*, p. 304.   82 *Por.*, p. 228.
83 *Por.*, p. 231.   84 *Por.*, p. 273.

one',[85] indicating that desire for elevation of view which, as we saw in Chapter II, is expressed in the imagery not only of several of the novels but also of passages from letters and essays where James talks admiringly about himself and the writers he likes.

James had a tolerant but patronizing conception of the narrowness of Emerson's intelligence, but it is hard not to see in the relationship between Isabel and Osmond a dramatization of what James was later to praise as the Emersonian vision 'of what we require and what we are capable of in the way of aspiration and independence'.[86] The consummate irony of *The Portrait of a Lady* is the degree to which Osmond is a mock version of the transcendentalist. He fits, so far as Isabel has any opportunity of knowing him, almost perfectly into the characterization which Emerson gives of the transcendental personality:

It is a sign of our times, conspicuous to the coarsest observer, that many intelligent and religious persons withdraw themselves from the common labors and competitions of the market and the caucus, and betake themselves to a certain solitary and critical way of living, from which no solid fruit has yet appeared to justify their separation. They hold themselves aloof: they feel the disproportion between their faculties and the work offered them, and they prefer to ramble in the country and perish of ennui, to the degradation of such charities and such ambitions as the city can propose to them . . . this part is chosen both from temperament and from principle; with some unwillingness too, and as a choice of the less of two evils. . . . With this passion for what is great and extraordinary, it cannot be wondered at that they are repelled by vulgarity and frivolity in people.[87]

The closeness of this description to the career of Osmond, even to his scorning the city of Rome to live in Florence, needs no comment in view of the quotations already made from the novel about him. To be aware of the similarity here is to make it less surprising that Isabel, whose mental processes are authentically Emersonian, should see an image of herself in the man she marries. Again, Emerson's description is a suitable characterization, but it is significant that the part of his essay

85 *Por.*, p. 371.   86 *Partial Portraits*, p. 9.
87 Emerson, 'The Transcendentalist', *Works*, I, 340–1, 342, 347.

which applies to Isabel is a description of mentality, while that which is relevant to Osmond describes merely the public evidences of such mentality:

> His [the transcendentalist's] thought, – that is the Universe. His experience inclines him to behold the procession of facts you call the world, as flowing perpetually outward from an invisible, unsounded centre in himself, centre alike of him and of them and necessitating him to regard all things as having a subjective or relative existence, relative to that aforesaid Unknown Centre of him.
>
> From this transfer of the world into the consciousness, this beholding of all things in the mind, follow easily his whole ethics. It is simpler to be self-dependent. The height, the deity of man is to be self-sustained, to need no gift, no foreign force. Society is good when it does not violate me, but best when it is likest to solitude. Everything real is self-existent.[88]

The first of these passages is a version of Isabel's difference with Madame Merle ('nothing else expresses me') when that lady, far from regarding 'all things as having a subjective or relative existence', declares that she has 'a great respect for *things*'.[89] The second, with its reference to 'the height' of man as being the condition of his self-subsistence, is not only a description of Isabel's 'aristocratic situation', but also a paraphrase of the idea of freedom, and its attendant imagery, which concerns James in most of the works we have considered. Given all this, it is extremely appropriate that when Mrs. Touchett finds Isabel in Albany the girl is 'trudging over the sandy plains of a history of German thought'.[90] At the time, no history of German philosophy would fail to make Kant as conspicuous to an American audience as Emerson already had.[91]

This connection between James and Emerson is worth attention because, as it has already been shown, the idealistic and romantic attitudes towards experience which are to be found in Emerson's essays are observable as well in the whole body of significant American fiction from Melville and Hawthorne to Faulkner. The relationship between James and Emerson is important within the larger fact that both of them

---

88 *Ibid.*, p. 334.   89 *Por.*, p. 175.   90 *Por.*, p. 20.
91 See, for example, Emerson's essay called 'Intellect,' *Works*, II, 342–7, but especially the passage in 'The Transcendentalist' where he derives the word 'Transcendental' from Kant's terminology, *Works*, I, 339–40.

subscribe to attitudes which are discernibly American, regardless of whether the literature derives from New England, New York, the South, or the West. It has often been said that Isabel Archer is an imitation of George Eliot's Dorothea Brooke, but it is apparent from all the novels of James which have no resemblance to *Middlemarch*, and from their Emersonian echoes, that *The Portrait of a Lady* could have brought the theme of aspiration to the point it does without the help of George Eliot.

Comparing, for example, the scenes wherein the heroine of each novel discovers within the atmosphere and landscape of the city of Rome a representation of her own feelings of disappointment, we can remark on the substantially greater vividness and resonance of George Eliot's imagery. In *Middlemarch* Rome *can* objectify and symbolize the nature of Dorothea's inner turmoil,[92] and it can do so in a way that considerably extends the historical as well as the personal significance of the failure of her marriage. By comparison, James's descriptions of the city in *The Portrait of a Lady* are misty, sentimental, and weakly suggestive. The city cannot adequately reflect the quality or the representative importance of Isabel's sense of failure and possible betrayal. A comparison between James and George Eliot along the lines being briefly sketched would require another study as full as this one. What I am offering is merely a specific instance to illustrate the literary consequences of James's temperamental bias towards a specifically American view of tragic experience – the discovery of the unsatisfactory correlation between the internal world of heroic imagination and the external, historical world. Santayana, speaking of American philosophers, including William James, summarizes the dilemma in ways that give Isabel's part in it a wider context. 'Each of them,' he writes in *Character and Opinion in the United States*, 'felt himself bound by two different responsibilities, that of describing things as they are, and that of finding them propitious to certain human preconceived desires'.[93] In James's novels, very often, the second of these is the happy

92 Chapter XX of *Middlemarch* provides relevant material for a comparison between George Eliot's use of Rome in her novel and such uses in *The Portrait* as are found, for instance, on p. 454.

93 George Santayana, *Character and Opinion in the United States* (New York, 1920), p. 61–2.

prelude to the first. This, at least, is the experience of his heroic characters, and it is ours in reading about them. For us as for Newman, Eugenia, Isabel, and Milly, there is the entertainment before there is the knowledge, the romance before the reality. In heading, as we are, towards a discussion of artful manners and glamorous deception in this novel, it is well to recall James's definition of 'romantic': '. . . the things that can reach us only through the beautiful circuit and subterfuge of our thought and desire'.[94]

IV

In each of the novels we have considered, there is a large element of artful manners in the represented social life. Deriving from this is much of the entertainment which the novels offer. The word 'entertainment', to elaborate on the significance with which I am using the word, refers here to any sort of action, including verbal action, which, as we witness it, is so absorbing as a phenomenon that we do not consciously try to make it coherent with our habitual experience of what ordinary life is like. When we read Dickens, for instance, we are often in the presence of such extraordinary, such inventive, such marvellously artificial imitations of peculiar humanity that to regard their conduct as if they were responsible to codes of everyday life is to violate the integrity of their fictional existence. In James, much of the verbal comedy makes us delight in characters or actions which are *essentially* reprehensible. But before we are faced with the essence of such characters, we 'feed', as James might say, on the extravagance, the overflow of their personalities. Eugenia, Madame de Bellegarde, and Sloper are theatrical experiences for us in the way that, say, Caspar Goodwood is not. His manners show us all that he is, which is what Isabel means when she thinks to herself that 'his passive surface, as well as his active, was large and firm'.[95]

On the other hand, Madame de Bellegarde does not, either in her conversation or in her gestures, offer a revelation of self. Rather, her manners are an exercise in the technical skill by which she projects the part she has chosen to play. Remote as

94 *The Art of the Novel*, p. 32.   95 *Por.*, p. 134.

the comparison may seem, we react to her during most of *The American* much as we do to Flem Snopes, the thorough-going scoundrel, in Faulkner's 'Spotted Horses'. 'You can't git ahead of Flem,' muses one of the characters, half in disgust, half in delight. 'You can't touch him. Ain't he a sight now?'[96] Our admiration for Flem, as for Madame de Belle-garde or her friend the Duchess, is, in part, the result of a natural delight in any kind of remarkably consistent technical skill that is beyond the capacity of ordinary humans: 'You can't git ahead' of any of them.

Such characters are glamorous and amusing because they are in some particular respects super-human. But by being so, they are also less than admirably human in the ways of love and charity and in the nature of the things they value. We prefer to laugh at them as long as possible because that is a way of keeping them foreign to the reality in which we live, just as their creators put them, by means of comedy, outside the context of ordinary life as it exists in the novel. In the comic scoundrel, both of the frontier and the drawing-room, we have an example of the way in which we choose to ignore essential knowledge about a human character in order to feel the un-bothered tolerance which comes from treating him as enter-tainment. In doing this we are roughly in the same position as Newman or Isabel or Milly Theale with respect to the events in the novel. If we experience the surface of the action and the language instead of confronting it as part of a nasty plot to hide the 'real' meaning, then we feel the glamour of things almost as much as they do.

James wrote no more glamorous novel than *The Portrait of a Lady*. It imparts an almost palpable quality to the extravagant and artful aspects of life which it presents, and it provokes the assumption that the glamorous possibilities of life are denied to no one capable of earning and appreciating them. The existence of glamour depends upon the suggestion that in some respect or other it allows the participation of anyone observing it, upon the very American illusion of self-creation, upon the possibilities of recreation, to make a pun about the connection between entertainment and one's imagination of the glamor-

---

96 William Faulkner, 'Spotted Horses', *Scribner's Magazine*, LXXXIX
(June 1931), 597.

ous. It matters a great deal, in terms of this definition, that everyone in the novel, except Warburton ('how I should object to myself if I were not myself, don't you know?'[97]), is a self-made man, a version of Emerson's self-subsistent man. This includes Daniel Touchett and Caspar in their business success, Mrs. Touchett in her strict and acquited emotional self-sufficiency, and Ralph, who literally keeps himself alive in order to gratify his imagination of Isabel. It has much to do with the magnificent manner and social charm of Madame Merle, both of which are learned and practised, and with the self-cultivation of Osmond, whose foolish sister is an indication, along with what is told of his mother, of how ineffectual he might have become.

Isabel, however, is, in the ways I am describing, the most glamorous of all, not merely because, as in a fairy-tale, she is rewarded with riches for being good, but, more importantly, because her whole effort at self-creation, the impulse which makes her into a kind of novelist of her own experience, presumes possibilities of achievement which incorporate and exceed those of all the other self-made people in the novel. In her career she adopts or admires the manners of other people on the basis of whether or not, to her eyes, they promise perpetual self-discovery or only, like Warburton's system, permanent self-protection.

By his rendering of artful manners and his illustrations of glamour in the lives of his characters, James tries to make us expatriates from the ordinary. Like Isabel, we drink of what James in his biography of a notable American expatriate, William Wetmore Story, calls the 'Borgia cup'. He is alluding to the Roman atmosphere which in his own experience had 'sweetened and drugged' the 'sterner realities'.[98] To give a similar experience of the European adventure to his readers, James can depend only upon the suggestiveness of his language. He does not intend, of course, to make us as wholly charmed as Isabel. Indeed, the assumption behind James's own relationship with us depends, as the tone of his narrative voice reveals, upon our feeling superior to Isabel even while we are deeply implicated in her situation and her attitudes. James is faced with the

97 *Por.*, p. 111.
98 *William Wetmore Story and His Friends* (Boston, 1903), I, 329.

difficult task of verifying her romantic responses by making us share them, while at the same time he must in each instance reveal her inexperience by making us more sceptical of the reality of romance than she is.

The excessiveness of the theatricality in certain crucial scenes is evidence of the trouble which James experienced in constantly moderating between his heroine and his audience. So pronounced is the effect of this theatricality that to a reader of any sophistication certain moments in the novel may seem unbecomingly close to an appeal to vulgar susceptibilities. Because of the discriminating social taste which is almost everywhere at play in James's presentation, the lapses, when they occur, leave us uncertain whether he intends them or not. When Isabel first meets Madame Merle, to give an example, it is hard to know whether we are to be amused or charmed or both at once. The circumstances and the dialogue are close to farce, and there is no certainty that James is aware of the effect. Mr. Touchett is dying in his apartment upstairs, and as Isabel descends from hers, noting through the house the 'perceptible hush which precedes a crisis', she hears the sound of 'low music' coming from the drawing-room. 'The drawing-room at Gardencourt was an apartment of great distances,' James tells us, but its impressiveness does not lend itself to the dialogue which follows:

'That is very beautiful, and your playing makes it more beautiful still,' said Isabel, with all the young radiance with which she usually uttered a truthful rapture.

'You don't think I disturbed Mr. Touchett, then?' the musician answered, as sweetly as the compliment deserved. 'The house is so large, and his room is so far away, that I thought I might venture – especially as I played just – just *du bout des doigts*'.

'She is a Frenchwoman,' Isabel said to herself; 'she says that as if she were French.' And this supposition made the stranger more interesting to our speculative heroine. 'I hope my uncle is doing well,' Isabel added. 'I should think that to hear such lovely music as that would really make him feel better'.

The lady gave a discriminating smile.

'I am afraid there are moments in life when even Beethoven has nothing to say to us. We must admit, however, that they are our worst moments'.[99]

99 *Por.*, pp. 149–50.

In his revision of the novel James changes the composer from
Beethoven to Schubert.[100] This small attempt to make Madame
Merle less impressively accomplished suggests that James was
mistakenly convinced that the earlier version communicated
the extraordinary attractiveness of this woman. The question
of intention and response in this instance does not allow for
certainty, however, and it is possible that James means to
reveal qualities in Madame Merle's performance which Isabel
does not recognize. We could, for example, put some special
weight on the phrase 'our speculative heroine,' and remember
that the opening of the novel calls for a reaction to uses of
language which makes Madame Merle's dialogue here as
suspiciously and comically pretentious as it is obviously intended to be elsewhere ('I came into the world in the Brooklyn
navy-yard. My father was a high officer in the United States
Navy, and had a post – a post of responsibility – in that
establishment at the time').[101] In his Preface to the novel,
however, James gives every indication that he meant the scene
at the piano to be conspicuous and to offer no suggestions of
tawdry sophistication. One of the two cases of 'rare chemistry'
in the novel, he claims,

> are the pages in which Isabel, coming into the drawing-room at
> Gardencourt, coming in from a wet walk or whatever, that rainy
> afternoon, finds Madame Merle in possession of the place, Madame
> Merle seated, all absorbed but all serene, at the piano, and deeply
> recognizes, in the striking of such an hour, in the presence there,
> among the gathering shades, of this personage, of whom a moment
> before she had never so much as heard, a turning-point in her life.[102]

James's description of what he meant to do is eloquently
phrased, but the scene, as it actually exists, reveals considerable
insecurity in determining the quality of experience which it
wants to present. This is more obvious here, and in other early
scenes involving Isabel with Madame Merle or with Osmond,
than at most places in the novel where attempts are made to
produce some of the sense of glamour which Isabel herself is
experiencing.

The shakiness at such moments is something that can be

100 *Por.* rev., I, 215.   101 *Por.*, p. 151.
102 *The Art of the Novel*, p. 56.

overlooked simply because the balances of tone in the presentation of Isabel are so extremely delicate that at certain points they necessarily become unmanageable. We have already noticed James's warning that those who 'judge' his heroine severely will find that she will become 'consistently wise only at the cost which will make a direct appeal to our sympathies' and his explicitness in admitting that 'she would be an easy victim of scientific criticism'. These unwonted appeals to the reader, like his curiously uncertain introduction of Madame Merle, attest to the difficulty of showing the great charm of things not only as Isabel but as he himself sees them, while, concurrently, he must hint at the qualities of moral dilapidation which Isabel is in no position to notice. The same situation obtains to some extent whenever James is dealing with sophisticated manners and with people capable of magnificent social accomplishment and cultivation.

The Portrait of a Lady is superior to *The American*, which gives a comparable emphasis to contrived social manners, partly because, as never before in his work, James is able to show the disastrous expenditure of feeling and intelligence, the waste of love and generosity when artfulness and 'technique' are used not to enrich human relationships, as in *The Europeans*, but to disguise their true nature. This situation can be dramatized with relatively little difficulty when the relationships among the characters involve natural and conventional assumptions about certain intensities and qualities of emotion. In *Washington Square* there is almost no element of choice or of judgment in the acceptance or rejection of love. Catherine simply deserves the love she is denied, and, because she receives irony instead of parental affection, she cannot be said to have chosen to accept the opportunity for love which Townsend offers her. It is the only chance she ever has. In dramatizing her problem James can depend upon a body of assumptions in his readers which is stimulated by the conventional, story-book motifs, discussed in the previous chapter, which help define Catherine's situation. No such assumptions apply to Isabel's relationships with the other characters in *The Portrait of a Lady*. There is no natural reason why she should love Madame Merle on first sight. James must show us the reality of Madame Merle's charm or expose his heroine to that criticism from the reader which he fears will be too severe; but he must also hint at her invidiousness, or lay himself open to the charge of surrendering his point of view to a girl who is often the victim of 'meagre knowledge' and 'inflated ideals'.[103] Necessarily, therefore, he feels compelled at some points simply to ask us not to make 'vulgar' judgments about Isabel, just as in making her enthusiasms attractive he must consciously or unconsciously make their object a curious mixture of the glamorous and the meretricious.

We are to admire Isabel's eager responsiveness to Madame Merle while feeling compassionate about the fact that the responses themselves are a function of her innocence. That this particular conjunction of feelings is within the ordinary daily capacity of mature people is beside the point. We are concerned not with the nature of human feelings but with the literary act by which these and not others are, at some specific point, created in us. In the effort of James's style to bring about this mixture of reactions, we can observe his desire to keep us from solidifying our attitudes about too uninclusive a manifestation of character. That the tone hovers close to vulgarity at some points and, at others, to a plaintive appeal for our tolerance is a relatively unimportant price which James pays for the ultimate success of making Isabel's freedom of response more beautiful to us than the self-satisfactions of our own sophistication. He accomplishes something for us as well as for her. He evolves a method for giving us the entertainment and enchantment which plays across the surface of what Isabel sees while simultaneously sharing with us hints of the knowledge that she misses. We are given the 'key', to use an image repeated throughout the novel, to the inner lives of the characters, but we are never allowed to forget that much of the time we belong outside, noticing the surface of things and sharing some of their ultimately dangerous allurement.

The things that both delight and deceive James's heroic characters always have a tinge of the theatrical. Images of the theatre and the term itself abound in all the novels. *Roderick Hudson*, *The American*, and *Washington Square* have, in particular, a dramatic movement which can be adequately summarized in a sentence which was added to the ending of the

103 *Por.*, p. 43.

first of these. Describing Rowland's feelings as he sits at the bottom of the cliff with Roderick's body, James explains that 'now that all was over, Rowland understood how up to the brim, for two years, his personal life had been filled. It looked to him at present as void and blank as a theatre bankrupt and closed'.[104] Christopher Newman, sitting in the Bellegardes' salon, feeling 'as if he were at a play, and as if his own speaking would be an interruption', and poor Catherine Sloper, victimized by a father who treats her as if she were a sort of 'straight man' and by an aunt who 'delighted of all things in a drama',[105] are characters who, like Rowland, eventually look back upon the experiences which promised delight and happiness as if they were part of a deceptive show with no more reality than one would find in a theatrical entertainment.

James's comedy always exploits the theatrical aspects of experience, particularly those which tend to disguise the processes that eventually betray the heroes and heroines. It is an evidence of his genius in the creation of character that except for foolish, melodramatic women like Mrs. Light and Aunt Lavinia, the comic pleasure that can be taken in the theatricality of his treasonable characters is not merely the result of the author's need to cheat us of knowledge in the interest of suspense. Ultimately, the surface of action and dialogue by which we find entertainment in Gloriani and Christina, in the Bellegardes, in Sloper, and in Madame Merle and Osmond, is not a mask behind which there is a totally different face. The mask reflects the most consciously pleasing, publicly deferential version of the real personality. If one were clairvoyant enough – though this would take the form of cynicism – it would be possible to see at once wherein the surface and the inner life were interchangeable and to find in the surface, however pleasing, a symptom of the potential evil in the background. Such insight would mean a destitution, however, of those very qualities of openness and responsiveness which are essential to the dramatic existence of James's novels. This is a way of saying that his creative energy draws upon an innocent hope, which each novel ultimately shows to be disappointed and betrayed, that the evident beauty and exorbitant charm of the glamorous life, particularly in Europe, is also its reality.

104 *R.H.* rev., p. 462.   105 *Wash.*, p. 64.

By the abrasions of comedy upon that surface James makes it less ideally glamorous for us than for his heroic dreamers. Yet, this very fact in itself provides us with a false lead, with the fiction of confident entertainment where there is to be the reality of pain.

James's continuous effort as a novelist involves the attempt through his style to catch and hold in simultaneity the charm and the threat of European high manners. By so doing he would modify a simplistic implication inherent in the plots of his novels. On the basis of a bare outline of many of his stories it would seem that everything which entertained in the first half is generally to be taken as a deception, that life is only a masked ball into which a Cinderella invariably wanders who must stay after midnight and do the cleaning up. As an extension of James's attempts to avoid a superficial reading of this kind, it can be supposed that the style of the later novels is a way of protecting characters like Kate Croy and Madame de Vionnet from those moralistic simplifications which he deflects in the early novels by comic use of language. Comedy makes us take pleasure in a Doctor Sloper, who is not nice, and it directs our satiric attitudes away from a character like Isabel, who so distinctly is. But in both instances comedy is an index of the complications about the creation of character which James is taking into account. Only in *The Europeans*, of all the early novels, does he succeed in making us feel deeply engaged with the emotional life of a glamorously mannered character while he simultaneously uses her for the purposes of theatrical entertainment. By contrast, most of the theatricality in *The Portrait of a Lady*, and it constitutes a very large element in the novel, is a reflection of that quality of emotional fixity in characters which qualifies them, more or less subtly, to be James's fools.

Innate limitation of sensibility in James's characters is almost always made a part of the comic entertainment which his novels offer. This is necessarily the case, since a 'fixed' characer is also usually a 'type', or like a figure in vaudeville. In *The Portrait of a Lady* a character may be theatrical in extremely subtle ways, and his 'fixity' need not make him simply a figure of fun. The theatricality of Osmond or of Madame Merle is of an obviously different quality from Henrietta's. Like Madame de Bellegarde, they resemble characters in a sophisticated romance. They are very much 'on-stage', both in posture and talk, as we notice in Madame Merle's first scene at the piano at Gardencourt, or in Osmond's attitudinizing at his 'Thursday nights' in Rome. Certain kinds of enclosed consciousness in this novel can take very attractive forms, and the manifestations of this offered by Osmond and Madame Merle are often ingratiating.

It is among the minor figures, however, that we must first look to see James most assiduously at work upon comically revelatory aspects of this type of character. Henrietta is the most delightful example. Like Roderick Hudson, she is the kind of character who believes certain things which James admires but who does so in a foolishly compulsive way. An illustration of this is her involvement in one of the central concerns of the novel – the relation between one's experience of the glamour of possibility and one's discovery of the reality of limitation. She arrives in England with a resolution not unlike Isabel's: 'to see as much as possible of the inner life'.[106] Almost at once, in some moments of highly comic dramatic engagement with Ralph and his mother, she reveals the incredible superficiality of her notion of privacy and of personal feeling. Not much later, and to Isabel's considerable relief, she decides to give up the project as too difficult. She turns to the continent for her material because 'on the continent there was the outer life, which was palpable and visible at every turn'.[107] Allowing so comic a view of the theme of perception serves to absolve the other characters in the novel, who are concerned with it, from suspicion of being as superficial as Henrietta. She draws off the poison, as it were. The comedy shows that the author knows how silly the matter *can* be and it therefore leaves him free to be as serious about it as he chooses.

What has been said about caricature as it develops about the figure of Henrietta applies as well to the elements in the novel of incidental social satire. If this were not so, the mention of figures like 'the Miss Climbers, two ladies from Wilmington',[108] might pass for a bit of Balzacian inclusiveness done *du bout des doigts*, as Madame Merle would say. Even with the

106 *Por.*, p. 69.   107 *Por.*, p. 246.   108 *Por.*, p. 124.

meagre attention, they receive, these two young ladies absorb, largely through their names, some of those stock suppositions about 'the American girl abroad' which would otherwise, James might rightly fear, attach themselves, in a reader's imagination, to Isabel. For a similar purpose, we are given apparently accidental glimpses of expatriate society. These moments in the novel serve to indicate the relative superiority of the people Isabel chooses for her close associates. This is a matter of some importance, since one feature of expatriate society in James's fiction is the extent to which it removes many of the aids, provided in a settled community, for knowing one's neighbours. The choice of friends among expatriates must have seemed to James relatively more temperamental than it was, say, in Cambridge, Massachusetts, more indicative of the kinds of personal life with which a person would choose to be associated if he were completely autonomous.

Expatriate society, with its implicit disavowal of customary public signs of personal identity in favour of more extemporized ones, is a fair testing ground, therefore, for Isabel's belief that external manifestations of character are fairly meaningless, 'a limit, a barrier, and a perfectly arbitrary one'.[109] James uses minor figures like the Luces partly to show that Isabel, depending as she does wholly on her intuition, avoids at least obvious failures of taste and judgment. Though Mrs. Touchett's friendship with the Luces might suggest, for example, that they are not wholly tiresome, James describes them with some of the supercilious wit which is reserved only for those towards whom he feels an enjoyable antipathy:

Mrs. Luce had been living in Paris since the days of Louis Philippe; she used to say jocosely that she was of the generation of 1830 – a joke of which the point was not always taken. When it failed Mrs. Luce used always to explain – 'oh yes, I am one of the romantics'. . . . The existence of Mr. Luce, her worthy husband, was somewhat more inscrutable. Superficially indeed, there was no mystery about it; the mystery lay deeper, and resided in the wonder of his supporting existence at all. [110]

Somewhat in the manner of Jane Austen, even in *Persuasion*, James in this passage takes delight in the very act of expressing witty contempt. Animus of this kind in both writers, is exercised almost as a relief from the passionate and exhausting imaginative activity by which a novelist does justice to the complexity of such characters as Isabel and Ralph. The novelist turns from his real work to stretch, as it were. It is significant of this fact that the description of Mr. Luce first implies that there is a 'mystery', an inner life, and then turns the implication into a joke: the 'mystery' is simply that he is capable even of sustaining his outer life, his 'surface', upon which James draws his satiric picture of the American abroad. Like Mr. Leavenworth and Mr. Striker, discussed in Chapter I, the Luces and the Miss Climbers are farcical 'types' to whom James explicitly denies an inner life.

The Portrait of a Lady includes a more interestingly compli- cated variety of circumscribed character than those we have just considered. These are figures, of whom Mrs. Touchett comes most readily to mind, who must be taken seriously and whose deficiencies encourage us to speculation rather than to merely amused observation. A character of this sort may be very imposing, and his 'surface', a word used to describe each of them, may give promise of rich emotional experience. None the less, all of them show, first almost imperceptibly and then through a gradually revealing series of gestures, that they have little capacity for and even an antipathy towards refine- ments of consciousness and the imagination of an impractical ideal. This deficiency has many versions, all of which elicit from James manifestations of feeling ranging from comic disparagement, which we have been considering, to a mixture of pity and disapproval. Countess Gemini receives very little affection in the novel, and yet, partly because of her opposition to Osmond, she deserves to be exonerated at least from calcu- lated meanness. With all her memories of amatory experience, she has managed to dissipate whatever awareness she might have had of the sanctity of human relationships. To Isabel she seemed 'to have no soul; she was like a bright shell; in which something would rattle when you shook it'.[111] Still another illustration of a character whose sensibilities have become deadened is Mrs. Touchett. Quite unlike the Countess Gemini, to whom she is demonstrably superior in tact and

111 *Por.*, p. 393.

intelligence, she is denied even the emotional excitations which come from memories – she has never been capable of emotionally involving herself with anyone. Madame Merle defines the matter adequately when she observes to Isabel that 'having no faults for your aunt, means that one is never late for dinner – that is for her dinner.'[112] Her personal relations are confined to social forms and punctiliousness, and even before the death of her husband and son she becomes for Isabel the object of undemonstrable pity. In expressing this, Isabel makes use of the image of 'surface' which has been prominent in all these characterizations:

. . . there seemed something so dreary in the condition of a person whose nature had, as it were, so little surface – offered so limited a face to the accretions of human contact. Nothing tender, nothing sympathetic, had ever had a chance to fasten upon it – no wind-sown blossom, no familiar moss. Her positive extent, in other words, was about that of a knife edge.[113]

As we saw in *The Europeans*, a large element of manner, of fabricated 'surface' that extends one's personality into social engagement with others, can be, regardless of how artful or contrived, the reverse of vacuity and deadness. This is apparent enough in Eugenia and equally so in Madame Merle, a later and corrupt version of the Baroness. 'Having a charming surface,' as Isabel observes of her, 'does not necessarily prove that one is superficial'.[114] Madame Merle herself claims that she is 'rather stout porcelain',[115] a remark that gives a particular pathos to her final scene with Osmond when, after he leaves her apartment, she takes down from the mantel the coffee-cup in which he had mentioned the existence of a crack and asks of herself, 'have I been so vile all for nothing?'[116] When Isabel was explaining to herself the charm of Madame Merle's 'surface' she had, without knowing it, hit upon the nature of the crack in the fact that Madame Merle 'existed only in her relations with her fellow-mortals'.[117] In this she escapes the emotional emptiness of Mrs. Touchett's life. But partly because her relationships depend upon her not recognizing Pansy as her own daughter, they exist at the expense of a natural capacity for love.

112 *Por.*, p. 169.   113 *Por.*, pp. 192–3.   114 *Por.*, p. 167.
115 *Por.*, p. 168.   116 *Por.*, p. 461.   117 *Por.*, p. 167.

Unlike Madame Merle, who in the interests of social ambition both for herself and for Pansy amputates her private life from the body of her presentably social manner, Isabel is determined 'to feel the continuity between the movements of her own heart and the agitations of the world'.[118] Her ideal, as she articulates it in her argument with Madame Merle about the relationship of outer to inner life, is that 'she would be what she appeared, and she would appear what she was'.[119] Her ambition fails to do justice to the possible value, as James sees it, of artful manner, of making use of external 'things', including cultivated personal gestures, as a means of self-expression. Ralph is a sufficient indication of the way manners can, as in the case of Eugenia, be liberating rather than restricting: 'His outward conformity to the manners that surrounded him was, none the less, the mask of a mind that greatly enjoyed its independence'.[120] Even the comedy in which he indulges is a social device, a way of releasing himself from anyone's odious supposition that his illness has mastered his spirit. Both his manners and his comedy protect in him what James calls his 'boundless liberty of appreciation'.[121]

Isabel's ideal makes sense only in a world which does not exist, where protections are not needed. And it is James's reiterated point about contrived 'surfaces' that while they may deaden and be a revelation of the stultification of feelings, they can also be an enrichment of them. Indirect self-expression, through 'things' outside oneself, like *objets d'art*, or through ceremonious social conduct, can be and often is the disguise of villainy in James. It can also, however, be the instrument of intelligent discrimination, the means for achieving a temporary detachment during which one can better observe and come to know the nature of another person and of one's self in relationship to him. This aspect of manners particularly recommends itself in the case of Isabel because 'the depths of this young girl's nature were a very out-of-the-way place, between which and the surface communication was interrupted by a dozen capricious forces'.[122] In light of this, her dilemma is a comment on the efficiency of the Emersonianism which she articulates;

118 *Por.*, p. 28.   119 *Por.*, p. 43.
120 *Por.*, p. 30.   121 *Ibid.*
122 *Por.*, p. 28.

it is exalting and admirable, but it has little to do either with
social or with psychological reality. Ralph represents that
admirable conjunction of idealism and worldly archness which
James has in mind when he refers to his predilection for
'adventure and irony',[123] It is one of the most revealing facts
in the novel, about which more will be said, that the character
who is most intelligently responsive to life is the one who is
also closest to actual death, while those who survive him are
more or less consumed by an inner deadness which invades
even the heroine. By his own admission he wants to stay alive
to see if Isabel will give life to that ideal of freedom with which
physical sickness imbues him and which he sees as the lost
cause among all the others in the novel, who are more
physically healthy, but also more spiritually dead, than he.

The relative 'fixity' or deadness of these others, and the
degree to which each of them is therefore a subject of James's
satiric comedy, is determined by how much of his 'surface',
of his actual social and articulated life, is in touch both with
other lives and with the spontaneous aspirations of his own.
Herein it can be observed that a taste for James is not incompat-
ible with an admiration for D. H. Lawrence. The concerns of
the best of Lawrence's short novels, *St. Mawr*, are very like
those of *The Portrait of a Lady*. Both novelists are preoccupied
with the various interruptions which deny to the human personality a free flow of vitality between its social, public existence
and the private life of deeply personal emotion. The similarity
is not merely one of theme. The idea of theme for both of them
is indistinguishable from its existence within the very quality
of their literary expression. Lawrence is unsurpassed in his
ability to represent emotional vacuity and its social concomi-
tants by giving us the experience of it in the prose style of his
characters. And as our continuing attention to theatricality in
James indicates, he, like Lawrence, will sometimes use the
conventions of fabricated expression, both social and literary,
as equivalents for the kinds of social deadness and conventionality within which his heroic characters are often trapped.

The trap is usually sprung when the heroes fall victim to
what Isabel calls, in commending Ralph for being absolved
of them, 'professional and official emotions'.[124] These have

123 *Por.* rev., I, 43.   124 *Por.*, p. 296.

been the undoing of all of James's favourites in each of the novels we have discussed: of Rowland, by the configuration of Roderick's romantic attitudinizing and, what drives them to excess, the insanely 'professional' attitude of Mrs. Light towards the marriage of her daughter; of Newman, by the traditional mystiques to which the Bellegardes can appeal in justification of the horrid machinations that destroy his romance; of Eugenia, by the smugness of Acton's final appeals to the shibboleths of his puritanical environment; and of Catherine, by the incapacity both of her father and her aunt to imagine her as more than a figure who must, being presumably as ineffectual as she seems, play whatever part either of them imagines for her. 'Official emotions', by tending to obstruct the expression of more enlivened, personal, and creative feeling, represent the line of defence by which the forces of conventionality, both emotional and social, keep the aspiring heroes of James from the prizes they seek. In James as a whole, restrictive conventionality of feeling is represented in various kinds of theatrical expression. This is vitally important in *The Portrait of a Lady*, where Isabel is, as Ralph remarks, 'ground in the very mill of the conventional'.[125] To see the connection between this remark and the theatrical aspects of the novel is to understand the ending in a way which has not heretofore been suggested.

V

Theatricality is a term which embraces many of the kinds of expression already discussed as characteristic of those people the contact of whose 'surface' with the world is limited and preconceived, and who express themselves in accordance with the public expectations which are attached to the rôles they have assumed. It was to have been Isabel's good fortune to escape this fate, even to the extent that James, as her creator, makes a considerable and unusual effort to protect her from being hemmed in by any too exclusive definitions of her character which may be inferred from the dramatic action. His language in the passages of analysis is general to the point of being abstract; he pleads with us not to judge her too readily; he nearly surrenders his own predilection for ambiguity

125 *Por.*, p. 506.

in the interest of rendering her uncomplicated sense of the glamorous; and he so encompasses her with conventionalized personalities that the reader is not apt to criticize in her certain of the characteristics which, in a small way, she shares with them.

The world of Gilbert Osmond may exploit the defects of Isabel's virtues and transform them to the uses of its conventions, but James in his presentation of her will not allow us to 'grind her' in the convenient typologies which literary and social convention provide for us. She gives Ralph the impression at Gardencourt that she is a girl who will not act the part which seems to be called for by her situation. An impoverished American girl who, when she first sees Lord Warburton, exclaims, 'Oh, I hoped there would be a lord; it's just like a novel!'[126] and who then proceeds to refuse his proposal of marriage, offers such a prospect of original accomplishment that bored and worldly Ralph Touchett is able to believe that here at last is something worth staying alive to witness. It is like a wholly new and different sort of drama which he has never before seen performed. When he convinces his father to leave her a fortune, the old man remarks that 'you speak as if it were for your entertainment', to which Ralph responds, "So it is, a good deal'.[127]

Reduced as Ralph is to 'mere spectatorship at the game of life', he literally dies when, having lost the freedom with which he tried to endow her, Isabel ceases to be capable of 'entertaining' him. On his first visit to Rome after her marriage, he reacts in terms which suggest how even at this point, after only two years with Osmond, she has begun to play the part which her husband requires of her. Instead of the free-spirited, individual self-expression which Ralph had hoped to foster, he finds, partly because she will not admit to him how miserable she is, that

if she wore a mask, it completely covered her face. There was something fixed and mechanical in the serenity painted upon it; this was not an expression, Ralph said – it was a representation. . . . Her light step drew a mass of drapery behind her; her intelligent head sustained a majesty of ornament. The free, keen girl had become quite another person; what he saw was a fine lady who was supposed to represent something.[128]

126 *Por.*, p. 12.   127 *Por.*, p. 160.   128 *Por.*, pp. 343–4.

The vocabulary is familiar enough – the images which make it sound as though she were engaged in a stage performance, the words 'fixed' and 'free', and the distinction made between 'expression' and 'representation'. Everywhere in the early fiction, providing indeed the foundation for this study of James, there is evidence of a profoundly felt concern about the distinction between those characters who 'express' themselves, and are within range only of James's gentlest irony, and those who 'represent' something and whose expression is, therefore, theatrical and conventionalized to the point of self-parody. The progress of the action in *The Portrait of a Lady* is in the direction of making Isabel into such a representative or 'fixed' character. There is some justice, therefore, in Isabel's remark to Henrietta that her career has become a comedy:

'I want to be alone', said Isabel.
'You won't be that so long as you have got so much company at home'.
'Ah, they are part of the comedy. You others are spectators'.
'Do you call it a comedy, Isabel Archer?' Henrietta inquired severely.
'The tragedy, then, if you like. You are all looking at me; it makes me uncomfortable'.[129]

This exchange occurs just before Henrietta is to escort Ralph back to Gardencourt. Despite his dismay at the changes in Isabel during his first visit, he has returned because, as James tells us:

What kept Ralph alive was simply the fact that he had not yet seen enough of his cousin; he was not yet satisfied. There was more to come; he wouldn't make up his mind to lose that. He wished to see what she would make of her husband – or what he would make of her. [The earlier visit] was only the first act of the drama, and he was determined to sit out the performance.[130]

The second 'act', eighteen months later, ends with Isabel's request to be left alone and without 'spectators'. The drama of freedom has become the tragi-comedy of her having 'suddenly found the infinite vista of a multiplied life to be a dark, narrow alley, with a dead wall at the end'.[131] Her intuition that

129 *Por.*, p. 439.   130 *Por.*, p. 346.   131 *Por.*, p. 371.

she is confronting a kind of deadness at the conclusion of some hopeful and confident movement is mirrored in Ralph's acceptance of the fact that, with so little left to appreciate in the drama of Isabel, he has no future prospect except death: 'The end of everything was at hand; it seemed to him that he could stretch out his hand and touch the goal'.[132] 'Everything' for Ralph not only includes Isabel but essentially *is* Isabel.

The implications of this need to be fully recognized, and they provide an astounding illustration of how the drama in the action of James's novels is an imitation of the drama of artistic creativity which goes into them. Ralph's death is to be taken as a metaphor for the fact that Isabel's freedom can no longer be imagined. It can no longer sustain the life of the imagination. She cannot provide for Ralph what Minny Temple, by actually dying, gave James: 'The positive relief', as he writes to William, 'in thinking of her being removed from her own heroic treatment and placed in kinder hands'.[133]

Isabel remains in the hands of Gilbert Osmond. Despite Ralph's last advice ('You must stay here'[134]), and Caspar Goodwood's warning, to which he says Ralph has subscribed ('It will cost you your life!'[135]), Isabel returns to 'the house of darkness, the house of dumbness, the house of suffocation'.[136] James's adoration, and it can be called that, for super-consciousness leads him at the end of *The Portrait of a Lady* to treat death in a curious way, as a preferable alternative to the deadness which encroaches upon life. There are similar expressions of this, all of them more direct, in his beautifully elegiac passages about the death of Minny Temple in *Notes of a Son and Brother*,[137] in the letters to his mother and to William about Minny,[138] to Grace Norton, after the death of his parents,[139]

132 *Por.*, p. 436.

133 See F. O. Matthiessen, *The James Family* (New York, 1947), p. 260.

134 *Por.*, p. 507.   135 *Por.*, p. 517.

136 *Por.*, p. 375.

137 See *Henry James Autobiography*, ed. Dupee, pp. 282–4; 504–44. Mary (Minny) Temple, James's cousin, died in March 1870, of tuberculosis. James remarks that he and William felt her death together 'as the end of our youth' (*Autobiography*, p. 544).

138 See James's letter to his mother, dated March 26, 1870 from Malvern, England, in *The Selected Letters of Henry James*, ed. Leon Edel (New York, 1955), pp. 32–6. Also see James's letter to his brother, dated March 29, 1870, also from Malvern, in Matthiessen, *The James Family*, pp. 259–63.

139 See *Letters*, I, 100–2.

and in the letter to Howells where, comforting him about the death of his daughter, he is brought to the admission that 'I can't talk of death without seeming to say too much – I think so kindly of it as compared with life – the only thing one can compare it to'.[140] Life finally denies Isabel the 'freedom and rest', to use James's words when he refers to Minny Temple's death, the 'eternal freedom'[141] which is given to Minny and to Ralph. With Ralph's death, Isabel ceases to live in the imagination of freedom, and he dies because her life no longer allows him to imagine the possibility that freedom and the life of the world are compatible. The end of the novel reverses the relationship between Isabel and Ralph. It is now she who carries his image in her mind, just as James carried the image of the dead Minny, 'as a sort of measure and standard', he wrote William, 'of brightness and repose'.[142]

The movement towards the end of the novel puts into juxtaposition the varieties of death and deadness which concerned James so deeply and all of those aspects of life which are tainted and deadened by the predictable, the conventional, the merely representative rather than the expressive. All the characters are at last *known* to us in some final way, as if they have become 'portraits' indeed, along the order of Browning's Duchess, rather than remained imaginatively alive and changing. Osmond is last seen making a drawing of an antique coin and spouting clichés about 'the honour of a thing'[143]; Madame Merle, totally isolated and defeated, decides that she is going to America, and thereby steps out of any associations in which we could continue to conceive of her; Henrietta and Mr. Bantling announce their engagement, as in the sentimental conclusion of a farce, making Isabel conclude that even they are now 'conventional'. When they tell her their plans, she feels, oddly, as if 'the dreariness of the world took on a deeper tinge'.[144] Mrs. Touchett, as undeviating and predictable as ever in her attitudes and responses, is even more deadened for us at the conclusion by Isabel's perception that the ageing and lonely woman 'saw herself in the future as an old woman without

140 Matthiessen, *The Major Phase*, p. 50. See also the little known essay by James entitled 'Is There a Life after Death?' reprinted in Matthiessen, *The James Family*, pp. 602–14.

141 Matthiessen, *The James Family*, p. 261.

142 *Ibid.*   143 *Por.*, p. 471.   144 *Por.*, p. 497.

memories'.[145] Warburton seems an exception to the general drift of the characters towards colourless inertia. He is at least to be married, though to a girl whose name is never even mentioned. The news makes Isabel feel 'as if she had heard of Lord Warburton's death'.[146]

Effectively, this leaves Pansy and Caspar as characters who might have a future that allows for expectation, and who could, if this were true, give us reason to imagine them rather than simply to 'know' them. But Caspar will, it is clear, continue in his by now stupefying hope of possessing Isabel, and Pansy, as we last saw her at the convent, had 'seen the reality. . . . She bowed her pretty head to authority, and only asked of authority to be merciful'.[147] While Isabel may promise to return to her, she does so without expectation of doing her much good. Pansy cannot be liberated from Osmond.

The world of possible freedom is, then, discouragingly left to Isabel, who sometimes on the trip 'envied Ralph his dying', and Ralph, who is dying in fact. Ironically, it is Caspar Goodwood, of all Isabel's suitors the one who gives the most distinct impression of narrowness of interest and feeling, who makes the final plea for freedom to Isabel: 'We can do absolutely as we please'.[148] Isabel's reaction to his passionate declaration of love testifies eloquently to the implication that the longing for freedom ultimately becomes, the world being what it is, the desire for death, for the 'freedom and rest' which James envied in Minny Temple. To let Caspar take her in his arms would be, Isabel believes in her momentary desire to let him help her,' the next best thing to dying'.[149]

Nothing in James is more movingly rendered, more calculated to extend and exalt our deepest emotions of pity than the scene in which Ralph Touchett dies in Isabel's arms. At last, and for the only time in the novel, two people speak to one another without a semblance of theatricality or shame or self-elevation. This is possible because neither one of them really feels, nor do we, that there is any promise of beauty left past the boundaries of this moment, either in the novel or in the life projected beyond it. Everything that matters to either of them has been done and done badly, but it is only

145 *Por.*, p. 501.   146 *Por.*, p. 502.   147 *Por.*, p. 488.
148 *Por.*, p. 518.   149 *Ibid.*

now that Isabel can cry in front of Ralph and can tell herself as well as him: 'Oh, Ralph, you have been everything!'[150] Here and only here, at the moment of undefensive anguish and the recognition of the futility and wastefulness of her life, Isabel finally achieves that absolute union of outward expression and inward feeling for which she has laboured. In neither their language nor in James's is there a touch of contrived insincerity or theatricality. Ralph, in particular, speaks with that endearing and direct kindness which, through all the various posturing among the other characters, he has consistently maintained:

'You won't lose me – you will keep me. Keep me in your heart; I shall be nearer to you than I have ever been. Dear Isabel, life is better; for in life there is love. Death is good – but there is no love'.[151]

His promise to be nearer her after his death and his assurance that she will grow young again and will not suffer too much are the final flickerings of his imagination, its last efforts to endow Isabel with some life beyond the point in it which she has reached and beyond, for that matter, the conclusions of the novel. But short of believing in spirits, our imagination cannot, in this matter, subscribe to Ralph's, nor does James expect that it should. Ralph's encouragement of Isabel is an indication of the pathos which James himself experiences when, having created a heroine about whom we are asked to be 'more purely expectant'[152] than we would be if she were an ordinary girl, he must see her reduced at last to telling Ralph, the man in the novel who has had for her the greatest expectations: 'I should like to stay, as long as seems right'.[153]

What has happened to Isabel? And why is it that Ralph's reassuring words tend to be less a prediction of her future than another example of his wonderful capacity, even as he dies, for hope, for loving comfort, even as he is himself most in need of it? These questions are really one question, in the sense that they are sufficiently answered by understanding the significance of Isabel's return to Osmond. Her reasons have been a source of repeated speculation and argument among readers of the novel, largely because the kind of answer usually

---

being sought is not the kind the novel offers to give. For in talking about her return we should be talking about a novel, not about a person, about the relation of her act to James's whole intention, more than about its revelation of her individual psychology. Consider, for example, the supposition that Caspar's kiss in the garden is what impels her to leave for Rome almost immediately. The suggestions of sexual fear in her reactions to Caspar begin very early, they are too recurrent to be ignored, and they reach a melodramatic climax at Gardencourt when he makes his final appeal for her love. Before their meeting, she is anxious to have an excuse for remaining awhile in England, and it is made apparent that her promise to Pansy is not a motive sufficient to make her return to Rome. After his kiss – it was 'like a flash of lightning'[154] – and her reflection that she had never really been loved before, she darts away from him, and we are told that 'she had not known where to turn; but she knew now. There was a very straight path'.[155] It takes her back to the husband whom she has heard Ralph describe as a 'sterile dilettante'.[156]

We have here another case where particular psychological suggestiveness is more inviting than the expressive rhythm of the whole novel allows us to admit. If Isabel is motivated by sexual fear in this scene, then all her previous acts of high principle might equally be explained, since Caspar figures in all of them, as evasions of psychological distress. From this point of view, the search for freedom becomes in reality the rationalization of an attempt to escape from those personal susceptibilities which, in fact, she is disappointed to find in Henrietta and Mr. Bantling. Henrietta has become subject to 'common passions', and her relationship with Mr. Bantling 'had not been completely original'.[157] It need not be argued that such a reaction to marriage is extremely odd. Just how 'original' can a human being afford to be? Admittedly, a case can be made for discussing the novel in terms of the psychological peculiarity of Isabel's conduct. In doing so a wholly new dimension is given to her idealism. It remains commendable, but it submits to consideration as an unconscious theoretical stratagem for avoiding life even as it illustrates its noble

154 *Por.*, p. 519.   155 *Ibid.*
156 *Por.*, p. 303.   157 *Por.*, p. 497.

possibilities. If we pushed the matter a bit further we would find the psychological basis for the attractiveness which Isabel finds in death and, if still further, the reason why James himself talks about death in his letters as if it offered the promise of freedom which the experience of life denies.

I have already indicated why, on the basis of James's treatment of Isabel throughout the novel, we are not requested to make intense psychological probings into the heroine. No novel can be read as it ought to be except on the principle that when we discover something covert it does not mean that we then give up or transform all that is obvious. Two things seem to me obvious about *The Portrait of a Lady*: first, that it reveals much more about Isabel and about James himself than the author ever intended or expected, and, second, that his actual intention is strongly enough felt over the full course of the narrative so that to put primary emphasis on its unintentional implications is simply to pretend that the experience which the novel offers as a whole is different from what it is. This is a novel of ideas more than of psychology, an imitation of moral action more than a drama of motive. Some may feel, as I do, that *The Portrait of a Lady* would be a greater accomplishment if some of its psychological implications were made a firmer part of the whole design.

James had a very tenuous and unorganized sense of the connection between sexual psychology, on the one hand, and, on the other, the desire for freedom and death. He had a very clear and conscious idea, however, about the relationship between freedom and death, and it is that which comes through to us from the final chapters. What Caspar offers her in the garden is an old call to action and freedom: 'The world is all before us'.[158] While the intensity of her reaction to Caspar deserves the closest attention, the reasons for her refusal to go away with him need no explanation. She is simply not deeply enough in love with him nor has she ever been. When she hurries away from him, however, she is also escaping his call to leave the 'garden' of her dreams now that, like Eden after the fall, it has become a place of desolation. The Miltonic echo in his plea is unmistakably placed there. The same line occurs much earlier in the novel when Isabel sees her relatives

158 *Por.*, p. 518.

off for America. Having done her duty by these figures out of her past, and in possession of what seems unhampered independence, she walks away from the station into the London fog: 'The world lay all before her – she could do whatever she chose'.[159] In James's use of the phraseology of *Paradise Lost* ('The world lay all before them, where to choose/Their place of rest…'), there is not only a Miltonic sadness, but also an irony derived from the fact that neither Isabel nor Caspar is free to choose anything. His life is in useless bondage to his love for her, while hers is dedicated to its errors. And there is nothing in her act which holds the promise, as does Adam and Eve's, of eventual happiness through suffering, even though Ralph assures her that there is. Her action is absolutely within the logic of her Emersonian idealism, so much so that the logic takes its vengeance. In effect she tells the reader, to borrow from 'The Transcendentalist', that 'you think me the child of my circumstances: I make my circumstance',[160] – including, one might add, 'my own misery.' It is of no importance to her that, in fact, she has been so calculatingly deceived by other people that it is preposterous to assume all the responsibility for her own past. To admit this would be finally to subscribe to Madame Merle's view that the 'self' is determined, in part, by 'an envelope of circumstances'[161] that one does not always create. Isabel's action at the end is fully consistent with everything she does earlier. Now, however, she asserts her idealism of self not in innocence but in full knowledge of the world. For that reason, freedom, which was the condition of self-creation, becomes a form of indifference to the fact that returning to Rome will, as Caspar admonishes, cost her her life.

159 *Por.*, p. 282.
160 Emerson, *Works*, I, 334. The similarity between the line from 'The Transcendentalist' and Madame Merle's remark is noticed by Philip Rahv, *Image and Idea* (New York, 1949), p. 53.
161 *Por.*, p. 175.

Conclusion

The Portrait of a Lady comes at the end of an exceptionally productive period in James's career during which, in the space of little more than five and a half years, he wrote all the fiction we have considered. For nearly three and a half years thereafter, he produced no major work whatever, only some short stories, some travel pieces and reviews, a dramatization of *Daisy Miller*. The pause allowed for revaluation and summation, indicative of which there appeared three collections of work written mostly in the seventies: *Portraits of Places* (1883), *Stories Revived* (1885), and the first, seldom noticed, *Collective Edition of 1883*. After writing five novels between 1875 and 1881, he did not turn again to a large effort in fiction until *The Bostonians*, published serially in 1885–86.

The reasons for this particular interruption in James's career as a novelist can, no doubt, be explained in several different ways. The explanation most important to an understanding of his work, however, is implicit in his use of comedy for purposes of sorting out his characters. How, he seems to be asking, may the most freely suggestive dramatic rendering of action be combined with the use of characters who exemplify certain predetermined categories of human experience? This is not a bothersome problem when it concerns characters other than the most central. We can be satisfied, for example, with the fact that the characterization of Osmond never permits a complication of his blackness, any more than does the characterization of Henrietta allow us to imagine anything about her deeper psychology. We are made happy with the likelihood that she does not have one. Characters of this sort need do no more than represent the static dimensions of the world within which more intricate sensibilities are active.

The matter is less satisfactorily handled, however, when it involves James's favourite characters, those who have an essentially religious attitude towards human possibility. Put simply, the problem is this: drama necessitates human engagement, and this, in turn, produces exactly those implications which bring the psychological motivations behind Isabel's sort of idealism under more searching attention than James intends to allow. It is but one indication of his intuitive mastery that in placing his heroes and heroines in dramatic action he creates those complexities which make his conclusions often seem evasive and morally theoretical. In *The Portrait of a Lady* he permits none of the suitors to present Isabel with a romantic challenge sufficient to make the fact of her rejections unreasonable. But the particular intensities that accompany her rejections allow the inference that she has isolated her emotions from her theories about human relationships. None the less, such inferences, even in the final scene between Isabel and Caspar, where they seem to point most specifically at the psychological perversity of the heroine, are not meant to deflect us from a primary concern for the more abstractly moral and idealistic nature of her conduct.

Something similar could be said about the characterizations of Roderick Hudson and Christopher Newman. Each of them represents a certain kind of moral attitude which is explained, despite the presence of astute psychological hints within the novel, in terms of more general conceptions about Will, in the case of Roderick, and about American innocence, in the case of Newman,. The weakest of James's novels, *Confidence*, bears witness to the fact that his dramatizations can create extremely suggestive localizations of unconcious motivation, and that these can then be lost in the interest of having the characters merely illustrate a general aspect of experience, in this case the absurdity of their attempts to experiment with one another's emotions. The story itself gives a dramatic focus to the artistic problem with which James was faced: How can one show the ideological quality of action and, at the same time, reveal the source of the action in feelings that are the reverse of that quality? How can a character be used to represent a certain type of humanity and yet express a very specific and individual psychology? Even in *Washington Square*, he leaves the connection between Sloper's cruelty and his earlier disappointments so much to inference drawn from so few details that many readers, who are not sensitive to contrary indications in the style of the comedy, choose to take the novel as a simple melodrama. Yet, James does manage in this novel, and in the case of Eugenia and Acton in *The Europeans*, to dramatize a connection, usually obscured in the other works, between the public manner of a character and, bearing little resemblance to it, his often unconscious psychological motivation.

The propositions about character which we are considering are inherent in the varieties of comic entertainment found in these novels. In each of them James can be found, to borrow his praise of Ernest Renan, making 'a formal, a sort of cheerfully hopeless protest in the name of the ideal'.[162] In doing so, he shows little of Renan's lack of dogmatism, however, and even less of what James calls 'the indifference of his opinions'[163] James, the least cynical of novelists, is also one of the roughest in his handling of a good number of his characters. His inherently idealistic temper is most active when least directly apparent, especially in his contemptuous attitude towards those he calls 'the fools who minister, at the particular crisis, to the intensity of the free spirit engaged with them.'[164]

His comedy in these instances is invariably used in defence of the human capacities which he sees being thwarted not *within* the fools but by them, in their dealings with his favourites. Considering this aspect of comedy in James, we come to recognize features of his style that are seldom noticed: the witty and pointed verbal play, the exaggerated expression, the hyperbole in description by which, as we saw in Chapter I, he satirizes all those who are not capable of reverence for impractical aspiration. Encouraged by James himself, we have been calling these characters 'fixed', and we are not allowed to find extenuations for their inadequacies. They may amuse and even please, but they are wholly incapable of those evidences of feeling and intelligence which would direct us to probe beyond their loudly apparent grotesqueness. If we are allowed to see beyond that, it is only because some of the 'fixed' characters have a deceptively promising manner, and even when we do look behind it, we discover only the dreary *fact* of their emotional limitation with nothing attendant to it that might excite compassion or imagination. The theatricality of expression which was blatant in Mrs. Light, of *Roderick Hudson*, is, for instance, fastidiously injected into Madame Merle's conversation. In her case, as in Osmond's, the very smoothness of verbal

162 Unsigned review of *The Reminiscences of Ernest Renan*, *Atlantic Monthly*, LII (August 1883), 279.
163 *Ibid.*, p. 274.   164 *The Art of the Novel*, p. 129.

and social facility reaches a point close to farce. Osmond, in particular, is an example of the most sophisticated form of 'fixity' which we find in the early novels. His manner, like Madame Merle's, is outwardly peculiar only because it is perpetually, almost inhumanly graceful, sometimes at the very moments when we are gazing into the utter drabness of his emotional paralysis. And, finally, even the irony expended upon the heroic figures themselves tends to be affectionately partial to their aspiring habits of mind. In his characterization of Isabel, James's humour is a way of protecting her from a kind of knowledgeable sarcasm which, in his direct appeals to the reader, he seems to anticipate.

It can be said that all the novelistic devices of comic entertainment are used in these works to show the beauty of people who are intensely conscious and who desire much that cannot be satisfied by practical social means. James's refusal to give us more than the superficial manifestations of characters he does not like is accompanied by a reluctance to go beyond the public surface of those he admires. He is shy of designating a motive, or even a configuration of them, which offers an explanation for their believing what they believe. Their motivations are, in a sense, taken care of by what he considers the pre-eminent value of their beliefs. His effort to allow them the most unrestricted freedom from imputations of motive can lead to difficulties in the dramatic resolution of the action, but it also has a purpose and a result which are morally and artistically admirable. It makes us pay attention, as this study has urged we should, as much to the outward evidence of things as to their less apparent implications. The virtues of such a procedure, in the presentation both of the different kinds of 'fixed' characters and of 'free' ones, is best described by James himself in a comment some ten years before the publication of *The Portrait of a Lady*, on an exhibition of Dutch and Flemish portraits in New York:

We are inclined to think that our modern degenerescence – we assume it to be incontestable – is less a loss of skill than a defect of original vision. We know more about human character, and we have less respect for human faces. We take liberties with those that are offered us; we analyze and theorize and rub off the bloom of their mystery, and when we attempt to reproduce them, are obliged to resolve a swarm of fine conflicting impressions back into the unity and gravity of fact. A painter like this quietly wise De Vries (and *a fortiori* a painter like Van Dyck or like Titian) seems to have received and retained a single massive yet flexible impression, which was part and parcel, somehow, of a certain natural deference for his subject.[165]

The prejudice against analysis in portraiture, against breaking up a massive impression in the interests of selected and 'experimental' probing of particular lineaments, is apparent in all the novels of the early period. It applies not only to those characters for whom he shows a 'certain natural deference', but also to those who are treated with the broadest caricature and satire. In their case especially, there is an effort to maintain the unity of impression even at the expense, which is worth paying, of flexibility. One consequence, however, of his attempt to avoid the 'degenerescence' which he describes in modern portraiture is that James creates more 'conflicting impressions', especially in the case of major characters, than he can or is willing to resolve back into the 'gravity of fact'. This is especially apparent in the characterization of a figure like Isabel, whose 'unity' consists in her pursuit of an ideal of knowledge and freedom to which James subscribes. The possibility that her idealism might be a rationalization of impulses which she does not understand is often suggested in the novel, but it is in no sense allowed to dominate our impression of her. This, for James, would be a form of cynicism. The achievement of bringing into conjunction an idealistic vision of life and the full complexity of emotional disturbances which can be its source awaited *The Bostonians*. Even there, it is true, he reaches a point in an analysis of Olive Chancellor where he remarks that 'there are mysteries into which I shall not attempt to enter'.[166] Much of his deference, however, is meant to stimulate our speculations, without too rigidly directing them, into those emotional abnormalities of the heroine which the novel itself abundantly assimilates.

It does not seem to me unlikely that to James's imagination Olive Chancellor is the 'portrait' of Isabel Archer seen from the

165 Unsigned, 'Art: The Dutch and Flemish Pictures in New York,' *Atlantic Monthly*, XXIX (June 1872), 759.
166 *The Bostonians* (London, 1921), II, 228.

back. Perhaps it would be fairer to say that when he turns the
portrait of Isabel over he discovers her anew in a composite
of Olive and her eager young friend Verena Tarrant. Of
Verena, Basil Ransom is essentially right in thinking that while
'she was made for love – she was profoundly unconscious of it,
and another ideal, crude and thin and artificial, had interposed
itself'.[167] The 'other ideal', which has its most literal representation in the suffragette movement, is revealed in a very
ambiguous light during Olive's emotionally overwrought
interview with Vernea at the beginning of the novel:

'Oh yes – I want to give my life!' [Verena] exclaimed, with a
vibrating voice; and then she added gravely, 'I want to do some-
thing great!'
'You will, you will, we both will!' Olive Chancellor cried, in
rapture. But after a little she went on: 'I wonder if you know
what it means, young and lovely as you are – giving your life!'
Verena looked down a moment in meditation.
'Well,' she replied, 'I guess I have thought more than I appear'.
'Do you understand German? Do you know "Faust"?' said
Olive. '"Entsagen sollst du, sollst entsagen"'
'I don't know German; I should like so to study it; I want to
know everything'.
'We will work at it together – we will study everything', Olive
almost panted. . . .[168]

The configuration of styles in this passage, involving the
unaffected simplicity of Verena, the sinister impulsiveness of
Olive, and the language of idealism and renunciation, abundantly indicates the extent to which James in *The Bostonians*
is willing to take risks with his characters and his preferred
themes that he did not take in *The Portrait of a Lady*. This may
explain why, after the latter, he waited so long before embark-
ing upon another major work. When he completed *The
Portrait of a Lady*, he had reached a point of crisis in his capacity to
imagine a character in all its fullness and yet to present her as
an object of more ideological than psychological interest.
  How close this problem was to his own living experience
is to be seen clearly enough in those passages from his letters
and reminiscences where he seems to weigh the advantages of

167 *Ibid.*, II, 133.   168 *Ibid.*, I, 102–3.

death, the ultimate state of abstraction, against life. One of the
most provocative instances of this occurs in a letter to Grace
Norton, in which there is some mention of *The Portrait of a
Lady*. His remarks are especially applicable to what concerns
us here because they have to do with marriage. This subject
provides the central dramatic circumstance in response to
which every major character in the early novels expresses the
degree to which he finds the offerings of daily experience
equivalent to his desires and ideals. In his letter to Miss Norton
James writes: 'I am unlikely ever to marry. . . . One's attitude
toward marriage is a fact – the most characteristic part doubtless of one's general attitude toward life. . . . If I were to marry
I should be guilty in my own eyes of inconsistency – I should
pretend to think quite a little better of life than I really do'.[169]
We should not allow ourselves to be so overwhelmed by the
large claims of this statement that we take it as a sufficient
explanation of matters for which, in fact, it can only serve as
an excuse. Perhaps Leon Edel's biography of James will, when
it is completed, provide the answer to some of the questions
which remarks of this kind ought to provoke.[170]

My interest in James's remark to Grace Norton is that it is
extremely relevant to the qualities of literary expression which
we find in the fiction. In James's statement about marriage, the
distance between the stated fact, 'I am unlikely ever to marry',
and the generalization about 'life' is so wide that we are more
interested in the space between than in the items on either end.
Similarly, there is in the fiction sometimes a curious dis-
continuity between the significances that are finally evoked
and the dramatic life that has been precedently created. When
James, after many years, returned in the later novels to the
theme of expectation and idealism, it is again, especially in
The Ambassadors, without the speculative psychological density
that he shows himself capable of incorporating into the structure of *The Bostonians*. Strether's return to Woollett can be
explained by using the terms that generally accompany discussion of the prevalence of renunciation in James. Thus, according

169 Quoted in Matthiessen, *The Major Phase*, p. 50.
170 Meanwhile, see Leon Edel, *The Untried Years* (New York, 1953), and
Saul Rosenzweig, 'The Ghost of Henry James,' in *Art and Psychoanalysis*, ed.
William Phillips (New York, 1957), pp. 89–111.

to Mr. Frederick Crews's recent book, Strether refuses to accept so limited an aspect of life as would be involved, presumably, in marrying Maria Gostrey because he has had an awakening that would make such an act an 'insufficient tribute to Life'.[171] The novel allows for such a reading, though I would myself begin to wonder if the word 'life', when it has to be spelled with a capital 'L', does not really mean death.

To find James's conclusion to *The Ambassadors* adequate, despite all that is suggested here and there in the preceding action about more interesting psychological possibility, is to be willing to accept schematic rather than dramatic resolutions. To prefer this is simply to value the concrete and accumulated dramatic life less than the ideas that can be deduced from them and less than the abstractions by which dramatic implication can be evaded. James's excuse for not marrying appeals to this preference. But it is, for all that, significant and moving for reasons which he would not have expected and would not like.

It is a touching statement because it asks us to disregard so much more than it asks us to notice. There is a grandeur and dignity, a kind of truth to whatever he says, because massed behind it is so much evidence of substantial creation that has the mark of genius. What could a man of such vitality and creativity have in mind when he speaks so of life and death? The source of his truly incredible productive energy, which went through a temporary but noticeable diminution after *The Portrait of a Lady*, rests, I believe, in the need to give validity to such statements as the one he makes to Grace Norton, to fill the emptiness between actual experience and idealistic rationalization with a self-justifying picture of life. This energy allowed him in the years from 1875 to 1881 to produce a series of novels, of which *The Portrait of a Lady* is the masterpiece, in which life is allowed to deceive innocence with romance and then to betray it with cynicism. But this happens only after James, with a loving hopelessness, has beguiled us, himself, and his characters with the fiction that the deadness inherent in social custom is comic and unnatural, rather than a horrid figure squatting at the heart of reality. His comedy is the partisan of freedom, the sworn enemy of all kinds of fixity, and yet his sincerities are quietly, almost pas-

171 Crews, *Tragedy of Manners*, p. 56.

sively, elegiac. Thus it is that his comic sense lays bare the urgency of his deeply personal commitment to the practice of his art. It is his best weapon in defence of a kind of freedom which, if defenceless in life, might, he fondly hoped, find an existence this side of death in the fictive world of his novels.

Index